day trips from new jersey

All photos licensed by Shutterstock.com.

Page 1: Trail to beach at Island Beach State Park, NJ.

Page 2 (top): Colorful Victorian style houses, Cape May, NJ; (bottom): Sandy Hook Lighthouse, Sandy Hook, NJ.

Page 3 (top): Sunset in Ocean City, NJ; (bottom left): Statue of Liberty National Monument, Liberty Island; (bottom right, upper): Waiting for high tide, Cape May, NJ; (bottom right, lower): The Great Hall in the Ellis Island Immigration Museum.

Page 4 (top): Mt. Tammany, Delaware Water Gap National Recreation Area; (bottom): Asbury Park Convention Hall, Asbury Park, NJ.

day trips® from
new jersey

POCONO MOUNTAINS VISITOR CENTERS
(1) lake wallenpaupack
(2) TANNERSVILLE *
(3) jim ThORpe
POCONO MOUNTAINS VISITOR BUREAU
STROUDSBURG

* I-80, EXit 299
The cROSSings premium outlets FOOd court
1000 premium outlets drive,
TANNERSVILLE, PA 18372
570-629-1703

help us keep this guide up to date

We would love to hear from you concerning your experiences with this guide and how you feel it could be improved and kept up to date. Please send your comments and suggestions to:

editorial@GlobePequot.com

Thanks for your input, and happy travels!

day trips® series

day trips® from new jersey

first edition

 getaway ideas for the local traveler

stephanie murphy-lupo

travel

Guilford, Connecticut

All the information in this guidebook is subject to change. We recommend that you call ahead to obtain current information before traveling.

Editor: Amy Lyons
Project Editor: Lynn Zelem
Layout: Joanna Beyer
Text Design: Linda R. Loiewski
Maps: Mapping Specialists Ltd. © Morris Book Publishing, LLC
Spot photography throughout © gary718/Shutterstock

ISBN 978-0-7627-7939-0

Printed in the United States of America
10 9 8 7 6 5 4 3 2

contents

about the author

Stephanie Murphy-Lupo is an author, freelance writer, photographer, and career journalist. She has explored many American destinations, and written about her travels to Cuba, Portugal, Italy, Australia, Finland, Sweden, and Canada.

Stephanie gained wide-ranging insight about the way people view their own journeys through interviews with tycoons and celebrities, scholars and scientists, musicians and artists, entertainers and athletes, analysts and policy-makers.

For three years, she coauthored *The Insiders' Guide to Boca Raton & the Palm Beaches*. Stephanie also wrote *Off the Record with Charles Calello,* a biography now in production.

She and her husband, Gerard Lupo, divide their time between Montville, NJ, and West Palm Beach, FL.

acknowledgments

Thank you, New Jersey, for a truly wild ride—from my first encounter with Newark Liberty Airport decades ago, through a recent twirl of the state from stem to stern.

I am grateful to editor Amy Lyons for the opportunity to relate these stories, and for all the professionals at Globe Pequot Press who helped produce the finished book.

In no particular order, thanks to the following for trusting a stranger to get it right: Sue Wheeler, Tom Edmunds, Robert E. Ruffolo Jr., John Battista, Nancy Miller, Prudence Pigott, Janet DiMauro, Mike Koblentz, Tony Sofia, Brian George, Tara Crocker, Jim McCook, Alecia Brooks, Caroline O'Toole, Joe "Ciid" Birardi, Tim McLoone, Thomas Stevens, Frank Walsh, Charlie the Waitress, Tom Minton, Rich Small, and Steve Marano.

Natives who shared valuable insight include John Scarpa, Frank Valvano, Donna Benelli, Kimm Zientek, Joe Ciraulo, Mike Papa, Anthony Tammaro, Irene Tammaro, and Frank Marino.

Thanks to Donald Trump, for his take on the liquid state of things in Atlantic City and the marvels of Manhattan.

Most importantly, my husband and travel bud Gerry deserves my eternal appreciation for his humor, patience, insight, and mapping skills. A Newark native, he enjoyed each fresh look at his home turf—even when a day trip scuttled his golf game.

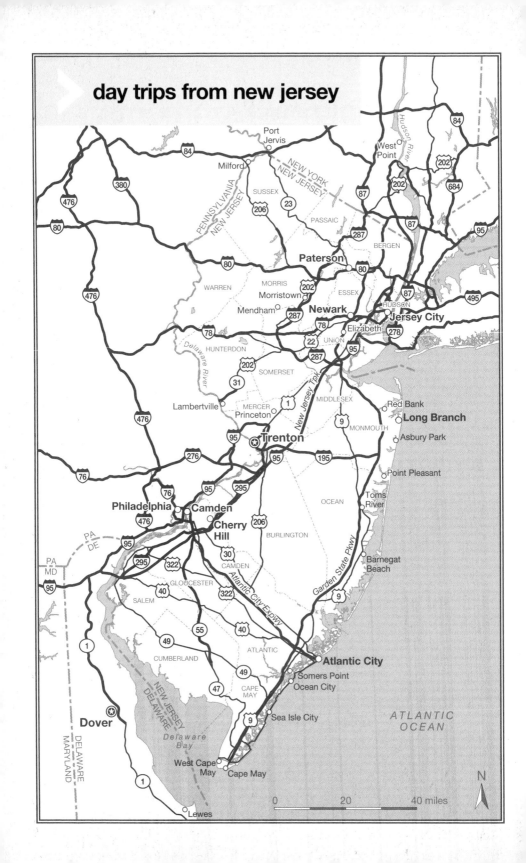

>> introduction

A tapestry of New Jersey would be threaded with rivers, embroidered with forests, studded with mountains, laced in orchards, tie-dyed in sea salt, and crocheted in coastal eco-fringe.

Its hourglass shape daring to be fully revealed, the state shoulders itself between the Hudson and Delaware Rivers, thrusts a hip into the Atlantic Ocean, and flexes a thigh at Philadelphia. It winks at the Appalachian Trail and wags its tail at Delaware.

The Lenni-Lenape Indians were right at home here for centuries before the Swedes, Dutch, and Brits were clutching at a hem. It was New Netherland before it was a province named for a Channel Island. And unlike most of the Thirteen Colonies at that time, Jersey was a popular place to relocate—drawing the disenchanted from New Amsterdam and New Haven. Eventually, New Jersey shrugged off those suitors and took charge of her destiny.

Should you like it wet, you've arrived, as the state is 15 percent water and gives you 130 miles of ocean beaches, plus lakes, streams, and beaucoup rivers. At only 70 miles wide and 170 miles long, New Jersey makes regional outings a breeze. Smaller than most states, yes, but the ambitious menu of its physical assets is authentic: waterways, mountains, valleys, woodlands, and wetlands.

History that happened here shaped the entire region and the nation—from its pivotal role in the Revolutionary War to its bearing on an emerging United States and the promising Industrial Era.

Culturally and religiously, New Jersey is diverse. Its people live in several big cities and more than 560 municipalities—yet the state is about 70 percent undeveloped by design.

There are outdoor wonders and indoor food for thought. Cities and villages have their own draw—from restored downtowns to retail gems, the music and arts scene, delectable cuisine, gaming and entertainment, historic monuments, museums, and architectural gems.

Simply take a ride to understand why New Jersey is called "The Garden State"—or why a trip on the Parkway is green on wheels. Dutch settlers chose this land to farm. They bought tracts from the Lenape, who taught them a thing or two about corn. The soil did not disappoint; hence, world-famous Jersey tomatoes. Tilled lands also deliver blueberries and cranberries, plus spinach, peaches, and peppers—creating ample demand at roadside stands across the state.

From the scenic peaks and forests of the Kittatinny Mountains to the inspirational Ellis Island Museum; from Sandy Hook to Cape May; and from Atlantic City across to "Pennsy," you can't go far without tripping over something interesting, entertaining, important, magnificent, or all of the above.

The Jersey Shore is largely distinct from the rest of the state and has little in common with the MTV reality show. Iconic towns, barrier islands, historic significance, and charm aside, you will find more than big naked guns at Gunnison Beach, and the bounty of Victoria's secret stash in Cape May.

Off-season in most regions, there is music that moves you, plays that inspire, engaging historic sites, shopping to renew, resorts and spas to restore, delightful dining, and lively recreation. Choose your passion among the scenic outdoors, stores, museums, food, wine tours, and betting against the dealer. Soak it up; sense it; and savor your way all 'round New Jersey.

>> using this guide

While many books in this series are geographically aligned by compass directions, *Day Trips from New Jersey* is laid out in six distinctive regions: Gateway, The Skylands, The Shore, Greater Atlantic City, The Southern Shore, and the Delaware River Region.

The Garden State is relatively petite and elongated—about 170 miles from head to toe, and about 70 miles wide at the waist. The book largely takes you up and down and across New Jersey, but some trips invite you across a state line into what is considered part of the neighborhood.

"Gateway" itineraries are in the state's northeast corridor, where some counties border the Hudson River and the Lower Bay. A few trips in this section will take you either into Manhattan or north into New York State.

"The Skylands" covers counties in the north-central and northwest, and we suggest some stops in neighboring Pennsylvania and New York.

"The Shore" in this case includes Monmouth and Ocean Counties, and stretches from Sandy Hook to Holgate along the Atlantic Ocean.

"Greater Atlantic City" takes in one county, from Brigantine to Longport, and the many barrier islands in and around AC. In addition, Ocean City appears in this section rather than the next, because its proximity to Atlantic City suggests a likely pairing.

"The Southern Shore" has its focus on Cape May County, especially the eastern towns and the iconic town at its tip. Also in this section are day trips to Lewes, DE, and Rehoboth Beach, DE, via a ferry ride across Delaware Bay.

"Delaware River Region" takes in the state capital of Trenton, historic Princeton, and Philadelphia, PA.

Although New Jersey is No. 47 among the states in land area, its dense population makes for busy roads. And many of the highways are toll roads.

hours of operation, prices & credit cards

Hours of operation and prices for attractions should be considered general guidelines. We strive to be accurate, yet this information is always subject to change. You should plan to call before you visit to get the latest details. The establishments listed accept major credit cards, except where noted.

pricing key

accommodations

The price code reflects the average cost of a double-occupancy room during peak season, excluding sales tax or extras. Be sure to ask whether there are discounts available for AAA members and/or seniors.

    $ less than $100

    $$ $100 to $175

    $$$ $175 plus

restaurants

The price code reflects the average tab for dinner for two (entrees), excluding cocktails, wine, appetizers, desserts, sales tax, and gratuity.

    $ less than $10 (per entree)

    $$ $10 to $25

    $$$ $25 plus

driving tips

The jug handle on a shard of porcelain may spark awe. The jug handle on your honey's mid-section may amuse or perplex. But a jug handle in New Jersey is likely to vex newcomers, because the state is plugged with them, and there is no getting around that. The department of transportation calls a jug handle an "at-grade ramp" at or between intersections. They exist because many roads do not allow left-hand turns or U-turns. In simple lingo, you move from the right lane onto a ramp that loops about 270 degrees, sending you on your way, sort of. The state acknowledges that jug handles are confusing to people from elsewhere, but it is often the only way to make a left turn.

Road trips to "The Shore" are a major headache any weekend in summer. In fact, if you hit the road after mid-morning on a Friday, you can expect to be in heavy traffic until you get off the Garden State Parkway (GSP). Seasoned travelers usually try to go on a Thursday evening and leave after the Sunday crush.

highway designations

The **New Jersey Turnpike (I-95)** runs for 148 miles from the Delaware Memorial Bridge toward New York City; (732) 750-5300; www.state.nj.us/turnpike. See the website to sign up for "MyNJ511" to receive traffic alerts by email or text.

The **Garden State Parkway** goes for 173 miles from Cape May to Bergen County, where it meets the New York State Thruway; (732) 442-8600; www.state.nj.us/turnpike.

The **Atlantic City Expressway** is 44 miles from Atlantic City to NJ 42 (toward Camden, NJ, and Philadelphia, PA); (609) 965-6060; www.acexpressway.com.

Major east-west arteries in the north part of the state include **I-80** from Fort Lee on the Hudson River west to the Delaware River; and **I-78,** from the Newark area west to Phillipsburg. Both go for about 68 miles.

I-287 is a north-south road that runs from the New York state line to make an L-shaped curve toward I-95. **I-195** gets you east-west between the GSP and I-295 into Trenton.

State routes are labeled NJ, PA, NY, or DE, followed by the number. County roads are referred to as Route, followed by the number.

Several major roads and highways have mile marker posts.

travel tips

alcohol

Many restaurants do not have a liquor license, but they welcome you to bring your own wine. However, grocery stores in New Jersey do not sell beer or wine. There are independent retailers and the major food chains sell alcohol in separate locations.

area codes

They vary among the six regions, and sometimes within a county. Expect to see the following: 732, 609, 973, 908, 856, and 201.

sales tax

Sales tax is 7 percent in New Jersey, excluding clothes and shoes, with additional local taxes on certain items in Atlantic City and Cape May County; 4 percent in New York, with additional local taxes in certain counties; 6 percent in Pennsylvania, plus local taxes, excluding food, clothing, and most footwear; no sales tax for consumers in Delaware. Hotel rates listed on websites do not usually include sales tax. In addition, the hotel bill may include a small "occupancy fee," $2 or so, and a tourism promotion fee.

seasonal issues

New Jersey celebrates mild weather and stamps its feet at the snow. With so many rivers running through the state, flooding is not uncommon in the spring. Winters can vary from benign to brutal, so plan your ski trips accordingly. If you visit during the Christmas holidays, make a point of driving through small towns in the early evening, for a remarkable Norman Rockwell-esque montage.

where to get more information

major highways

New Jersey Turnpike. For road conditions: (732) 247-0900 or (800) 336-5875; for the status of construction: www.state.nj.us/turnpike.

Garden State Parkway. (732) 727-5929; www.state.nj.us/turnpike.

train service

An overview of rail service appears in the Theme chapter, Train Yourself (p. 259).

Train travel is available through NJ Transit. The rail division has 11 lines and more than 160 stations, mostly in northern New Jersey. With more than 950 route miles, its weekday ridership is fourth in the United States. The Hoboken Division runs from Hoboken Terminal and Newark–Broad Street. The Newark Division runs through Newark Penn Station and operates the Atlantic City Line as well. Stations run the gamut—from the mini-city at New York Penn Station to solo platforms in a one-horse township.

NJ Transit also operates a series of light-rail lines:

- **PATH.** (800) 234-7284; www.panynj.info. Rail service from the Newark metro area into Lower Manhattan is available on the Port Authority Trans-Hudson, operated by The Port Authority of New York and New Jersey. There are 13 stations spanning 14 miles, and trains run 24 hours a day. There are three terminals in New Jersey and two in Manhattan.

- **Newark Light Rail** goes from Newark Penn Station to Broad Street Station.

- **River Line** gets you around Camden and Trenton; (800) 626-7433; www.riverline.com.

- **Hudson-Bergen Light Rail** connects Bayonne, Jersey City, and Manhattan; (973) 275-5555; www.njtransit.com.

The Delaware River Port Authority operates the **PATCO Speedline** between Camden County, NJ, and Center City in Philadelphia. There are four stations on the line in Philly and nine stations in New Jersey, where you will find park and ride facilities. A primary stop at Woodcrest Station connects you directly with I-295 exit 31. PATCO Speedline runs 24 hours a day.

ferry/boat service

Ferry service is described in the three chapters that require this form of transport: Ellis Island (see p. 4), Liberty State Park (see p. 6), and Lewes, DE (see p. 220). For boaters looking to locate a marina, see www.jerseymarinas.com.

airports

Newark Liberty International: (800) 247-7433; www.panynj.gov/airports/newark-liberty

Teterboro Airport: (201) 288-1775; www.teb.com

LaGuardia International: (800) 247-7433; www.laguardiaairport.com

Atlantic City International: (609) 645-7895; www.acairport.com

Philadelphia International: (215) 937-6937; www.phl.org

where to get more information

This inaugural edition of *Day Trips from New Jersey* has both broad strokes to get you started and details on much to explore. If you want some information on a topic we did not provide, here are some resources to contact:

new jersey welcome centers: www.visitnj.org

Pleasantville. Atlantic City Expressway, mile marker 3.5; (609) 383-2727.

Farley Travel Plaza. Atlantic City Expressway, mile marker 21, Hammonton; (609) 965-6316.

Deepwater. Route 295 North, exit 2B; (856) 351-0194.

Jackson Premium Outlets. Route 537 near I-195 exit 16, Jackson; (732) 833-0503.

Jersey Gardens Outlet Mall Information Center. Lower Level, Elizabeth; (908) 436-3005.

Jersey Shore Premium Outlets. Tinton Falls; (732) 918-1700.

John Fenwick Plaza. New Jersey Turnpike, mile marker 5.4, Penns Grove; (908) 354-5900.

Knowlton Welcome Center. Route 80 East, Mile Marker 7, Columbia; (908) 496-4994.

Liberty State Park. New Jersey Turnpike exit 14B, Central Railroad Terminal; (201) 915-3440.

Liberty Village Premium Outlets. Church Street, Flemington; (908) 782-8550.

Molly Pitcher Travel Plaza. New Jersey Turnpike, mile marker 71.9; (609) 655-1610.

Monmouth Travel Plaza. Garden State Parkway, mile marker 100, Belmar; (732) 681-4314.

Montvale Travel Plaza. Garden State Parkway, mile marker 172; (201) 391-5737.

Newark Liberty Airport. Satellite Information Center, Concierge Desk; Terminal B; international arrivals, lower level; (973) 623-5052.

New Jersey State House. 125 W. State St., Trenton; (609) 777-2719.

Ocean View Tourist Center. Garden State Parkway, mile marker 18.3; (609) 624-0918.

Rutgers University Bush Campus Visitors Center. Piscataway; (732) 445-1000.

Somerset Tourist Center. 360 Grove St. at Route 22 East, Bridgewater; (908) 725-1552.

Trenton Transit Center. 72 S. Clinton Ave., Trenton; (609) 292-2261.

Vince Lombardi Information Center. New Jersey Turnpike, mile marker 116, Ridgefield; (201) 943-8757.

other good resources

Jersey Shore Convention & Visitors Bureau. Toms River; (732) 244-9283; www .visitthejerseyshore.com.

New Jersey Division of Fish & Wildlife. (609) 292-2965; www.state.nj.us/dep. Check this site for fishing and hunting license regulations.

New Jersey Sports and Exposition Authority. www.njsea.com. Look here for the rules on off-track wagering at various facilities run by this state agency.

New Jersey Office of Travel & Tourism. (800) 847-4865; www.visitnj.org.

acting with "atticus"

Let's say you want to know what Mary Badham had to say about acting with Gregory Peck in To Kill a Mockingbird, *the 1962 classic film based on Harper Lee's novel. Badham, who played the role of Atticus Finch's 10-year-old daughter, Scout, gave talks about her experiences in 2011 to coincide with a production of the play performed at The Shakespeare Theatre of New Jersey in Madison. For information on related topics, see www.jerseyarts.com.*

Pennsylvania Department of Transportation. (888) 783-6783 or (215) 567-5678; www.dot.state.pa.us. Look here for information on a ferry ride on the Delaware River near Camden and Philadelphia.

Delaware Tourism Office. (866) 284-7483; www.visitdelaware.com.

New York State. www.nystatetourism.com.

campgrounds
gateway

Liberty Harbor Marina & RV Park. (201) 386-7500; www.libertyharborrv.com.

Ramapo Valley County Reservation. (201) 327-3500; www.co.bergen.nj.us/bcparks (does not have RV hookups).

Sun Air Lakeside Campground. Oak Ridge; (973) 697-3489; www.sunairlakesidecamp .com.

the skylands

Beaver Hill Campground. Hardyston; (800) 229-2267; www.beaverhill.com.

Cedar Ridge Family Campground. Montague; (973) 293-3512; www.cedarridge campground.net.

Delaware River Family Campground. Delaware; (908) 475-4517; www.njcamping.com.

Harmony Ridge Farm & Campground. Branchville; (973) 948-4941; www .harmonyridge.com.

Panther Lake Camping Resort. Andover; (973) 347-4440; www.njcamping.com/ panther.

the shore

Atlantic City North Family Campground. Tuckerton; (609) 296-9163; www.campacn .com.

Baker's Acres Campground. Little Egg Harbor; (609) 296-2664; www.bakersacres .com.

Pine Cone Campground. Freehold; (732) 462-2230; www.pineconenj.com.

greater atlantic city

Shady Pines Campground. Galloway; (609) 652-1516; www.carefreervresorts.com.

Wharton State Forest. Hammonton; (609) 561-0024; www.njparksandforests.org.

the southern shore

Depot Travel Park. West Cape May; (609) 884-2533; www.gocampingamerica.com.

Holly Shores Camping Resort. Cape May; (609) 886-1234; www.hollyshores.com.

King Nummy Trail Campground. Cape May Court House; (609) 465-4242; www .kingnummytrail.com.

delaware river region

Four Seasons Family Campground. Pilesgrove; (888) 372-2267; www.fourseasons camping.com.

Turtle Run Campground. Wading River; (609) 965-5343; www.turtleruncampground .com.

Wading Pines Camping Resort. Chatsworth; (609) 726-1313; www.wadingpines.com.

gateway

day trip 01

gateway

>>> **steerage sans upgrades:**
ellis island

Who do you think you are? Really—not reality television. Thanks to the pull of pop culture and some boldfaced names onscreen, TV viewers are familiar with that expression. And many who seek answers find them at Ellis Island—once "square one" for immigrants seeking the promise perceived in a new frontier.

This chunk of rock in New York Harbor was the official gateway for millions of born-elsewheres who chose America during the pivotal decades between 1892 and 1924. An estimated 100 million Americans are related to someone registered at Ellis Island during peak operation.

The first soul documented at the federal depot was Annie Moore, 17, of County Cork, Ireland. And thanks to a record bank of ship-passenger manifests, Christina Deroche, a hotel executive in Coronado, CA, found the name of her grandfather. Giuseppe Lupo also was 17 when he arrived from Italy on Dec. 23, 1898.

A lot of people expect to explore Ellis Island at the same time they visit the Statue of Liberty. It can be done, as the same vessels take you to both places. But separate trips are a must to truly experience what each destination has to offer.

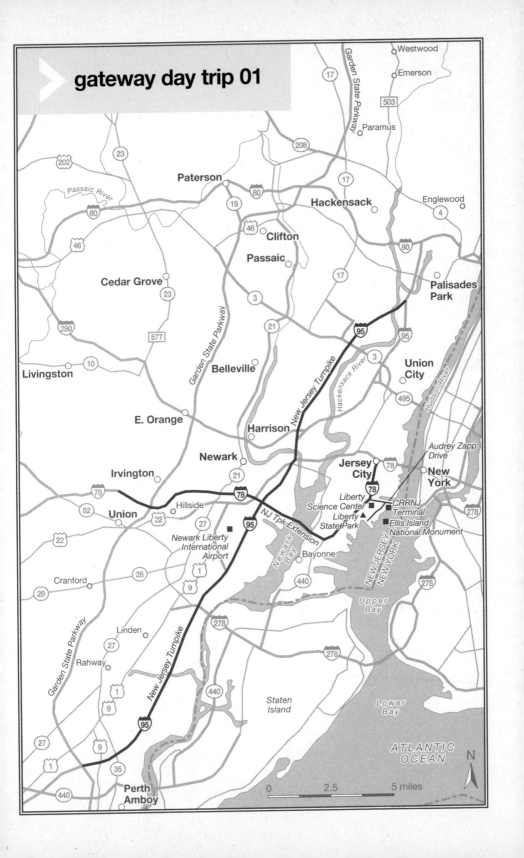

gateway day trip 01

ellis island

getting there

Ferry service is your sole option, and it's available from Jersey City, NJ, and Castle Clinton in Battery Park, NY. From the New Jersey Turnpike, take exit 14B and go east on the New Jersey Turnpike Extension (also called I-78); after the toll, bear left and follow signs to Liberty State Park. Go straight through one traffic light and turn left at the traffic circle. Turn right onto Audrey Zapp Drive and go straight to the CRRNJ Terminal; park on the right. If some-one in your party isn't up for a healthy trek to the terminal, you may drop off passengers closer to the terminal before parking. Inside, ferry passengers must go through airport-style security screenings. The ride takes about 15 minutes and ferries run every 40 minutes. To fully explore the exhibits, expect to stay 2 or 3 hours. A 45-minute audio tour is available in nine languages.

where to go

The American Family Immigration Center. www.ellisisland.org. Located on the first floor of the west wing of the museum; see photos of more than 900 ships and historic data on more than 6,500 vessels. Opened in spring 2001, this research facility contains ship pas-senger records of tens of millions who entered the country during Ellis Island's peak years. It is possible to view and obtain copies of ship manifests and photos of the vessels. The website gives advice about how to prepare for a search before you begin.

The Ellis Island Immigration Museum. Based in the Great Hall—which was created in 1900 and converted to a museum in 1990—the building has been restored to the way it

face to face

Ellis Island became a federal property in 1808, when the island was bought from New York. It had been a private island in the 1700s, and was originally settled by Native Americans. In 1890, President Benjamin Harrison decreed that Ellis Island would become the registry for immigration. The largest period for receiving immi-grants was between 1892 and 1924, when it was the primary platform for people of all national, racial, cultural, and religious origins to meet the United States face to face. Ellis Island is only half an hour from Newark, yet light-years in terms of the journey so many made to get here.

a whisker on the map, eyes on a wall

Rimming a circular field outside the main building at Ellis Island is an astonishing and very personal postcard from the edge of hope. Silvery panels making up The American Immigrant Wall of Honor hold the names of more than 700,000 people who represent the spirit of what it means to choose this country as one's home. And this is the only place in these United States where you can honor someone at a national monument. The wall has names of deceased ancestors, people alive today—even new citizens celebrating their naturalization. Famous people and the everyday anonymous have posted names—anyone can. It doesn't take political influence or magic to be on the wall—although Harry Houdini is up there. What it takes to immortalize someone is $150. And so on a summer day in 2011, Gerard Anthony Lupo visited Ellis Island with a lead and some details from his cousin, Christina Deroche—whom he saw in the spring after more than 50 years. He paid the $150 and looks forward to an upcoming visit when he and his brother Jack can see the name of their grandfather on the Wall of Honor. Giuseppe Lupo will have arrived in a different way—114 years after his ship came in, right before Christmas 1898. He left his home in Salerno, Italy, and booked passage on the Karamania, which set out from Naples.

looked during its busiest days. Linger in front of the baggage exhibit to get a feel for the atmosphere as it was.

where to eat

The Ellis Island Cafe. Outdoor seats and benches make for a casual refreshment stop between various points of interest. It is unlikely that a visitor would take the ferry just for the food, but it's plenty tasty, affordable, and varied enough to satisfy most palates. Salads, sandwiches, panini, and pizza are some of the offerings. If you want a burger, choose among beef, turkey, or veggie style. Fish and chips, shrimp, chicken wraps, and barbecue are up for grabs. $.

day trip 02

gateway

>>> **don't keep the lady waiting:**
liberty state park

The Statue of Liberty National Monument merits another visit for anyone, especially if you haven't made the trek since Liberty Weekend in 1986, which marked the centennial of this gift from France to glorify the ideal of American democracy. Yes, we know—Americans upon occasion don't see eye to eye with the French. But don't let that deter you from getting reacquainted with this magnificent Lady—who waits, patiently, for you to play catch-up.

The monument is a World Heritage Site in the United States, and is listed on the National Register of Historic Places. The statue stands within an 11-point star, the original footprint for Fort Hood, on Liberty Island—formerly Bedloe's Island.

This trip could be accomplished with a companion stop at Ellis Island if time is a critical factor. Ideally, however, separate the two outings. Each is a unique experience that can keep you engaged and occupied for hours.

liberty state park

getting there

Ferry service is your sole option, and it's available from Jersey City, NJ, and Castle Clinton in Battery Park, NY. (According to the ferry firm Statue Cruises, expect faster processing and boarding—ample parking and convenience—if you opt for a Jersey City departure.) From the New Jersey Turnpike, take exit 14B; after the toll, bear left and follow signs to

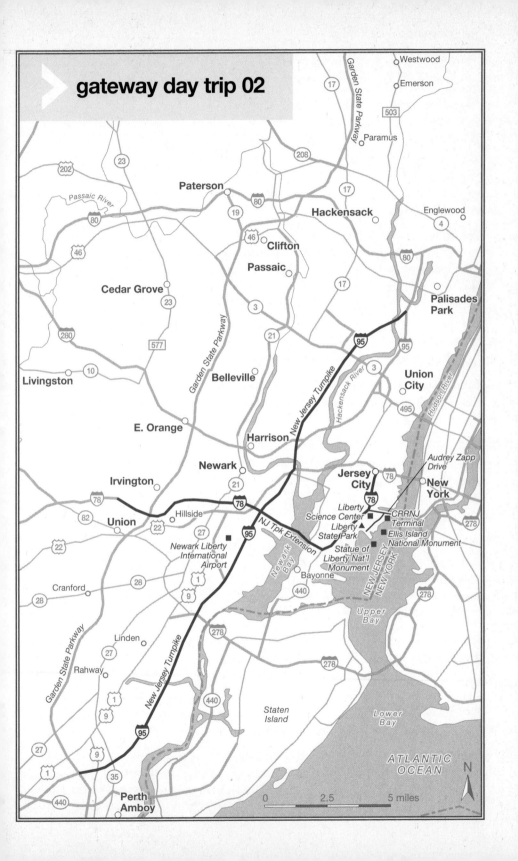

Liberty State Park. Go straight through one traffic light and turn left at the traffic circle. Turn right onto Audrey Zapp Drive and go straight to the CRRNJ Terminal; park on the right. If someone in your party isn't up for a healthy trek to the terminal, you may drop off passengers closer to the terminal before parking. Inside, passengers must go through airport-style electronic security screenings. Ferries run every 40 minutes.

where to go

The Statue of Liberty Grounds. (201) 604-2800; www.libertystatepark.com. Ideal for someone who has seen other aspects and simply wants to bask in the environment, admire the harbor sights and fresh air, and get reacquainted with the statue's exterior elements. For such an imposing icon, the Lady is surprisingly engaging from all angles. She frankly seems nonplussed at the denouement of it all. And that might be what the sculptor intended when he wrote that, "The surfaces should be broad and simple, defined by a bold and clear design, accentuated in the important places." For this visit, either book Reserve tickets or 3-Day Flex tickets, good for one visit within a three-day period.

Statue of Liberty Museum and Pedestal. Essential for the visitor who hasn't been here in a while, this pass lets you enter the pedestal and the museum exhibits, and lets you view the interior structure of Liberty from below. The ticket is the same price as the Reserve or 3-Day Flex, but availability is limited.

Statue of Liberty Crown. An exciting prospect for first-time visitors, this pass includes access to the museum and pedestal. Availability is limited and advance purchase is required. (For all current ticket prices, see www.statuecruises.com.) Verify the dates when the Statue of Liberty will be off-limits for construction of a second staircase.

***Calypso* Sailing Adventures.** 150 Audrey Zapp Dr., Jersey City; (908) 377-1202; www.sailcalypsonyc.com. *Calypso* is a 36-foot luxury sailboat available for charter for up to 6 passengers. Choose among afternoon, sunset, and evening cruises of New York Harbor. You can take the wheel or let the skipper do all the work. Charters are available from Apr through Oct. Rates for a 2-hour sail are $75 each (2-person minimum), $150 for a couple, and $400 for 6. For weekend rates, holidays, and longer excursions, ask for a quote.

***Sea Fever* Excursions.** 80 Audrey Zapp Dr., Jersey City; (201) 887-8700; www.sailthehudson.com. Among the many options available to cruise, sail, or ride a ferry around the harbor, *Sea Fever* sets sail for 2-hour tours from the Liberty Landing Marina in Liberty State Park. Rates are $79; $149 for a couple; and $399 for the 6-person "fill the boat" special. Snacks and meals are available for separate purchase.

Statue Cruises. Liberty State Park; (877) 523-9849; www.statuecruises.com. The same company that runs ferry service to Ellis Island and the Statue of Liberty offers a Liberty Harbor Cruise. It includes those sites as well as Governors Island, the September 11 Memorial, the Brooklyn Bridge, and Battery Park. Stay tuned to the company's website for updates on the launch of its *Hornblower Hybrid,* a new vessel being built in Bridgeport, CT. It should be worth the wait, as the cruise line brags about its design of the world's first hydrogen-fueled hybrid ferry.

Central Railroad of NJ Terminal. 1 Audrey Zapp Dr. (Liberty State Park), Jersey City; (201) 915-3440; www.njparksandforests.org. If you have no sea legs or are otherwise not up for a water voyage to one of the monuments, the historic terminal is worth a visit anyway.

muse for a monumental maiden

For 125 years, the countenance of Libertas, *better known as the Statue of Liberty, has been associated with New York Harbor—even though she lives in New Jersey waters. From the beginning, however, Lady Liberty was a well-traveled grand dame. The idea for her creation was born at a dinner party in Versailles, France, where sculptor Frédéric Auguste Bartholdi overheard his host, law professor Édouard René de Laboulaye, pose the notion that any monument to American independence should involve both nations. Bartholdi formed the Franco-American Union—to raise money in France for the statue, and in America for its pedestal. While still a gleam in the artist's eye, Liberty was the hook for the premiere of a new* cantata *by composer Charles Gounod at the Paris Opera. Liberty's arm—the first part completed—traveled to Philadelphia for the 1876 Centennial Exposition and lingered in New York for several years. Her face got around, too, at various international venues. Metal merchants Japy Frères donated the copper sheets for the statue's skin, and rumor says the metal was mined in Norway. Bartholdi chose copper beaten in the* repoussé *method to lighten the statue's weight—a process he spelled out in sketches and diaries inside the pedestal museum. Posters show the iron-truss tower under Liberty's skirt—a brilliant solution by designer Alexandre-Gustave Eiffel—featuring a metal frame with "saddles" attached with rivets to the copper skin. Bartholdi's sketch of Liberty became a logo of sorts that picnicked all over France—on cheese and wine labels—as people opened their wallets in support. In America, publisher Joseph Pulitzer campaigned for pedestal money. Liberty was built in France before her ocean voyage in crates to Bedloe's Island. Her copper and iron features were assembled on the pedestal for a dedication that included remarks by President Grover Cleveland, a New Jersey native. During a parade, excited Wall Street traders launched the tradition of throwing ticker-tape out the windows of the New York Stock Exchange.*

It was built in 1889 and has been partially restored to reflect its decades as a hub for daily commuters and newly arrived immigrants. Inside is a small museum of local history.

Jersey City Museum. 350 Montgomery St., Jersey City; (201) 413-0303; www.jerseycity museum.org. Talk about a checkered past! The museum was founded in 1901 as a teaching institution and was part of the Jersey City Free Public Library for a century. Its focus was art, science, industry, and history. After hitting some bumps in the road—and having to put its collections into storage—the museum separated from the library and moved into a restored 1920s building. The 30,000-square-foot layout has eight galleries, the152-seat Caroline L. Guarini Theater, two state-of-the-art classrooms, and an atrium lobby with skylight. Since the move, the museum is considered the premier presenter of contemporary art in New Jersey. Open Wed through Sat, noon to 5 p.m. To do research in one of the galleries, make an appointment. Admission is $5 for adults and $3 for seniors and students.

where to eat

The Chart House. Lincoln Harbor Pier D-T, Weehawken; (201) 348-6628; www.chart-house .com. The view is the true attraction here, with terraces, dining rooms, and bars on the Hudson River facing the Manhattan skyline. There are numerous Chart House locations around the United States, including one in Atlantic City, but few can compete with this vista. It is the perfect location for a special-occasion cocktail or meal. On our last visit, the food was surprisingly wanting—yet food is almost always secondary to the setting—and the restaurant has had its share of positive reviews over the years. Owned by Texas-based Landry's Restaurants, the Chart House menu provides plenty of choices, from fresh seafood to prime rib, steaks, and chicken. Open daily for dinner, Sat for lunch, and Sun for brunch. $$$.

Liberty House Restaurant. 76 Audrey Zapp Dr., Jersey City; (201) 395-0300; www.liberty houserestaurant.com. The "view with a room" overlooks the Manhattan skyline and serves food to compete with the dynamic vista. Open for lunch, dinner, and Sunday brunch, Liberty House is closed on Mon. It also is much-in-demand for weddings and other special events. Dine indoors at tables and banquettes, or outside on the terrace. The cuisine is contemporary American, plus sushi and raw-bar favorites. There is a full bar, wine list, and beer selections. $$.

The Restaurants at Newport. Hudson River waterfront, Jersey City; www.newportnj .com/restaurants. Choose among 13 places to eat, whether you favor American, Chinese, Cuban, Indian, Italian, Japanese, or Mexican food; pub grub, sandwiches, ice cream, courtyard fare, or Starbucks to spare. $–$$$.

The Statue of Liberty Crown Cafe. On Liberty Island. Select from sandwiches and burgers, panini, pizza, and salads. Chicken, pork, tilapia, lobster roll, shrimp, and crab. Outdoor tables are plentiful, and many chairs and benches are under shade trees. The facility is an award-winner—selected for *Event Solutions* magazine's 2010 Spotlight Award for Event

pyrotechnic passionistas

New Jersey pops, all by itself. And anytime there is a fireworks display in New York Harbor, you can see, hear, or feel the excitement on this side of the Hudson. Plenty of time, the magic is courtesy of Fireworks by Grucci, a family-owned, multi-generational enterprise that began in Italy in 1850. Two decades later, founder Angelo Lanzetta moved his incendiary innovations to Long Island. In the 1920s, his son recruited Lanzetta's nephew, Felix Grucci Sr., as an apprentice, launching a new generation of energy and dedication to the ancient science of celebration. Felix met and married Concetta DiDio, and their three children—James, Donna, and Felix Jr.—joined the family business. Their success remained largely regional, in the tri-state area of New Jersey, Connecticut, and New York, until the nation's centennial in 1976. Then, television viewers nationwide witnessed the images of Fireworks by Grucci as they appeared over the Charles River, with music by the Boston Pops. Later kudos prompted the press to call the company "America's First Family of Fireworks." Donna Grucci Butler continues to run the company, along with her son, Felix "Phil" Grucci. These days, shows are in several price ranges. They reflect the time and scope of the display and other factors—so you can choose between $5,000 and $175,000 worth of kaboom.

Site of the Year. More interesting, however, is the background of said company. As of 2011, Evelyn Hill Inc. has been providing food and merchandise to the Statue of Liberty and Ellis Island for 80-plus years. Aaron Hill and his wife, Evelyn, were so successful from the outset that their son, James I. Hill, continued the operation for 46 years. Now, his son, Bradford A. Hill, runs the ever-evolving show under a National Park Service contract. The menu is tasty and affordable. $.

where to shop

Hudson Mall. 701 Rt. 440 South, Jersey City; (201) 432-0119; www.shophudsonmall .com. This regional mall has 50 stores—Marshalls, Staples, and Old Navy, for example, plus Good Fortune Feng Shui & Gifts, and the Shoe Dept. There are nine restaurants and a seven-screen cinema.

Newport Centre Mall. 30 Mall Dr. West, Jersey City; (201) 626-2025; www.simon.com. Newport is a major merchandising center with 130 specialty stores on three levels. Kohl's and Macy's are two of the anchors. It has an 11-screen cinema, a food court, and 15 other places to eat in the mall.

Newport River Market. River Drive, Jersey City; www.newportnj.com. The upscale market along the waterfront is a central feature of Newport, an upscale mixed-use community across the Hudson River from the World Financial Center of Manhattan. There are 50 outdoor shops.

worth more time

Liberty Science Center. 222 Jersey City Blvd., Jersey City; (201) 200-1000; www.lsc .org. LSC is all about connecting the dots among nature, humanity, and technology. It first opened in 1993 and needed to expand after attracting millions of visitors in the first dozen years. It reopened in 2007 after two years of makeover—a $109 million renovation with hundreds of exhibits in eight new galleries and the nation's largest IMAX Dome Theater. What goes on at LSC is said to be a model in the global science museum field. To get here, take the New Jersey Turnpike to exit 14C and stay in the right lanes at the toll; the exit to Liberty State Park is immediately after the toll. Take the first right onto Jersey City Boulevard, then a prompt left into the parking lot.

day trip 03

gateway

>>> **billets-doux to broadway:**
manhattan

Forever plaid, checked, striped, solid—woven, knit, tie-dyed, embossed, and embroidered onto the psyche of live-theater buffs—"The Great White Way" is just around the corner from northern New Jersey. The GWW moniker was coined in 1902 in a headline in *The New York Evening Telegram,* to refer to the bright lights of box office marquees.

More than half a century later, the same stretches of sidewalk were readily identified as a red-light district. But today, people are hanging up the stereotypes. You wanna sit on the edge of your seat? C'mon down to Broadway for cutting-edge drama, quirky satire, and the most feel-good musicals ever to debut.

manhattan

getting there

From northern New Jersey, exit the Garden State Parkway or the New Jersey Turnpike onto NJ 3 east; merge onto NJ 495 (a partial toll road formerly called I-495) and follow signs to Weehawken for a short ferry ride to West 39th Street in New York. The NY Waterway fare includes bus service to countless points near your chosen venue. If you prefer to drive into the city, stay on NJ 495 through the Lincoln Tunnel; locate a parking garage and choose your magic.

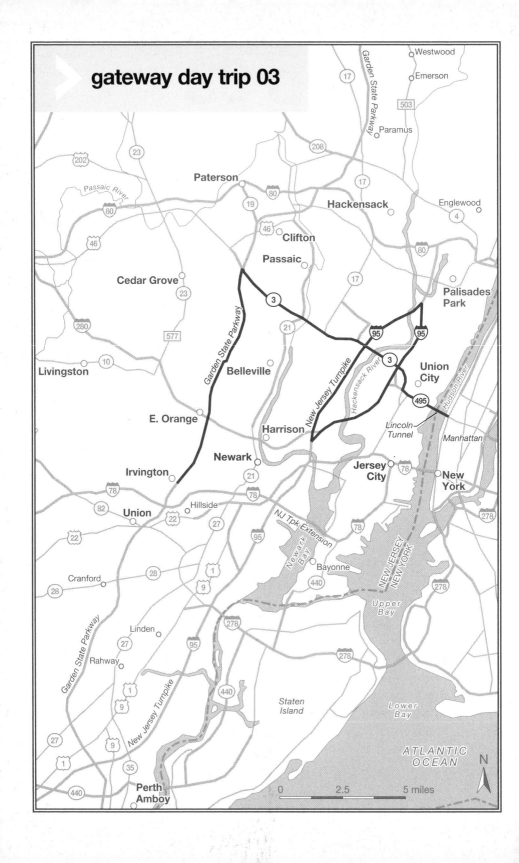

gateway day trip 03

where to go

Broadway and Off-Broadway. www.broadway.com. Say you can't get enough of *Jersey Boys*: To reach the August Wilson Theatre, 247 W. 52nd St., stay on 40th Street, turn left onto 8th Avenue, and turn right onto 52nd Street. There is a parking garage next to the theater. Nostalgic for another dose of a classic such as *The Phantom of the Opera*? Find the Majestic Theater, 247 W. 44th St., where the production continues as the longest-running show in Broadway history—since 1988. Newer titles on the marquees include *Master Class, The Book of Mormon, All New People,* and *Venus in Fur.* For current schedules and venues, check the website.

***Intrepid* Sea, Air and Space Museum.** 1 Intrepid Square, New York; (212) 245-0072; www.intrepidmuseum.org. Docked at 46th Street and 12th Avenue, the ship is very handy to the ferry terminal at 39th Street. The US Navy's aircraft carrier *Intrepid* is a National Historic Landmark, an interesting outing, an education, and an adventure. A famous platform for fighter pilots during World War II and Vietnam—and essential to NASA recovery missions—it became a museum in 1982. You can see amazing artifacts, sit in an A-6 cockpit, tour the inside of the Concorde, and visit a Virtual Flight Zone. Take children to the Exploreum Hall for lively lessons; and put in at Pier 86 for a snack at the Au Bon Pain Cafe and browsing in the museum store. Pier 86 also houses the Intrepid Welcome Center and Box Office.

Trump Tower. 725 Fifth Ave., New York. The late architect Der Scutt designed this 58-story, mixed-use skyscraper, which opened in 1983 with retail, commercial, and residential components. Being next door to Tiffany & Company is interesting, but Trump Tower has other noteworthy tidbits. There is, of course, the visually engaging multistory atrium with waterfalls, restaurants and bars, a Starbucks location, and pristine "comfort stations"—even if you didn't buy a souvenir, a cocktail, or a salad. There is the Gucci flagship retail store on the ground floor; and the fact that billionaire real estate developer Donald Trump lives here with his wife, Melania, and their son Barron; and that Trump, as host and executive producer of the NBC reality show *The Apprentice,* finds it convenient for show creator Mark Burnett to film the episodes here; and that fans show up in droves on a daily basis to see who is on first—or, gasp, on the pink path. Tenants in Trump Tower include a hemispheric football conference, Qatar Airlines, Prince Mutaib bin Abdul-Aziz of the Saudi royal family, maybe Bruce Willis chillin'—or Beyoncé regroupin'—and Erik Prince, who definitely knows where to park his gear.

where to shop

The Shops at Columbus Circle. 10 Columbus Circle, New York; (212) 823-6300; www.shopsatcolumbuscircle.com. This very upscale chic destination comprises 40 style-centric luxury retailers, cutting-edge restaurants, a Whole Foods market, and the nearness of Jazz at Lincoln Center—all within the Time Warner Center. For the most magnificent views of southern Central Park, find a window table at the MObar in the Mandarin Oriental. Restaurants in the center with superb views include A Voce Columbus (modern Italian), Asiate (contemporary Asian), and Porter House New York (a steak house). Celebrity chefs who have set up shop here include Thomas Keller, Masayoshi Takayama, Michael Lomonaco, March Murphy, and Missy Robbins.

where to eat

Daniel. 60 E. 65th St., New York; (212) 288-0033; www.danielnyc.com. If the ultimate gourmet dining experience is on your bucket list for the day, you have arrived at the right address. The flagship restaurant of Daniel Boulud, this bastion of French delicacies reflects every aspect of his passion for food, wine, decor, tableware, and atmosphere. The très entrepreneurial Daniel also creates lines of cookware and kitchen implements for serious foodies. A protégé, Lyon-native Jean François Bruel, is the executive chef. $$$.

db Bistro Moderne. 55 W. 44th St., New York; (212) 391-2400; www.danielnyc.com. Part of Daniel Boulud's empire, this contemporary and more casual den is still upscale—in fact it was here that Boulud introduced his now famous db Burger. Then, $28; today, $32, but well worth the price to experience this premium sirloin patty stuffed with braised beef short ribs and black truffle and served on a parmesan bun with *pommes frites*. Check out his website for the Broadway Matinee Brunch specials. $$$.

Gallagher's. 228 W. 52nd St., New York; (212) 245-5366; www.gallaghersnysteakhouse .com. The legend lives on, as it has since Prohibition, when people in the know knew where to find an illicit beverage to go with a fine charcoal-charred steak. Open since 1927, Gallagher's reeks of history and still packs in the public. $$.

Nougatine at Jean Georges. 1 Central Park West, New York; (212) 299-3900; www .jean-georges.com. Operated by star chef/restaurateur Jean-Georges Vongerichten, this restaurant and the more formal Jean Georges have very high-profile locations off the lobby of the Trump International Hotel & Tower. Vongerichten operates many spots all over the city—each one accentuating a local neighborhood with a combination of French techniques and his fondness for Asian-fusion dishes. See his website for all the locations. $$$.

Patsy's Italian Restaurant. 236 W. 56th St., New York; (212) 247-3491; www.patsys .com. This family-owned, traditional Neapolitan landmark in the theater district has been drawing repeat customers since 1944. Talk about vertical integration! Only three chefs have presided over the menu for all that time: Pasquale "Patsy" Scognamillo, his son Joe, and Joe's son Sal. It also is a celebrity favorite. $$.

Primola. 1226 2nd Ave., near 64th St., New York; (212) 758-1775. East Siders who seek out like company seem to love this neighborhood-y Italian place with an intimate bilevel dining layout and cozy bar. Owner Giuliano Zuliani offers both *prix-fixe* and *a la carte* menus.

Maybe another attraction in recent years is that it was Bernie Madoff's favorite—and his victims like to dine while keeping in mind that he misses Primolo like crazy. Try the Gli Apri Bocca di Franco, an array of seasonal vegetables, and the seafood risotto. $$$.

Swifty's Restaurant. 1007 Lexington Ave. (between 72nd and 73rd Streets), New York; (212) 535-6000; www.swiftysnyc.com. Renowned for its American and Euro-accented menu, Swifty's attracts people who are attracted to style and substance without a second helping of pretension. Patrons rave about the luscious lobster roll—so why argue? Open for lunch and dinner. $$.

Uncle Jack's Steakhouse. 440 9th Ave., New York; (212) 244-0005; and 44 W. 56th St., New York; (212) 245-1550; www.unclejacks.com. With two locations in Manhattan, you can't take a wrong turn at Jack's. USDA Prime beef and Kobe steaks are the passwords here, but count on seafood choices such as lobster, Alaskan crab, salmon, and sea bass. The lunch menu is equally superb—offering Jack's version of a French dip, known as the Kobe Rib Club. While making reservations online, check out logo items, cutlery, and Uncle Jack's small-batch custom sauces in the gift shop. If you enjoy upscale, elegant dining, you will enjoy this splurge. $$$.

where to stay

The Mandarin Oriental. 80 Columbus Circle (35th floor, Time Warner Center), New York; (212) 805-8800; www.mandarinoriental.com/newyork. Recently, the luxury hotel was offering a great deal, "Wine, Dine & Delight." The promotion included a night's accommodation and a chef's tasting at one of Time Warner's restaurants. $$$$.

Trump International Hotel & Tower. 1 Central Park West, New York; (212) 299-1000; www.trumpintl.com. A plum perch, *mais non*?—across the street from Central Park; steps from Broadway, and a short cab ride to the theater district; also near Lincoln Center and the Time Warner Center. If you crave an indulgence, book a luxury room or suite, dawdle in the spa, dine well without leaving the premises, and take in the vista of New York's skyline. Donald Trump understands living large, whether the stay is for just the two of you or a special occasion for the whole family. See the website for seasonal specials such as complimentary breakfast and a third night for free. $$$$.

day trip 04

gateway

the hudson in a bottleneck:
west point, ny (including highland falls); stony point, ny; haverstraw, ny; central valley, ny

Here, at a 90-degree angle in the Hudson River, the history of the new republic took a leap of faith. And shortly, fresh cadets will become West Point plebes. But first, they will experience some toughening up—research, recreation, reconnoitering, and an oh-mi-god regimen of physical and mental preparedness. While it isn't easy to get accepted and receive a free education at the United States Military Academy, the bonus is four years in the history-laden lap of heroes and heroines.

West Point is literally across the street from Highland Falls. And Haverstraw, situated on the widest part of the river, has some unique sites and stories to tell.

west point, ny (including highland falls)

getting there

From the Newark area, the trip takes about 1 hour and 30 minutes. Take the New Jersey Turnpike (I-95) to exit 73, right before the George Washington Bridge. Turn left at Lemoine Avenue for 0.5 mile, bearing right onto the Palisades Interstate Parkway. Go north for 37 miles until the highway ends at the Bear Mountain Bridge traffic circle. Go ¾ of the way

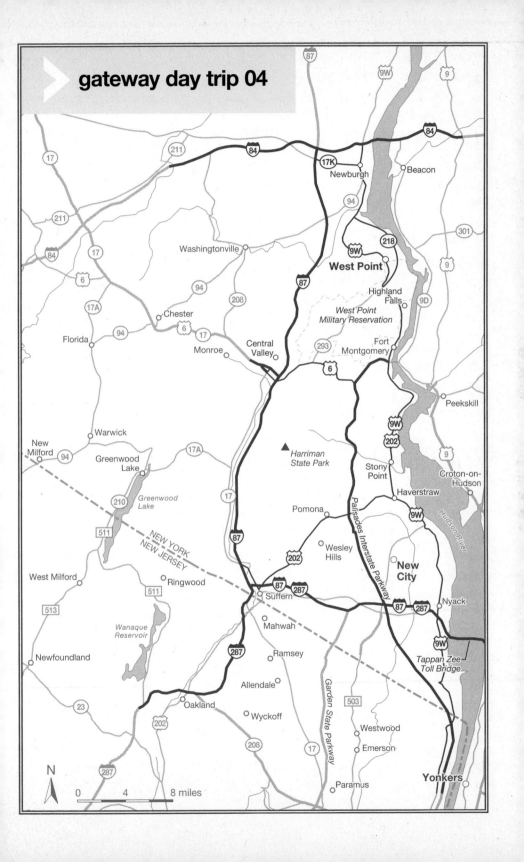

gateway day trip 04

around the circle onto US 9W north. Go about 3 miles, then turn right onto NY 218 north, toward Highland Falls. Follow signs for the West Point Visitor Center.

As long as you have a photo ID, visitors are welcome to be among half a million a year at this amazing National Historic Landmark and working Army base. In addition to tours of the stunning campus, the surrounding countryside offers abundant historic sites, magnificent outdoor activities, quaint towns, and plenty of reasons to linger for several hours or days.

where to go

West Point Museum. Pershing Center, West Point Military Reservation; (845) 938-3590; www.usma.edu/museum. The oldest military museum in the United States has the largest collections devoted to military history. The museum is adjacent to the West Point Visitor Center and a short distance south of the main entrance to West Point (Thayer Gate). The impetus for its collection was courtesy of the British after their defeat at Saratoga in 1777. British materials confiscated there were stashed at "Fortress West Point," and were among the first Revolutionary War trophies to be used for cadet instruction when West Point was founded in 1802.

United States Military Academy. Pershing Center, West Point Military Reservation; (845) 938-2638; www.westpointtours.com. Begin your excursion at the West Point Visitors Center just south of the Thayer Gate. Hours are 9 a.m. to 4:45 p.m., except for Thanksgiving, Christmas, and New Year's Day. There are fascinating exhibits, and the staff makes it easy for you to plan your "maneuvers"—opting for a 1-hour or 2-hour bus tour of West Point. One-hour tours cost $12 for adults and $9 for children; 2-hour tours cost $14 and $12. There is some walking involved, when you get off the bus and walk around Trophy Point. West Point as a whole is a paradox, in that the surrounding terrain is both calming and awe-inspiring while the institution's purpose for two centuries-plus has been to hone the nation's military edge. Fort Putnam—in place almost a quarter century before the Academy opened—was key to defending "Fortress West Point." Its cannons protected land up and down the Hudson. The fort is on Delafield Road north of Michie Stadium. Admission to Fort Putnam is free. It is open seasonally and is not wheelchair accessible.

Trophy Point Concerts. Trophy Point overlooks the Hudson River facing north at West Point; www.westpointonhudson.com. Each Sunday in summer through Labor Day, lawn concerts are free and open to the public. The band shell backs up to what is called West Point's "million-dollar view," and various ensembles perform light classics, opera overtures, John Philip Sousa marches, hits from Broadway musicals, and soundtracks from Hollywood movies. Bring a picnic and something to sit on.

Constitution Island. In the Hudson River off West Point; (845) 446-8676; www.consti tutionisland.org. Tours of the historic isle leave from West Point's South Dock. Originally

quoins of the realm

When you visit West Point, know this going in: The motto here is "Duty, Honor, Country," and it is a recurring theme chiseled into the quoins of many campus buildings. Other symbols you see frequently are carvings of an American eagle, the national shield, and the helmet of Pallas Athena, Greek war goddess. The military-Gothic buildings are impressive, from the cadets' chapel to Pershing Barracks. Faculty residences on Professors Row include the dean's digs, a Victorian-style villa, circa 1857, built in the Hudson Valley vernacular. Numerous statues of heroes bring you into the take-away of this heritage—and its startling continuity from the 18th century to right this minute. If you are lucky, you will see teenage cadets toting weapons and bedrolls, climbing out of trucks, and walking around landmarks to learn about their new home. They look impressed—much as visitors do.

named Martelaer's Rock, and renamed Constitution Island in 1775, it is a few football fields east of West Point. As seen from Sherburne Battery at Trophy Point, the island lines up almost perfectly with the mountains beyond it. The island and the mainland were anchors for the famous Great Chain, a heavy system of metal links attached to a log boom and placed across the Hudson River. General Washington and his team created the ploy to keep British naval vessels from gaining river access during the Revolutionary War. An original remnant is on display at Trophy Point. Polish-born Col. Thaddeus Kosciuszko directed the chain construction at West Point and on Constitution Island.

where to shop

Daughters of the US Army Gift Shop. Inside the West Point Museum; www.dusagiftshop .org. This is insignia-centric, with apparel for men, women, and children, tabletop items such as placemats and bottle-stoppers, plus gifts for the home and office.

West Point Gift Shop. Inside the Visitors Center; (845) 938-2638; www.westpointgiftstore .com. The specialty is fitness and athletic wear for men, women, and children, as well as books, charts, souvenirs, and West Point–themed gift items. There are home decor items, hats and visors, towels and blankets, and golf gear such as towels and head covers.

West Point Wines & Spirits. 521 Main St., Highland Falls; (845) 446-7777. The shop sells all the usual suspects, along with baskets and gift items. If you're trying a new wine, it may as well be the one with the "West Point" label.

where to eat

Most restaurants near West Point are in historic Highland Falls, a village just across the street from the visitor's center. (Also see dining options inside The Thayer Hotel in the "Where to Stay" section below.)

Highland Falls Market. 447 Main St., Highland Falls; (845) 446-3992; www.highlandfalls market.com. This restaurant and market opens at 6 a.m. daily. You can order breakfast all day long, sample lunch specials, and stop by until 11 p.m. or midnight on weekends. The brand is Boar's Head, and the market offers free delivery and catering. $.

The Park Restaurant. 451 Main St., Highland Falls; (845) 446-8709; www.parkrest.com. Anna and John Pozo opened the place in 1956 in a building that was already a century old. It had housed a hotel, then a bar, before the Pozos posed the motto "Good food, good friends, and a good place to be." The family's third generation uses the same bragging rights today. Steaks—plain, Cajun or Montreal-style—are among the grill choices. Choose among seafood and chicken specials, barbecue rib combos, pasta dishes, salads, sandwiches, Southwest wraps, and baskets of fried shrimp or clams. Open for breakfast, lunch, and dinner; closed Mon. $.

Schade's Restaurant. 457 Main St., Highland Falls; (845) 446-2626; www.schades restaurant.com. This family outfit draws people from the village and around the West Point reservation. The menu is meant to please: pizza, calzones, steaks, seafood, pasta, salads, soups, sandwiches, and wraps, plus beer, wine, and cocktails. $.

Sushi King and Deli. 323 Main St., Highland Falls; (845) 446-1458; www.sushikingonline .com. This ambitious operation covers its bases, with sushi a la carte, rolls, hand rolls, and specialty rolls, plus sashimi boats, Korean dishes, and Western classics such as grilled sandwiches and wraps, hoagies, and salads. They serve a Southern Italian combo, as well as Northern Italian, plus the Crazy Randy—piles of turkey, ham, salami, Muenster, lettuce, onion, and honey mustard on a hero roll. Sushi King serves lunch and dinner six days and closes Sun. $.

where to stay

Bear Mountain Inn. The Palisades Region; www.visitbearmountain.com. Check on the renovation schedule of the main inn. Alternatives include the Overlook Lodge and the Stone Cottages at Bear Mountain Inn.

The Thayer Hotel. 674 Thayer Rd., just inside West Point's main gate; (845) 446-4731; www.thethayerhotel.com. It opened in 1926 as lodgings for Academy personnel and their guests, and today is the only private property at West Point. The hotel was named for Colonel Sylvanius Thayer, superintendent of the Military Academy from 1817 to 1833. It's a full-service luxury hotel, listed on the National Registry, with 149 guest rooms and suites and a restaurant and lounge on the premises. The Thomas Jefferson Patio opens in the summer for *alfresco* dining on the deck overlooking the Hudson. MacArthur's Restaurant, the newly renovated Gothic-style main dining room, serves breakfast, lunch, dinner, and Sunday brunch. For lighter meals and cocktails, there is General Patton's Tavern, where complimentary hors d'oeuvres on Friday are a real bargain. Energetic night owls might consider the hotel's rooftop ZuluTime Lounge. All in all, The Thayer is a unique perch from which to tour West Point or take in the surrounding attractions and activities—from skiing and snowboarding to golf, fishing, and cruises on the Hudson. $$.

stony point, ny

Stony Point is home to many historical markers such as the Springsteel Farm House, which was built in 1779, Washington Wayne Lookout, the Stony Point Lighthouse, and the Iona Island & Marsh. Gothic-style gates mark the entrance to Stony Point State Park.

getting there

This rural berg is about 15 miles south of West Point off US 9W. It is Rockland County's most rural town.

where to go

Harriman State Park. Stony Point, just south of West Point, NY; (845) 786-2701; www .nysparks.com. Less than an hour from Newark, Harriman State Park borders Bear Mountain State Park and the 16,000-acre forest reserve at West Point. Harriman partly borders Sterling Forest. Hiking trails are maintained by the New York-New Jersey Trail Conference. Harriman has more than 46,000 acres and is New York's second largest state park. Hikers may enjoy more than 200 miles of trails—including more than half of the Appalachian Trail. There are more than three dozen lakes, plus streams, camping areas, and scenic views.

Bear Mountain State Park. Bear Mountain, NY; (845) 786-2701; www.nysparks.state.ny .us/parks. This 5,000-acre mountainous state park on the west bank of the Hudson River, just south of West Point, is a scenic trove for a shady picnic, fishing, swimming, bike riding, hiking, and cross-country ski trails. The roadway to Bear Mountain takes you past several Roman-style stone bridge overpasses. Ice skaters may glide on an outdoor rink from late October through mid-March. The Perkins Memorial Tower atop Bear Mountain—1,305 feet above the Hudson—is a dynamite viewing ground of the park and the whole 16-mile run of the Hudson Highlands. The tower is open from April through late November, weather permitting. For a truly breathtaking view up and down the Hudson, ride over the Bear Mountain Bridge.

Stony Point Battlefield. Route 9 West and Park Road, Stony Point; (845) 786-2521; www .nysparks.com/historic-sites. This historic site, museum, and lighthouse are about 14 miles south of West Point. By summer 1779, both the Americans and the British were weary of the Revolutionary War's toll. Gen. Washington was intent on outwitting Gen. Henry Clinton, who had attempted to force his foe into a final battle for river domination. When Clinton zeroed in on Stony Point, Washington put Brigadier Gen. Anthony Wayne in charge of lead- ing an attack. Carrying only bayonets, Wayne's infantry completed a successful late-night raid to confiscate Clinton's site and take his soldiers prisoner. Stony Point ended British control of the river and was one of the last battles of the war. Its museum has exhibits on the battle and the Stony Point Lighthouse, plus reenactments of 18th-century military life, displays, and children's activities. The 1826 Stony Point Lighthouse is the oldest beacon on the Hudson River, where it fulfilled its mission for almost a century. Tours inside the lighthouse are available Wed through Fri during museum hours, depending on weather and staff availability. Picnic facilities are available.

where to eat

Fireside Steak Pub. 84 N. Liberty Dr., Stony Point; (845) 429-0484. A year-round opera- tion serving lunch and dinner. $.

The River Barge & Grill. Stony Point Bay Marina, 36 Hudson Dr., Stony Point; www.stony pointbaymarina.com. There is a restaurant separate from the marina and it has indoor and outdoor dining and spectacular views of the Hudson River. $.

haverstraw, ny

So what do Babe Ruth, the Hitchcock thriller *Psycho,* and treason have in common? The answer is Haverstraw (originally Haverstroo, the Dutch phrase for "oat straw"). This is the town where American traitor Benedict Arnold and British Major John André went to hammer out a deal to swap detailed plans of "Fortress West Point."

getting there

Take the Palisades Interstate Parkway to exit 12, US 303 North; go to US 9W and ride north to New Main Street.

where to go

Haverstraw Brick Museum. 12 Main St., Haverstraw; (845) 947-3505; www.haverstraw brickmuseum.org. Inasmuch as the village was known as "the brick-making capital of the world" for more than a century—and supplied materials for trophy buildings in New Jersey and New York—the museum honors this legacy. The industry began in 1771 when Jacob

Van Dyke made bricks by hand from yellow and bluish clay beds along the river. This was more than a century after Henry Hudson anchored the *Half Moon* here during his explorations. Hours are 1 to 4 p.m. Wed, Sat, and Sun, or by appointment; donation $2.

M/V Commander. Haverstraw Marina, Haverstraw; (845) 534-7245; www.commander boat.com. You may charter the legendary *Commander* for private parties, and it is available for group excursions from May through Oct. The vessel is rare and something of a hybrid— a design link between heavy, late-19th-century steamboats and lighter craft in the century that followed. *Commander* was listed in 1984 on both the National and New York registers of historic places, the *International Register of Historic Ships, Great American Ships,* and *The Dictionary of American Naval Fighting Ships.* She is the last operating vessel in the US Navy that dates to World War I and bears a Victory medal for combat service. *Commander* takes passengers to and from Haverstraw, West Point, and Peekskill. Rates are $18 for adults and $16 for seniors and students. Reservations are required.

where to eat

Civile's Venice on the Hudson. 16 Front St., Haverstraw; (845) 428-3891; www.civiles .net. Capitalizing on its waterfront location at Emeline Park, the restaurant opened in 1998 and specializes in contemporary Italian fare. As a devotee of *alfresco* dining, owner Tom Civile is a happy man. The restaurant is open for lunch and dinner daily during the summer and for dinner on weekends in the winter. The fall, spring, and holiday schedule adjusts to customer clamor. Murals of Venice decorate the inside dining room; outdoor dining lasts well into October, with a heated tent for chilly days. Much of the time, you may bring your own wine without a corkage fee. There also is an ample wine list, thanks to a 3,500-bottle cellar. There is a new boat docking facility. $$.

Union Restaurant & Latino Bar. 22–24 New Main St., Haverstraw; (845) 429-4354; www.unionrestaurant.net. Located in the historic Pressler Building, Union is co-owned by Chef David Martinez and Maitre d' Paulo Feteira. They cater to locals and visitors who love recipes from south of the border, some creative Latin-fusion, and a patio to relax over the

inspiration for art & film

On US 9W just north of New Main Street in Haverstraw, a house stands defiantly, and it poses a spooky sense of déjà vu. And not because it was interpreted in Edward Hopper's painting, The House By The Railroad. *The house also inspired the creeped-out digs of the film character Norman Bates, played by Anthony Perkins, in Alfred Hitchcock's 1960 movie thriller* Psycho.

meal. The restaurant opened in 2007 and a year later was getting lots of ink: "Best New Restaurant" in the *Hudson Valley News,* and "Best Restaurant of the Year" in *Rockland Magazine.* Also, Martinez got kudos in *Hudson Valley Magazine,* which called him one of the "Hot New Chefs of the Hudson Valley." Union is open for lunch and dinner and closes Mon. Bar Latino has live music on Friday. $$.

where to stay

The Bricktown Inn. 112 Hudson St., Haverstraw; (845) 429-8447; www.bricktowninnbnb .com. A Victorian-era bed-and-breakfast, circa 1885, the building originated as the home of a prominent family who owned a local brickyard. The innkeepers are Michelle and Joe Natale, and guests sing their praises for clean, comfortable, charming rooms and delicious meals. Breakfast is a big hit—can you say poached-pear pancakes three times real fast? The inn's recent renovation added today-friendly amenities while retaining the historic high ceilings, plaster moldings, and mahogany staircase. Guest rooms are decorated with heirloom-quality antiques. The parlor has an inviting baby grand player piano, and there's a library plugged with books and collectibles. Swing on the porch, or rock, if you prefer, on wicker chairs. There is on-site parking. $.

central valley, ny

One big draw here is outlet shopping. Nearby towns and villages also draw browsers interested in exploring local antiques shops, art galleries, and novelty retailers.

getting there

Take the Palisades Interstate Parkway north to exit 18 (US 6 west); exit onto NY 32 north (right turn at traffic light).

where to shop

Woodbury Common Premium Outlets. 498 Red Apple Court, Central Valley; (845) 928-4000; www.premiumoutlets.com. The complex has 220 stores touting routine savings on upscale and name-brand merchandise. Designer apparel for the whole family; shoe salons that would have made Imelda swoon; children's boutiques; leather and luggage; accessories and jewelry; and home furnishings and accessories. At least 17 food purveyors mean you won't shop hungry.

where to eat

Cosimo's Woodbury. 100 Route 32, Central Valley; (845) 928-5222; www.cosimoswood bury.com. A wood-burning brick oven is the chef's secret to authentic Tuscan flavor and innovations made possible from fresh, local produce. Handmade mozzarella is a tradition here, as it is in all the restaurants owned by this company. Cosimo's is close to the shops at Woodbury Common Premium Outlets described above. $–$$.

worth more time

Storm King Art Center. 1 Museum Rd., New Windsor, NY; www.stormking.org. This unusual museum devoted to sculpture and nature is northwest of West Point, east of US 87, and west of Route 32. A visit here could be combined with either a West Point tour or a Newburgh outing. Storm King comprises 500 acres of lawns and wooded outdoors devoted to the display of post-World War II sculpture. Many are large-scale abstracts, and the media range from steel to stone and clay. Sky is the limit at Storm King, where the viewer takes in each work of art in an "exhibit space" sans walls or artificial lighting; the ground, the sky, and the surrounding Hudson Highlands are the props for each center stage. The grounds are open from Apr to Nov. Admission is $12 for adults, $10 for seniors, and $8 for students. Storm King provides trams for visitors with limited mobility and young children, who may be given priority over other visitors. Visitors may disembark, walk, and reboard at designated points throughout the grounds. Storm King Cafe is located in the Art Center's outdoor pavilion. Managed by Fresh Company, it offers salads, sandwiches, snacks, and seasonal specials. $.

day trip 05

gateway

>>> **derailing a conspiracy:**
newburgh, ny; beacon, ny

Roller skates would have helped George Washington during the pivotal 16 months he stayed here. That busy bee oversaw the wind-down of the Revolutionary War from here; dissuaded a well-intentioned but misguided notion that he should become a king, here; pre-empted a military coup of the government, here; and created and awarded the first Badge of Military Merit, now called the Purple Heart, here. Also in Newburgh, Washington wrote to state governors about penning the US Constitution.

This was about a century after Dutch settlers staked claim to lands occupied by the Waoranek Indians. In 1609 British navigator Henry Hudson—sponsored by the Dutch East India Company—wrote that this perch on the river would be a nice spot for a town.

German Lutherans, the first European settlers, named it Palatine Parish. The Brits and Scots renamed it Newburgh.

newburgh, ny

getting there

From the greater Newark area, the trip takes about 1 hour and 45 minutes. Take the New Jersey Turnpike (I-95) to exit 73, right before the George Washington Bridge. Turn left at Lemoine Avenue and go half a mile, bearing right onto the Palisades Interstate Parkway. Go north for 37 miles until the highway ends at the Bear Mountain Bridge traffic circle. Go ¾

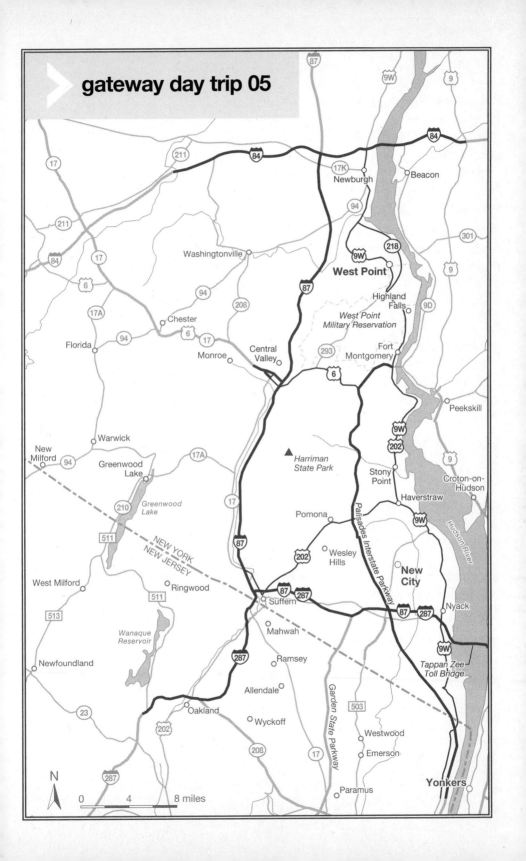

gateway day trip 05

of the way around the circle onto US 9W north. Newburgh is about a 15-minute ride north of West Point.

The Newburgh Waterfront is home to a dozen or more restaurants serving contemporary American fare, as well as theme menus and ethnic varieties. Many are situated in former industrial sites making good on the savvy strategy of adaptive re-uses.

where to go

East End Historic District. This section of Newburgh covers 445 acres and more than 2,000 notable properties, reflecting the architectural styles of various eras: mid-rise Italianate townhouses, Federal bungalows, Dutch Colonial digs, and Gothic-Revival. Even so, Hudson's sentiment is alive today: it was a nice place to start a town. The revived waterfront is a bustling rendezvous—with appealing stops created in abandoned buildings from the Industrial era.

Hudson River Adventures. Torches Landing on Front Street, Newburgh; (845) 220-2120; www.prideofthehudson.com. To get an overview of the splendid Hudson Highlands, there's nothing like a river cruise. Aboard the *Pride of the Hudson,* the captain narrates landmarks on the voyage such as Mount Beacon, Pollepel Island, and Bannerman's Castle. The schedule is May to Oct. This vessel is one good way to see bunches and choose the nuggets you favor. It's advisable to book cruises in advance, as the company adjusts the schedule for private charters. The main salon with wraparound windows is air-conditioned and heated. A topside sundeck and intimate foredeck are great for fresh-air buffs. The top and main decks have bar service. A companion vessel, the motor launch *Pollepel,* takes adventurers for a rugged hike to Pollepel Island near Beacon, which was named for a freighter that crashed on the rocks. There, you can see the skeleton of Bannerman's Castle. Its ruins are testimony to the region's harsh winters, but there is a campaign afoot to rescue what is left of Francis Bannerman VI's folly. The New York City munitions merchant built the castle in the early 1900s for his powder stores and as an island getaway for the family. For updates on access to the castle, visit www.bannermancastle.org.

Washington's Headquarters State Historic Site. At Liberty and Washington Streets, Newburgh; (845) 562-1195; www.nysparks.com/historic-sites. The centerpiece here is the Dutch-style Hasbrouck House, the long-serving headquarters of George Washington during the Revolutionary War. Washington stayed at Jonathan Hasbrouck's home for 16 months. In 1850, the sturdy stone house became the first publicly operated historic site in the United States. It is furnished with period pieces and reproductions to reflect Washington's stay, and is the oldest house in Newburgh. An adjacent redbrick museum has military artifacts. It was here that Washington deflected a proposal that he create and lead an American monarchy, simultaneously preempting a mutiny of officers disgruntled over pay and pensions. Hasbrouck and his wife, Trintje, built the existing structure on the original foundation in 1750. The house was enlarged twice in the next two decades—and has three original jambs-less fireplaces—meaning no sides, just a fire-back and hood. Admission is $4 for adults, $3 for seniors and students.

The Captain David Crawford House. 189 Montgomery St., Newburgh; (845) 561-2585; www.newburghhistoricalsociety.com. Captain Crawford and his wife, Fanny Belknap, built the house in 1830 as a home for their two daughters. Crawford was a prominent maritime entrepreneur and instrumental in the town's 19th-century vogue. With Newburgh's position on the Hudson, it prospered from shipping and transportation for its many industries. The Crawford House took a page from English country homes inspired by Italian designer Andrea Palladio, and capitalized on its perch on 500 acres above Newburgh Bay. Design features include 40-foot Ionic columns, Palladian windows, ornate woodworking, and black marble fireplaces—even a carved mahogany dolphin newel-post on the staircase. The house is open Sunday, 1 to 4 p.m., May through Oct. Admission is $5. There is a gift shop on the main level featuring Hudson Valley items and books about the region.

where to eat

Torches on the Hudson. 120 Front St., Newburgh; (845) 568-0100; www.torchesonthehudson.com. The restaurant is on the northern end of the Newburgh Waterfront. You'll be tempted to head for an outdoor seat for panoramic views up and down the river; but don't neglect a tour of the dining room with its 6,000-square-foot saltwater aquarium, 25-foot ceilings, mahogany built-ins, and charming maritime decor. The restaurant opened in 2001 and is one of five properties owned by Cosimo Restaurant Group (a legacy of the late Cosimo di Brizzi). Torches' menu is democratic—steaks, seafood, pasta, salads, and sandwiches. There is a full bar and good wine selection. $$.

beacon, ny

Beacon was named for the signal fires on the mountains above Fishkill Landing, summits that alerted the Continental Army about the whereabouts of British troops. It is about 6 miles from Newburgh on the east side of the Hudson River.

When people tip their bonnets to Beacon, it's partly because it once was known as the "Hat Making Capital of the US." And if you are a fan of Paul Newman and/or Bruce Willis, much of *Nobody's Fool* was filmed on streets and in homes in Beacon.

getting there

To reach the Newburgh-Beacon Bridge over the Hudson, drive north on the New York State Thruway (I-87) to I-84 east/NY 52; take the exit to NY 9D south. A fun alternative is to take a ferry from the docks on Front Street in Newburgh to Waterfront Park in Beacon.

where to go

Dia: Beacon. 3 Beekman St., Beacon; (845) 440-0100; www.diabeacon.org. Open since 2003, Dia: Beacon, Riggio Galleries houses its permanent collection of major works of art from the 1960s to the present. Overlooking the Hudson River, it occupies almost 300,000 square feet of space in a former printing factory. The galleries' namesakes are patrons Louise and Leonard Riggio. Admission is $10 for adults, $7 for seniors and students. In addition to the galleries, there is a bookstore and cafe that serves sandwiches, salads and soups, coffee and pastries.

Madame Brett Homestead. 50 Van Nydeck Ave., Beacon; (845) 831-6533. The white clapboard house is the oldest original home in Duchess County. Listed on the National Register, the bungalow was built in 1709 and was home to seven generations of one family, until 1954. Catheryna Brett, the daughter of Francis Rombout and Helena Teller, inherited the land from her father. Her husband was Roger Brett, a lieutenant in the British navy. When they moved in, people said she was the first white woman to settle in the Hudson Highlands. During the Revolutionary War, their guests included General Washington, the French strategist and nobleman Marie Joseph Paul Yves Roche Gilbert du Motier—better known in America as the young Marquis de Lafayette—and Baron von Steuben. Its 17 rooms house a museum furnished with original 18th- and 19th-century pieces. On display is the grant giving Catheryna more than 28,000 acres of the Rombout Patent. The house has hand-hewn beams, scalloped cedar shingles, wide-board floor planks, sloped dormers, Dutch doors, and a native stone foundation. A garden and brook round out the 6-acre wooded homestead. The house is open the second Saturday of each month, 1 to 4 p.m., Apr through Dec and by appointment. Docents are members of the Melzingah Chapter of the Daughters of the American Revolution. Admission is $5 for adults and $2 for students.

worth more time

Hudson Highlands State Park. New York State took over lands in 1988 that included archaeological sites and ruins of buildings from assorted industries, especially brick-making. One site, Dennings Point, is off-shore from Beacon, and was named for the Dennings Point Brick Works established around 1885. Bricks made there from river clay remain today in the Empire State Building and Rockefeller Center, among others. The Hudson River Valley Ramble is an annual fall event which celebrates the landscape, culture, history, and industries of the region; www.hudsonrivervalleyramble.com.

day trip 06

gateway

>>> **fertile fields, a feisty flock:**
newark, nj (including elizabeth
& livingston)

The hub of the Gateway region is full of reminders that past transgressors don't get to have the last word. Today, downtown Newark is, because the city was, all about belief; about taking risks on faith. Newark was selected in 1666 by Puritans from the New Haven Colony, outraged by a royal decree allowing the Connecticut Colony to absorb them.

Robert Treat led these pioneers to a basin framed by the Passaic River and the marshes of Newark Bay. Many historic churches still standing—built in prominent architectural styles—reveal the role religion played.

Westward toward the Watchung Mountains was fecundity itself—lush, fruitful land as green as sunlight and water can make it. As the Dutch already understood, becoming the Garden State was New Jersey's destiny. Before long, shipping and rail heads made Newark the busiest transportation hub in the United States.

Until urban crises of the 1960s, Newark was as much a bastion of prosperity as nearby Manhattan. Notable piles of bricks are well-represented—Beaux Arts, Gothic, and Georgian styles among them. Art Deco buildings include several 1920s-era skyscrapers, such as the National Newark Building, the restored Newark Penn Station, and Arts High School. Moorish Revival buildings include Newark Symphony Hall and the Prince Street Synagogue, one of the oldest synagogues in New Jersey.

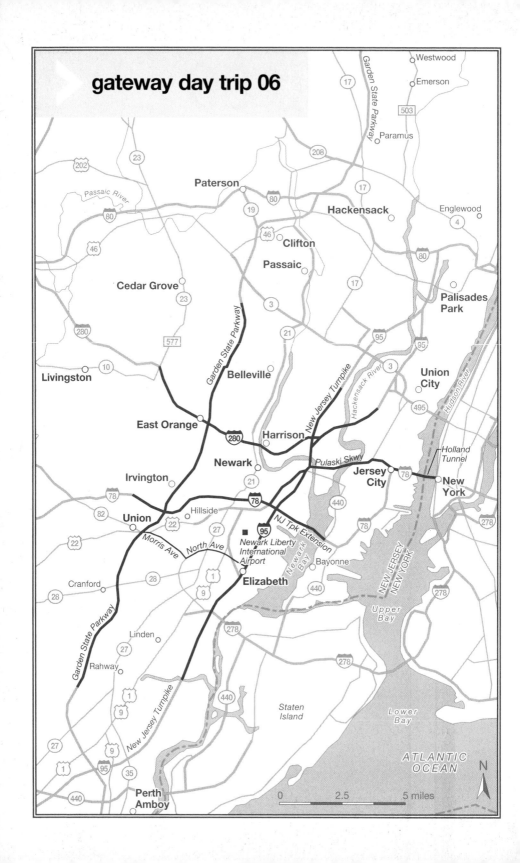

gateway day trip 06

newark, nj (including elizabeth & livingston)

getting there

From northern New Jersey and from the shore, use the Garden State Parkway; exit on I-280 east for Downtown Newark. From Manhattan, pretend you are Tony Soprano on a detour; exit on the west side of the Holland Tunnel to the General Pulaski Skyway; follow the signs for downtown Newark.

In 2011, Sundance Channel aired the second season—second chance, perhaps—of *Brick City,* a documentary about efforts to backpedal half a century of corruption and crime. It reveals a city able to go toe-to-toe with world-class culture and historic landmarks—all new reasons to visit Downtown. The city is changing—clawing back—for the better. As a result, Jersey boys and girls, even Newark natives, are taking notice anew.

where to go

Four Corners Historic District. The corner of Broad and Market Streets in Newark is "square one" for discerning the evolution of the city and is one of seven historic districts. This is where founder Robert Treat built his home in the 1600s. Today, Four Corners comprises 22 square blocks bounded by Raymond Boulevard, Mulberry Street, Hill and Washington Streets, and University Avenue.

New Jersey Performing Arts Center. 1 Center St., Newark; (888) 466-5722; www.njpac .org. Since it opened in 1997, NJPAC has been credited as the main catalyst for a growing Downtown revival. In addition to its headliner menu of cultural virtuosos and top entertainers, the center's 3-acre Theater Square hosts a free outdoor summer music series, "Sounds of the City," which has drawn upwards of 3,000 spectators to the Thursday evening hangs. The *New York Times* called the series " . . . Newark's town social." See the website for a calendar of pop and classical offerings.

Prudential Center. 165 Mulberry St., Newark; (973) 757-6000; www.prucenter.com. The multipurpose sports-entertainment arena is home to the National Hockey League's New Jersey Devils. When it opened in 2007, it was the first new major league sports venue in the New York-New Jersey Metropolitan area in more than 25 years. The center has attracted major reinvestment in the area and is credited with some of Downtown's optimism. On a summer night in 2011, a handful of tractor trailers idled a few blocks away—the ads on their container skins confirming what the paying public already knew: Taylor Swift was most definitely in the house.

Aljira, a Center for Contemporary Art. 591 Broad St., Newark; (973) 622-1600; www .aljira.org. Aljira has been exhibiting the work of emerging artists for more than a quarter of a century. Their origins are broad, and some are New Jersey natives. The center hosts an annual auction of fine art in the spring, as well. In its online shop, you can browse books, fine art, prints, and catalogs.

City Without Walls Gallery. 6 Crawford St., Newark; (973) 622-1188; www.cwow.org. The state's oldest nonprofit contemporary art gallery was founded in 1975. In recent years, cWOW has added a new cultural education program, "City Murals," which invites artists of all ages to design and create public murals in various neighborhoods. For example, a wall on Hawthorne Avenue in the South Ward was chosen to depict a tribute to bygone jazz clubs.

Branch Brook Park. Bloomfield Avenue at Lake Street, Newark; (973) 268-2300; www .branchbrookpark.org. The nation's first county park, Branch Brook Park dates to 1895— mainly because it took more than 30 years of legislation and debate to make it happen. In 1862, the Old Blue Jay Swamp was commandeered as a training ground for New Jersey volunteers during the Civil War. Five years later, Frederick Law Olmsted—the visionary of Central Park in Manhattan—chose the site for a park. It is about 4 miles long and 0.25 mile wide, covering 360 acres. In 1895, Essex County set aside the tract for a park. The swamp became a lake flanked by lawns and gardens. The park has more than 2,000 cherry trees, surpassing the variety in Washington DC, and its Cherry Blossom Festival in April attracts more than 10,000 people a day. Inside the Cherry Blossom Center, you will find a two-story atrium with a replica of a cherry tree, murals of cherry trees, and a painting of blossoms by a bridge in Japan. The park is open daily year-round and admission is free. Lakes, ponds, streams, and a threading brook form the backdrop for 19 bridges. There are fields for play- ing softball, bocce, and tennis; walking and biking trails, and a roller-skating rink. Seasonal events include concerts and outdoor movies.

Military Park. Broad Street at Park Place, Newark. Established in 1667 as a training ground for local militia—and later, a drill field for Colonial and Continental armies—Military Park is outwardly nondescript. A slim triangle, it hosts an iconic sculpture among several statues. In the center is *Wars of America,* a large bronze work by sculptor Gutzon Borglum, a native of Idaho who created the granite countenances of four US presidents on Mount Rushmore in the Black Hills of South Dakota. Borglum unveiled *Wars of America* in Newark in 1926. It interprets 42 human figures and two horses, and represents major US conflicts through World War I. Interesting to aficionados of art and history is the fact that Borglum included the faces of himself, his wife, and his son among the 42.

Old First Presbyterian Church. 820 Broad St., Newark; (973) 642-0260. Not just the oldest church in Newark (circa 1667), First Presbyterian was the village's first public building when it was founded as a Congregational Church. For the first four decades of village life, it was the seat of all discussion—the only legitimate forum for public, military, and religious affairs. Later generations reflected a budding religious tolerance, and in 1720, the members renamed it First Presbyterian Church. The current stone Georgian-style building was completed in 1791.

The Cathedral Basilica of the Sacred Heart. 89 Ridge St., Newark; (973) 484-4600; www.cathedralbasilica.org. Conveying undiluted Gothic grandeur, the fifth-largest cathedral in North America is among the largest in the Gothic style. Moreover, it has enough stained glass to shatter records at Chartres. On the flank of Branch Brook Park, it is the seat of Newark's Roman Catholic Diocese. Begun in 1899, the edifice was completed in the French Gothic vernacular half a century later. In 1995, when the late Pope John Paul II held services here, he elevated the status to basilica. When the public attends concerts throughout the year, they can enjoy music played on an organ featuring 154 ranks playable from dual consoles.

Essex County Courthouse. West Market Street at Dr. Martin Luther King Jr. Boulevard, Newark. Cass Gilbert, especially famous for the Woolworth Building in New York City, designed this Beaux Arts edifice, which dates to 1906. Situated on a tier below the Hall of Records, the plaza hosts Newark's second work by Mount Rushmore sculptor Gutzon Borglum—*Seated Lincoln.*

New Jersey Historical Society. 52 Park Place, Newark; (973) 596-8500; www.jerseyhistory.org. Established in 1845, the society is the oldest cultural institution in the state. Take in current exhibits and visit the research library containing documents, photographs, and maps. The society hosts walking tours, workshops, festivals, and occasional film series. Hours are Tues through Sat, 10 a.m. to 5 p.m.; $4 is the suggested donation.

Newark Museum. 49 Washington St., Newark; (973) 596-6550; www.newarkmuseum .org. The largest such complex in New Jersey, the Beaux Arts–style facility dates to 1909. In 2011 the museum marked the centennial of one of its most revered treasures—as it famously houses the most extensive collection of secular and religious Tibetan art outside of Tibet. Equally well-known for its exhibits of American, African-American, and Asian art, the museum comprises 80 arts and science galleries with permanent national and international collections, a mini-zoo with more than 100 animals, the Dreyfuss Planetarium, an auditorium, sculpture garden, and schoolhouse. Architect Michael Graves designed a $29 million expansion in 1989. Admission is $10 for adults, $6 for seniors, students, and children. Hours are Wed through Sun, noon to 5 p.m.; the Museum Cafe serves snacks and beverages from noon to 3:30 p.m. The Museum Shop sells jewelry and gifts. $.

Ballantine House. 43 Washington St., Newark; www.newarkmuseum.org/ballantinehouse .html. The 3-story brick and limestone mansion was built in 1885 for Jeannette and John Holme Ballantine. His father, Peter, founded Ballantine Brewers. Originally 27 rooms, Ballantine House is a lone reminder of the Victorian manses that rimmed Washington Park during the heyday of the Industrial Age. The home became a wing of the Newark Museum in 1937 and was restored in 1975. Featuring two floors of rooms decorated with authentic accoutrements of the Ballantines' luxurious lifestyle, the site is open during regular Newark Museum hours.

where to shop

Jersey Gardens Mall. 651 Kapkowski Rd., Elizabeth; (908) 354-5900; www.jerseygardens .com. It's located east of the New Jersey Turnpike, exit 13A. There are more than 200 stores under one roof, and one of the draws is tax-free shopping on clothes and shoes. There's a food court, kids' play area, and some restaurants.

William S. Rich & Son. 857 Broad St., Newark; (973) 623-1616; and 1089 Elizabeth Ave., Elizabeth; (908) 351-1110; www.richpawnnj.com. This jewelry business dates to 1890, and Frank Valvano has owned it since 1985. The company specializes in new and estate jewelry. Other locations are in Belleville, Union, Edison, Union City, and North Plainfield—making Rich & Son the state's largest fully licensed pawnbroker. The merchandise is gorgeous and the staff is friendly and professional.

where to eat

Fornos of Spain Restaurant. 47 Ferry St., Newark; (973) 589-4767; www.fornosrestau rant.com. Fans come here for tasty tapas such as gambas al ajillo (shrimp in garlic sauce) or to linger over a luscious paella Valenciana—a one-dish mélange of shellfish, chicken, sausage, rice, and saffron, most often ordered for two or more. Lunch and dinner. $.

Iberia Peninsula Restaurant. 63 Ferry St., Newark; (973) 344-5611; www.iberiaresta urants.com. Named for the peninsula that contains Spain and Portugal, this is two estab-lishments, plus a seasonal patio. Iberia Tavern was the original; the owners built Iberia Peninsula to meet demand. The newer restaurant is a cavernous temple to the rodizio experience—a prix-fixe way of enjoying all-you-can-eat barbecued meats, poultry, ribs, sausage, and more. One of the seafood favorites is Parrilhada, featuring shellfish, garlic, rice, and saffron. If you want to make friends with a 24-ounce lobster tail, you can do so here; lunch and dinner. $$.

The Ironbound. East of Penn Station; www.goironbound.com. Several streets in the district are considered hot spots for food and beverage. The draw here is authentic ethnic cuisine—mainly Portuguese, Spanish, and Brazilian restaurants—although there are a few Italian holdouts from the days when Ironbound spoke the lingo. Sip a Caipirinha, chow down on rodizio, nibble on some bacalhau, or buy a margherita pie. This moniker for part of Newark's East Ward is a nod to its location by multiple rail lines. Another nickname is Down Neck, because it borders an Adam's apple-bend in the Passaic River. Ferry Street is one main attraction—as witnessed when Spain beat Germany 1–0 in the World Cup of soccer. Cars pulled over to acknowledge a solid wall of dancing, cheering humanity in the street. Here are a few dining suggestions in the Ironbound:

> **Maize.** Located on the ground floor of the Robert Treat Hotel, 50 Park Place, Newark; (973) 733-2202. The original dwellers of Newark were the Lenape

Indians, who taught Colonial farmers what they knew about raising corn. So it's apropos that a hotel named for Newark's founder would name its restaurant Maize. It serves breakfast, lunch, and dinner, with tables and banquette seating. The Maize Lounge is clubby and cozy, with sofas and wing chairs. $$.

Pizza Villagio Cafe. 311 Ferry St., Newark; (973) 344-0707. The owner has been serving pizza and pasta here since the early 1970s. The pies make you wonder how soon you can come back, so it's very popular with locals. The stromboli is full of flavor, too. Service is friendly and prompt; lunch and dinner. $.

Tony da Caneca. 72 Elm St., Newark; (9973) 589-6882. One of the longest-established restaurants in the Ironbound, this family-owned Portuguese restaurant serves lunch and dinner. The menu also has some Spanish dishes, seafood, steaks, pasta, and sandwiches. $$.

where to stay

Robert Treat Hotel. 50 Park Place, Newark; (973) 622-1000; www.rthotel.com. This 15-story upscale hotel is owned by The Berger Organization and sports a Best Western flag. After a renovation, there are 176 rooms, a fitness center, the Maize restaurant and lounge, and facilities for meetings, conferences, and banquets. $$.

The Westminster Hotel. 550 W. Mount Pleasant Ave., Livingston; (973) 533-0600; www .westminsterhotel.net. This luxury hotel is about 13 miles west of Newark off Route 280. There are 183 guest rooms, the Deluxe Spa, and The Strip House—an upscale steak house and lounge. Westminster also has banquet and meeting space. Dining at the Strip House is expensive, but worth the splurge. $$$.

worth more time

Riker Hill Complex. 284 Beaufort Ave., Livingston; (973) 533-9433; www.essex-countynj .org. More than 200 acres surround this hill crest, which gives amazing views of Essex County topography. In the complex is Becker Park, with 147 acres of undeveloped land. The Riker Hill Art Park takes up 42 acres, with studios and galleries housed in a former Nike missile base. There are studios for painting, ceramics, and graphic arts; and a craft center for glass blowing, woodworking, and sculpture. A valuable collection of outdoor sculptures decorates the grounds. A portion of the complex no longer open to the public is Walter Kidde Dinosaur Park, a 16-acre paleontological site significant as a major repository of preserved dinosaur tracks. The original Roseland Quarry was declared a National Natural Landmark in 1971. That was a year after two local teenagers sent President Richard Nixon a fiberglass cast of a footprint made 200 million years earlier by a *Eubrontes giganteus* dinosaur. To find the complex, take Route 280 West to exit 4A (Eisenhower Parkway South); turn left onto Beaufort Avenue; enter on the left.

day trip 07

gateway

>>> **falling for power on the silk road:**
paterson, nj

Bright lad that he was, Alexander Hamilton positioned the cradle of American industry right here in 1791, when he and a group of investors created the Society for Establishing Useful Manufactures. And just like that, a town later named for Gov. William Paterson reflected the "SUM" of its parts: water power from the Passaic Great Falls, abundant capital, innovative machinery, and handy labor. The combination of those assets and the investors' vision created the first designed-for-industry town in the young republic.

Hamilton's team hired Pierre Charles L'Enfant to design a canal system of "raceways" to divert water from the 77-foot-high falls above the Passaic River to mills lining its banks—no mean feat back in the day. Among Paterson's firsts—cotton duck cloth for sails, paper on a continuous roll, Samuel Colt's first marketable revolver, Rogers Locomotives, and John Holland's first practical submarine. Early aviation also got a boost in Paterson, where Wright Aeronautical built engines from 1920 to 1945.

Paterson's second natural landmark is Garret Mountain. The city also is famously known as "The Silk City" for its dominant role in silk production during the latter half of the 19th century. It is New Jersey's third largest city and one of the largest in the metropolitan New York area.

You will find numerous locations on the National Register of Historic Places: museums, civic buildings, private homes, vintage commercial buildings, Hinchliffe Stadium, Public School Number Two, the Danforth Memorial Library, the Cathedral of St. John the Baptist, and St. Michael's Roman Catholic Church.

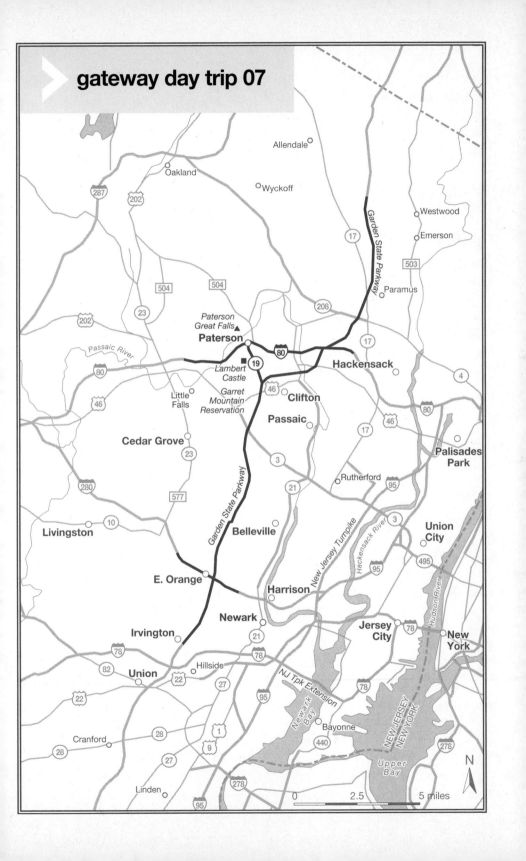

Downtown Paterson reflects a number of architectural gems, including 19th-century Beaux Arts–style buildings. The well-known New York firm Carrère and Hastings designed City Hall in 1894. It was modeled after the Hôtel de Ville ("city hall") in Lyon, France, which was Europe's capital of the silk industry.

paterson, nj

getting there

Paterson is less than half an hour from Newark; from the Garden State Parkway, take NJ 19; from I-80, take exit 57 toward downtown.

With municipal, state, and federal efforts, surviving mills and remnants of the water-works have been salvaged. They are considered unique and critical to the area's heritage tourism. A national architectural competition is addressing better ways to showcase the Great Falls and their surroundings. Today, Paterson poses a fun skate through history with a magnificent natural phenomenon as the backdrop.

where to go

Paterson Great Falls National Park. 65 McBride Ave. Extension, Paterson; (973) 279-9587; www.patersongreatfalls.org. The Great Falls Historic District Visitor Center is the best place to get an overview of the falls and their place in the history of both Paterson and American manufacturing. The site covers 139 acres of national park and 112 acres of state park.

tribute to tribal turf

Paterson got the current name in 1792, but it was incorporated a century earlier as Acquackanonk Township, named for Lenape Indians who spoke the same Algonquian dialect as neighboring tribes. Acquackanonk was situated in what is now northern Essex County. The land was owned at one time by Jacques Cortelyou, the surveyor general of New Netherland—who bought 12,000 morgens (several thousand acres) from the Indians. In 1679 Jasper Danckaerts, an explorer from Zeeland, spelled the place "Ackquekenon." Alternate pronunciations sound like stray script from an AFLAC commercial. So what does the word mean? One source calls it "a place in a rapid stream where fishing is done with a net." Another uses the indigenous form, axkwaakahnung, *to mean "a lamprey stream." Clearly, these "ungs" predated the era of texting.*

The Great Falls of the Passaic River. At Spruce and McBride Avenues, Paterson. The falls emerged thousands of years ago as the Ice Age ended. Melting glaciers overloaded the Passaic River so that it pushed its way around the basalt of the northern Watchung Mountains. The Great Falls emerged as shale and sandstone, displacing the harder stone to become the second largest waterfall by volume east of the Mississippi River. View this phenomenon from Haines Overlook Park or a bridge downriver from the falls.

The Paterson Museum. 2 Market St., Paterson; (973) 321-1260; www.paterson museum.com. The museum was founded in 1925 and is owned and operated by the city. Since 1982, it has been housed in the Thomas Rogers Building, formerly the erecting shop of Rogers Locomotive and Machine Works, a major 19th-century locomotive manufacturer. Two engines are on the premises. Other main exhibits pay tribute to industrial pioneers such as John Holland's submarines; the Colt Paterson revolver and other firearms Sam invented here; and leaders in silk, cotton, and other textiles—some who toyed with the Jacquard loom to fashion brocade, damask, and matelassé patterns. Tues through Fri, 10 a.m. to 4 p.m.; weekends, 10:30 a.m. to 4:30 p.m. Admission is $2 for adults. For more about a newer permanent exhibit, see the sidebar in this chapter, "A Need for Speed."

Garret Mountain Reservation. Valley Road, Paterson; (973) 247-0085; www.passaic countynj.org. The mountain sits on 568 acres of public recreation area near I-80 and Route 19. The peak elevation is about 500 feet—giving visitors views of northern New Jersey and New York City. On clear days, the vista from its sheer cliffs takes in Bear Mountain, NY, the George Washington Bridge, and the Verrazano-Narrows Bridge—all the way to Sandy Hook. There are fields, walking and running trails, picnic areas, hoops courts, and Barbour's Pond for fishing. There also is an equestrian center where you can take horseback riding lessons. Birding is famous here, drawing aficionados from the tri-state area to view more than 150 species, including migrating songbirds. The reservation is named for Garret Hobart Jr., son of Vice President Garret Hobart, a Paterson native who served with President William McKinley. The younger Hobart established the reservation as a public park.

Lambert Castle Museum. 3 Valley Rd., Paterson; (973) 247-0085; www.lambertcastle .org. Belle Vista, locally known as Lambert Castle, was made of sandstone from Garret Mountain, where it sits just off Route 19. The fortress was built in 1892 as the home of Catholina Lambert, a prominent, self-made silk manufacturer in Paterson's textile industry heyday. Lambert had emigrated from Yorkshire, England, as a teenager whose father worked in a mill. After getting his start in a Boston silk mill, he moved to New York to run his company's interests there—along with his new wife, Isabella Shattuck, daughter of a well-to-do Massachusetts farmer. Soon, he landed in Paterson and got busy producing silk ribbon from imported Italian fabric. The land for the castle on the cliffs was Isabella's gift to her husband. After telephone connections reached Lambert in the late 1870s, he

a need for speed

In the 1930s, a California craze called midget-car racing made its way east, and the years after World War II saw midget races becoming a daily pastime. At Hinchliffe Stadium in Paterson, midgets scorched the track. Many were owned by or built by locals, and the process of tooling and priming those beauties took place in an unlikely part of town—a double row of garages behind East 29th Street at 17th and 18th Avenues. These lean-tos and sturdier structures were erected to store newfangled automobiles being bought to replace horses at the early part of the last century. That locale, coupled with local racing history, inspired Joe Ruffilo to coordinate an exhibit touting the vroom-vroom of it all. New in 2011, and now a permanent exhibit at The Paterson Museum, "Gasoline Alley" is a nod to an unassuming area of town laden with legend and lore from the days of midget and stock-car racing at the nearby track. Whether the Gasoline Alley comic strip took its name from Paterson, or vice versa, "Garage Row" certainly earned its nickname. West Coast racer Ted Horn came east, which helped to fuel interest here. He last raced at Hinchliffe in 1947, the year before he died. Other drivers known around Paterson were Al Keller, Johnny Ritter, Bill Schindler, Johnny Ringger, Art Cross (Indy Rookie of the Year in 1952), and Len Duncan— who once was assigned to drive President Harry Truman around London. Racing buffs sing about one particular model of midgets, "Sugar Blues." One was built in Paterson for Jerry Willetts. For its first race, on Easter Sunday 1946 at Hinchliffe, the driver was Rex Records.

worked there instead of his silk mills—forerunner of the home office. After he died in 1923, the Lamberts sold the castle to the city. Today, the edifice is home to the Passaic County Historical Society, which completed a multimillion-dollar restoration in the 1990s, devoting four floors to museum and library uses. Lambert Castle Museum features historical period rooms, rotating exhibits, long-term gallery shows, a research library and archives, and educational programs. A 75-foot observation tower stands at the mountain peak and has been renovated to its 1896 condition. The museum is open Wed through Sun, noon to 4 p.m.; the grounds and Garret Mountain are open daily until dusk.

Eastside Park Historic District. Paterson; (973) 345-2700; www.eastsideneighborhood .org. The draw to this area is residential architecture, about 1,000 mansions and homes in numerous styles—including Tudor, Georgian, Victorian, Italianate, and Dutch-Colonial. Other points of interest include the Civil War Monument, The Plaza of Memories, General

Pulaski Statue, Christopher Columbus statue, Charles Curie Monument, the Gazebo, and the Alice Weight Memorial Fountain.

where to shop

Paterson Farmers Market. 449 E. Railway Ave., Paterson; (973) 742-1019; www.pat ersonfarmersmarket.com. Located in the south part of town, along the old Erie Railroad line, the market has operated here since it opened in September 1932. It created a hub for local farmers' produce and has supplied smaller fruit and vegetable vendors, hospitals, and supermarkets for decades. During World War II, US Army troops at 38 camps in the East ate fruits and vegetables sent from Paterson. Today, arriving trucks bear goods from remaining farms—fruits, vegetables, plants, flowers, and assorted foods. In addition, there are butcher shops and ethnic restaurants. The market invested $2.14 million in a renovation—gaining a new façade, lighting, paved streets, sidewalks, awnings, canopies, and signage. Look for seasonal produce and baked goods; and during the winter holidays, wreaths, Christmas trees, and poinsettias.

where to eat

The Bonfire Restaurant. 999 Market St., Paterson; (973) 278-2400; www.bonfirerestau rant.com. The tagline "After 50 years, we're almost perfect" will have to be revised at some point—but updating websites can be expensive, so what's one decade here or there? The format is lunch weekdays and dinner daily. The menu is Continental—both European classics and American favorites. There is a good wine list, with plenty of selections by the glass. $$.

Duffy's Riverside Grill. 855 River St., Paterson; (973) 357-8100. This breakfast and lunch place is open until 4 p.m. Mon through Sat. The menu is mostly straightforward—flapjacks, burgers, hot dogs, and chicken wings—but you might find escarole soup or some other comfort food from time to time. $.

Ralph Piccolo's Pizza. 312 Union Ave., Paterson; (973) 942-0282. This old-fashioned storefront was established in 1964, and regular customers rave about the world-class pizza, pasta, and sandwiches. Ralph and Madeline are the owners, and their restaurant got some high-profile notoriety when it showed up in an episode of *The Sopranos.* Open for lunch and dinner Tues through Sun; closed Mon. $.

where to stay

The Clinton Inn Hotel. 145 Dean Dr., Tenafly; (201) 871-3200; www.clinton-inn.com. With access from I-80, the New Jersey Turnpike, the Garden State Parkway, and the Palisades Interstate Parkway, the hotel is about 15 miles east and north of Paterson. There are 119 guest rooms, both king and queen suites. The in-house restaurant at The Clinton Inn is Palmer's Crossing, for breakfast, lunch, and dinner. $$.

The Renaissance Meadowlands. 801 Rutherford Ave., Rutherford; (201) 231-3100. This hotel has a relationship with the Marriott Vacation Club and is close to Route 3, the New Jersey Turnpike, and the Garden State Parkway. The hotel is only 1 mile from MetLife Stadium, a few minutes from the Prudential Center and NJPAC in Newark, and 6 miles from New York City. Newly renovated, the hotel has 167 rooms and suites. For beef and seafood, the in-house restaurant is CK's Steakhouse. $$.

day trip 08

gateway

>>> **don't sweat the flakes—
prepare for snow-motion:**
east rutherford (meadowlands), nj

Once upon a time, you had Giants Stadium in East Rutherford. It was renamed Meadowlands Stadium to reflect its use by the New York Jets as well. When the aged arena went to that great touchdown in the sky, a new one was built next door. In 2011, the New Meadowlands Stadium caught a newer password, MetLife Stadium—prompting the notion that insurance might be a good thing.

That's because tourism and sports honchos had already decided to tempt the gods and schedule Super Bowl XLVIII for February 2, 2014—the first-ever cold-weather Super Bowl to be played in an open-air arena. In fact the centerpiece of the host committee's logo is the George Washington Bridge and a snowflake.

That National Football League championship game also will be the first Super Bowl to be played in the New York metropolitan area. And while pigskin aficionados will be closely attuned to game-day preparations closer to countdown, visitors are already mapping out where to stay and what to do for the rest of that trip. But that will be then.

For now, the Meadowlands Liberty Region, a manageable bite of the Gateway, remains a big draw for the scope of its attractions. Aside from events at the Meadowlands Sports Complex, including the stadium, there are entertainment venues, hotels and restaurants, museums, nature trails, and monumental shopping choices.

Situated between the Hackensack and Hudson Rivers, from the George Washington Bridge to Liberty State Park, the region is about 15 miles from Newark Liberty International Airport, and minutes from Midtown Manhattan.

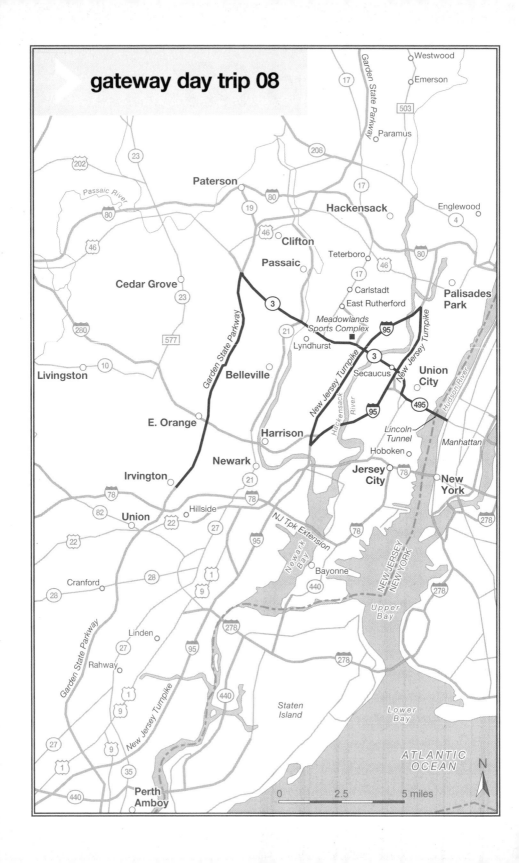

gateway day trip 08

Did someone say Xanadu, or was it Xana-Who? Further along, you'll read about the new "American Dream at the Meadowlands."

east rutherford (meadowlands), nj

getting there

Take the New Jersey Turnpike (I-95) to exit 16W (NJ 3 west); the Meadowlands Sports Complex, including MetLife Stadium and The Izod Center, will be on your right; from the Garden State Parkway, take exit 153 and go east on NJ 3; the complex will be on your left, so watch for signs for a jug-handle.

where to go

MetLife Stadium. Route 3, East Rutherford; (201) 559-1515; www.meadowlands.com. This is the main stage for home games for the New York Giants and the New York Jets. In the off-season, you might see soccer here or a headliner concert. The stadium has a 23,000-space parking lot, and fees vary by event.

The IZOD Center at the Meadowlands. Route 3, East Rutherford; (201) 925-8500; www.izodcenter.com. This 20,000-seat venue is a popular choice for major entertainers. *American Idol* held auditions here in 2011, and the Fordham University men's basketball team plays here. Professional basketball and hockey teams who used to play here now compete at the Prudential Center in Newark. Sizeable, with good acoustics, it remains in demand, presenting shows featuring Jay-Z and Kanye West, Guns N' Roses, Ticketcity Legends Classic, Disney on Ice, Sesame Street Live—Elmo Makes Music, and The Harlem Globetrotters World Tour.

Meadowlands Racetrack. 50 State Route 120, East Rutherford; (201) 843-2446; www .thebigm.com. This harness-racing destination is home to the $1.5 million Hambletonian Stakes and numerous other special events.

Aviation Hall of Fame of New Jersey. 400 Fred Wehran Dr., Teterboro; (201) 288-6344; www.njahof.org. Among the unique exhibits here are the rocket engine that propelled the X-15 toward records for speed and height, and the American hovercraft invented by Charles Fletcher. Located on the east side of Teterboro Airport, the museum displays helicopters, a restored OV1 Grumman Mohawk, airplane models, and air and space artifacts. You'll also see photographs, fine art, and aviation models. The library has thousands of volumes and hundreds of videos, and the facility is available to researchers by appointment. Admission

up, up & away

The first recorded aviation exercise in the Western Hemisphere lasted 45 minutes and covered 15 miles. Daring French balloonist Jean-Pierre Blanchard departed from Philadelphia, traveled across the Delaware River, and landed in Deptford, NJ, on January 9, 1793—about 180 years before the founding of the Aviation Museum. In other Jersey-linked highlights, the Wittemann brothers built the Bar-ling Bomber at Teterboro in 1922; Charles Lindbergh flew across the Atlantic in 1927 in the Spirit of St. Louis *powered by a Wright Whirlwind engine; also in 1927, Clarence Chamberlin flew to Germany in a Wright-Blanca built in Princeton, also with a Whirlwind; Amelia Earhart prepared for her solo transatlantic flight at Teterboro in 1932; the German zeppelin* Hindenburg *exploded at Lakehurst Naval Air Station in 1937; during World War II, General Motors' Eastern Aircraft Division built 13,500 Grumman fighter planes at plants in Linden and Trenton, and the Curtiss-Wright Corp. built 281,164 engines and 146,468 electric propellers in New Jersey plants; in 1968, Wally Schirra, of Oradell, became the only astronaut to fly in all three spacecraft—Mercury, Gemini, and Apollo; and in 1984, the first woman to walk in space was astronaut Kathryn Sullivan, a native of Paterson.*

is $7 for adults and $5 for seniors and children. Check the website for special events, such as Open Cockpit Days.

New Jersey Naval Museum. 78 River St., Hackensack; (201) 342-3268; www.njnm.com. Several important vessels are housed here. The primary exhibit is the USS *Ling 297,* a Balao-class diesel-electric submarine, one of 122 built for the US Navy during World War II. The Patrol Boat *Riverine,* the only one on view in the Northeast, was among hundreds used in the Vietnam War. Enemy artifacts from World War II include a Japanese Kaiten IIs ("turned toward Heaven") suicide torpedo; and a German Seehund ("seadog"), a 39-foot, two-man coastal defense submarine used in shallow waters. There are evening events and educational tours. Hours are 10 a.m. to 4 p.m. Sat and Sun. Admission is $9 for adults and $4 for children.

Medieval Times Dinner & Tournament. 149 Polito Ave., Lyndhurst; (201) 933-2220; www.medievaltimes.com. Similar to operations in Chicago, Dallas, Atlanta, and Orlando, this experience includes a four-course dinner followed by a jousting tournament. The venue is a castle built in the style of 11th-century Spain. A handful of daredevils dressed in knightly armor, swords, and mail prance on horseback, competing to be king's champions. Prices for dinner and the show are $59.95 for adults and $35.95 for children 12 and under. From Route 3, take exit 17 south.

Favorites at Woodbridge. 3 Lafayette Road, Fords; (201) 935-8500; www.njsea.com. This off-track wagering facility is run by the New Jersey Sports and Exposition Authority. In an oversize sports bar, with TVs at every angle, you can wager on live horse races while watching games in the National Football League, the National Hockey League, Major League Baseball, and college football.

River Barge Park. Outwater Lane, Carlstadt; (201) 460-1700; www.njmeadowlands.gov/environment. Once a neglected marsh along the Hackensack River, marred by an abandoned restaurant, this new 5.5-acre public park and marina makes a firm declaration that urban sites can reclaim and celebrate patches of nature. The New Jersey Meadowlands Commission bought the site of the former Barge Club eatery and built two new facilities—a 650-square-foot education pavilion and a 2,400-square-foot paddle center. The pavilion was named for Robert Ceberio, a former executive director of the commission. With a vista of the New York skyline in the distance, you can launch a boat or canoe from the paddle

x out xanadu, pencil in american dream

When your daily commute takes you past a failed real estate venture with aesthetics best forgotten, the best news possible is that it will go away and emerge as something better than the old concept. Here, the consensus is that the half-baked boondoggle formerly named Xanadu won't be missed. Situated near MetLife Stadium, the entertainment/retail complex was renamed "American Dream at Meadowlands" in 2011. The new developer, Triple Five, the banks that own the property, and Gov. Chris Christie announced a redesign to forge a hub for tourism, entertainment, and high-end retail. Triple Five owns part of Mall of America in Minnesota. Christie said the project could boost the state's whole economy. He cited a more appealing design, the new name, and a solid timeline for completion as the key to a much-needed makeover. American Dream will have an enclosed amusement park, indoor water park, ice rink, cinema, aquarium, comedy club, a dinner theater, performing arts venue, and restaurant variety. The only indoor ski slope in North America—with manufactured flakes drifting in the chilled air—makes it unique. Triple Five Chairman Nader Ghermezian, who grew up in Canada, cited benefits of job creation, tourism revenue, tax revenues, and a place to meet, shop, dine, play, and be entertained. His father was born in Azerbaijan, where Orthodox Jews were a minority, and immigrated to Canada in the 1950s. Triple Five Worldwide has hundreds of companies in North America, England, Japan, Taiwan, and the Middle East. To find out when you can visit, see www.americandream.com.

center. The river was dredged, making way for a new bulkhead, ramp, and docks. There is a boathouse, winter storage for vessels, and a promenade near the water.

where to shop

Big Fun Toys. 602 Washington St., Hoboken; (201) 714-9575; www.bigfuntoys.com. A few miles east of the Meadowlands, off Frank Sinatra Drive, you'll find this quirky store with unusual toys and gift ideas. Consider the "Super Rolling Art Cart" for $239.99—a bargain, if it keeps your child engaged in creative, sans-media activities for a few hours.

Harmon Cove Outlet Center. 20 Enterprise Dr., Secaucus; (201) 348-4780; www.harmon meadow.com. Harmon Cove has 55 stores in an enclosed outlet mall, featuring designer brands and a food court. Bass, Reebok, and Perry Ellis are in the mix.

The Mall at Mill Creek. 3 Mill Creek Dr., Secaucus; (201) 348-4780; www.harmon meadow.com. You will find discount stores here such as T.J. Maxx and Sam's Club, plus Marshalls, Kohl's, Sports Authority, and Toys "R" Us.

The Plaza at Harmon Meadow. 700 Plaza Dr., Secaucus; (201) 348-4780; www.harmon meadow.com. Shops, restaurants, hotels, L.A. Fitness, and the Kerasotes Showplace 14-cinema complex make up this segment of the Secaucus shopping hub. It's easy to find from Route 3 west of the New Jersey Turnpike.

The Secaucus Outlets. Meadowlands Parkway, Secaucus; (201) 348-4780; www.har monmeadow.com. The idea of outlet shopping cut its teeth here, which is why the layout is behind the times. You need your car to get from store to store, but bargain-hunters will love the choices. Keep in mind that there is no sales tax on clothes and shoes in New Jersey.

where to eat

McLoone's Woodbridge. 3 Lafayette Rd., Fords; (732) 512-5025; www.mclooneswood bridgegrille.com. This 175-seat dining room is located inside Favorites, the off-track wagering facility described above. It serves lunch and dinner seven days. The menu includes "backstretch quesadilla," a raw bar, burgers, sandwiches, salads, pasta, carne asada, fajitas, salmon parilla, and McLoone's Meatloaf (bacon wrapped). Sides include Parmesan mashed potatoes, grilled asparagus, wild rice, sautéed spinach, onions, mushrooms, and frizzled onions. $$.

Redd's Restaurant & Bar. 317 Washington Ave., Carlstadt; (201) 933-0015; www.redds restaurant.com. Located near the Meadowlands Sports Complex, this upscale-casual establishment has a Jersey menu that thinks for you—from appetizers and small plates to pizza, sandwiches, salads, wraps, burgers, and a full range of entrees. There are 25 flat-screen TVs for game day, in case your team is playing out of town. Redd's also offers patrons shuttle service to events at MetLife Stadium and the Izod Center. $$.

where to stay

The Renaissance Meadowlands. 801 Rutherford Ave., Rutherford; (201) 231-3100; www.marriott.com. This hotel has a relationship with the Marriott Vacation Club. It's a good spot from which to roam northern New Jersey and Manhattan, with ready access to Route 3, the New Jersey Turnpike, and the Garden State Parkway. The hotel is only 1 mile from MetLife Stadium, a few minutes from the Prudential Center and NJPAC in Newark, and 6 miles from New York City. Newly renovated, the hotel has 167 rooms and suites. For beef and seafood, the in-house restaurant is CK's Steakhouse. $$.

the skylands

day trip 01

the skylands

a peak peek & serendipitous summit:
montague, franklin, vernon & sussex, nj

The Skylands is a state of mind, inviting you to revel in a bundle of natural and cultivated assets—a runaway train of good times. This corner of northwestern New Jersey has magnificent outdoor splendor, marvelous historic and cultural treasures, paramount sports and recreation for all seasons, delightful dining, and a trove for shoppers.

If you dig ravines, waterfalls, red shale cliffs, and untouched forests, The Skylands delivers. You can wind through and across mountains such as Hamburg, Kittatinny, and Musconetcong—where the Lost River Caverns anchor the Pennsylvania side. The Appalachian Trail (the AT) beguiles you here as it teasingly intersects regional trails.

High Point, the highest peak in the Kittatinny Mountains, charges nothing extra for panoramic views of three states—New Jersey, New York, and Pennsylvania. The ridge runs northeast to southwest in vivid scenic splendor. And when falls are involved, pick and choose among them but don't pass up on Buttermilk.

No matter where you are in the Garden State, you are not far from a roadside stand selling tomatoes, corn, blueberries, and other seasonal produce. Prepare to grin at dwindling symbols of another time, such as working farms, silos, grazing pastures, cows, and horses.

Ski, swim, snowboard, or float your boat; hike, stroll, wander, then meander. In The Skylands, the perfect pace is your own.

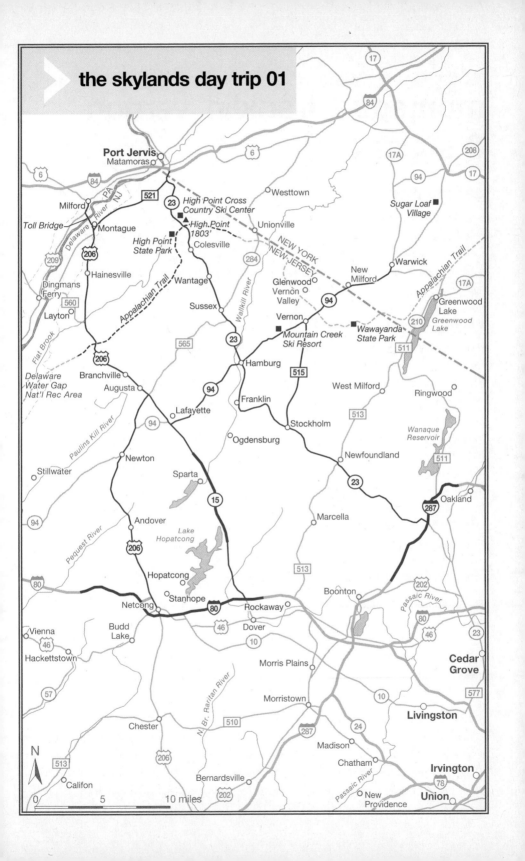

the skylands day trip 01

montague, franklin, vernon & sussex, nj

getting there

From the Garden State Parkway, take I-280 north to exit 42 onto I-287 north; take exit 52-B onto NJ 23 north, a divided curving two-lane road; in several places, you will see 35 mph speed-limit signs: a good call, given curves and altitude shifts in the mountains. Watch for a rest area after Echo Lake Road, and be on the lookout for jug handles on NJ 23, in case you miss a turn.

where to go

High Point State Park. 1480 State Route 23, Sussex; (973) 875-4800; www.njparksand forests.org. This 16,000-acre expanse just east of the Delaware River runs for about 8 miles from the New York state line southwest to Stokes State Forest. Col. Anthony R. Kuser and his wife, Susie Dryden Kuser, donated the land, which was dedicated a nature preserve in 1923. The Olmsted Brothers of Boston, sons of Central Park designer Frederick Law Olmsted, designed the High Point landscape. The site along the crest of the Kittatinny Mountains will challenge and delight hikers and skiers; yet there is plenty of lush-leaf quietude for picnics and fishing for trout and largemouth bass. Lake Marcia is a 20-acre spring-fed natural lake for swimming. Lifeguards are on duty; nearby are dressing rooms and a food concession. More than 50 miles of trails, from 0.5 mile to 18 miles, offer variety in each season. Designated multiple-use trails are for hiking, mountain biking, horseback riding, cross-country skiing, snowshoeing, dogsledding, and snowmobiling. There are ridgetops with 360-degree views, dense forests, fields, and wetlands. Boat launches are at Sawmill Lake and Steenykill Lake—subject to state regs and park rules.

The Monument at High Point State Park. This 220-foot spire honors New Jersey's war heroes. The top marks the state's peak elevation of 1,803 feet. Vantage points at the top of the tower and the base provide vistas of the Poconos, the Catskills, and the Wallkill River Valley. Completed in 1930, the tower's face is New Hampshire granite and New Jersey quartzite. You can climb the stairs for the best views. Only the first floor is accessible for people with limited mobility.

High Point Cross-Country Ski Center. 1480 Route 23, Sussex; (973) 702-1222; www.xc skihighpoint.com. With an elevation of more than 1,600 feet promising powdery precipitation, and more than 10 miles of groomed trails, High Point calls itself "New England nearby." Snowier than elsewhere in the area, bouncing reflections of the High Point monument off your goggles, it delivers an alpine hollow to embrace. Even in the lean years, the center on

blue hue is barely a clue

New Jersey brags about its wildlife, especially the mighty black bear. Yet not all "black bears" are black. The gray ones appear blue. Brown ones abound; the albino, not so much. And when you see a black bear all aglow in a warm shade of cinnamon, it may—or may not—mean those honey buns are missing from your picnic basket.

Lake Marcia has snowmaking capabilities to keep you gliding. Rent skis and snowshoes here, as well as baby-backpacks. To warm you up, seek out the fireside, soup, and cider. Hours from Dec through Apr are 9 a.m. to 4 p.m. weekdays, 8 a.m. to 4 p.m. on weekends.

Dryden Kuser Natural Area. 1480 Route 23, Sussex; www.njparksandforests.org. Named for New Jersey politician and conservationist Dryden Kuser (first husband of Brooke Astor), this 800-acre natural area is part of High Point State Park. It includes a rare, distinctive bog. You can hike a trail along a ridge surrounding the swamp, which has mature hemlocks, white pine, and a unique stand of mature Atlantic white cedar. At 1,500 feet above sea level, it is the highest-elevation swamp of its kind in the world. Pick up a self-guided trail booklet at the park office. Endangered species include the three-tooth cinquefoil and Cooper's hawk.

Foster-Armstrong House. 320 River Rd. (Route 521), Montague; (973) 293-3106; www .montaguehistory.org. Julius Foster built the original structure with a Dutch gambrel roof circa 1790. Brother-in-law James B. Armstrong completed the addition in 1820. Every room has a fireplace. There are Victorian-era rooms, complete with a tea service, and furnishings of several periods. You can see the beehive oven and learn how it was used. In the military room you will see uniforms, newspaper accounts, and handwritten notes from soldiers who fought in the Civil War and both World Wars. On display is a rope bed, hand-loomed linens, weaving looms, and quilts. One special exhibit shows scale-model covered bridges. This house is on the National Register. You may tour on Sun in the summer between 1 and 4 p.m., or by appointment from Jan through Oct. The house is open on the second and fourth Wednesday of each month from 9:30 to 11 a.m.

Nelden-Roberts Stonehouse. 501 Route 206 North, Montague; (973) 293-3106; www .montaguehistory.org. This house dates to the early 1800s and was named for George Nelden, who settled here in 1820. The Roberts family owned the farm across the road. The house has been a home to many families and was a schoolhouse with a teacher's apartment on the second floor. You will see original wide-plank wooden floors, the fireplace, and deep windows. The display here will show much about 19th-century Montague life. Note the herb garden.

Stokes State Forest. 1 Coursen Rd., Branchville; (973) 948-3820; www.njparksandforests
.org. Two stars vie for one's attention here. Sunrise Mountain gives you heart-stopping,
panoramic views of two valleys. And a 50-foot waterfall known as Tillmans Ravine takes
you on a mental leap following the path of Tillmans Creek flowing through a gorge of giant
hemlock trees, mountain laurels, and ferns. The ravine's chilly air creates a microclimate that
nurtures plants better suited to a more northern environment. At the falls, the creek bursts
into an ebullient cascade over red rocks—in one case, a 10-foot free fall. The falls are at
the south end of Stokes State Forest, and you can walk there from the ravine's parking lot.
If you are up for a climb to the top of Sunrise Mountain, elevation 1,653 feet, a 12.5-mile
section of the Appalachian Trail follows the Kittatinny Ridge through the forest. Plant life
here includes mountain laurel, wild blueberry, pitch pine, and scrub oak. If you are not up
to a mountain climb, you can drive to the pavilion at the summit. Besides the narrow, often
rocky AT, the forest has more than 33 miles of marked trails, and many cross each other.
Terrain varies from lowlands to rocky mountains. Stony Lake and Kittle Field have picnic
areas. You may launch a small boat with an electric motor at Lake Ocquittunk—but check
the park rules, and there is no boat ramp. Lifeguards are on duty in summer at Stony Lake.
You will find changing areas, restrooms, and a first-aid station.

Green Valley Farms. 997 Route 23 North, Wantage; (973) 875-5213; www.greenvalley
farms.us. This family-owned produce market and ice cream store is located on a 250-acre
farm operating in Sussex County for more than a century. Shop here for fresh fruit and
vegetables, the rancher's beef and pork, homemade ice cream, and cut flowers. During the
holidays, they sell Christmas trees and decorations. The farm has a Christmas in July event
when it sells quilts. The market is open Mon through Fri, 10 a.m. to 6 p.m., and Sat from 9
a.m. to 6 p.m. Call for the seasonal schedule.

Franklin Mineral Museum. 32 Evans St., Franklin; (973) 827-3481; www.franklinmineral
museum.com. New Jersey rocks, and not just with music. Franklin calls itself "the mineral
capital of the world," and this museum makes you a believer. A new exhibit is Welsh Hall,
with more than 5,000 mineral specimens from the collection of Wilfred R. Welsh. Another
new exhibit shows antique microscopes that date to the 1850s from the Liedy Microscopi-
cal Society. In one room, you'll see a 33-foot-long exhibit of brilliant fluorescent minerals.
There is a mine replica, an exhibit of American Indian tools and artifacts, and fossils. You
may tour the museum, as well as poke around the 3.5-acre Buckwheat Dump, where visitors often collect mineral specimens. Museum admission is $7 for adults, $5 for seniors,
and $4 for children. The same fees apply to mineral collecting, plus $1.50 per pound for
specimens.

Sterling Hill Mining Museum. 30 Plant St., Ogdensburg; (973) 209-7212; www.sterling
hillminingmuseum.org. This zinc mine operated from the 1830s to the mid-1980s, when
the price of zinc left its owner with diminished options. The New Jersey Zinc Company left
the mine to the borough in lieu of paying back taxes, and it sold at public auction. Brothers

renewed interest

In 1942 Amelia Stickney Decker wrote That Ancient Trail (The Old Mine Road), *describing the first road of any length built in America. It ran for 104 miles from what is now Kingston, NY, to Port Jervis, and along the eastern shore of the Delaware River for 40 miles through Sussex County to the Pahaquarry Copper Mines. The book was out of print for decades and then reprinted. The Montague Association for the Restoration of Community History made it available for a while at a bargain price. See www.montaguehistory.org for history books of local interest.*

Richard and Robert Hauck were high bidders. They turned the property into a museum, where you can take a 1,300-foot underground mine walking tour, view historical equipment, and see exhibits. There is a lamp room, shaft station, galleries, a rock discovery center, fossils, fluorescent minerals, gemstones, and carvings. This attraction will engage children but is not recommended for those younger than age 6.

Mountain Creek Ski Resort. 200 Route 94, Vernon; (973) 827-2000; www.mountain creek.com. This destination only 47 miles from New York City is the metropolitan area's closest ski resort, with 167 acres of ski area on four peaks. Mountain Creek merged with Crystal Springs Golf Resort in 2010—creating a four-season destination. Amusements include Mountain Creek Water Park, and Diablo Freeride Park. This mini-city is spread over 5 miles of Vernon Valley, where you will find seven golf courses, two luxury day spas, fine dining, skiing, snowboarding, snow-tubing, mountain biking, a water park, and special events. The Zoom Zipline Adventure and Mountain Coaster were to open in summer 2012. Mountain Creek also boasts that it has the nation's largest wine cellar. See the "Where to Stay" section for lodging information.

Skylands Ice World. 2765 Route 23, Stockholm; (973) 697-1600; www.skylandsice worldnj.com. The rink uses a Zamboni ice resurfacer to keep the facility customer-ready. Check the schedule for public skating and hockey times.

Buttermilk Falls. South of Walpack Center in Sussex County; (570) 426-2452; www.nps .gov/dewa. New Jersey's highest waterfall is part of the Delaware Water Gap National Recreation Area and a favorite among experienced hikers. You can see Buttermilk Falls without that much exertion, however; just climb some intricate stairs around the falls. Experts suggest you stop at Tillmans Ravine on the way to taking in the vista at Buttermilk Falls. Ask park rangers for directions to a gravel road south of Walpack Center. At the falls, water cascades down the red shale jawline of the Kittatinny Ridge. Apart from the Great Falls in Paterson, this is the only waterfall in New Jersey with a developed viewing area.

appalachian aptitude

The Appalachian Trail dips into New Jersey at the Wawayanda State Park and snakes westward along the New York border until it hangs a left into High Point State Park. There, "AT" follows a rocky ridge giving you scenic views of valleys and mountains. The trail zigzags through hemlock gorges into fields that used to be farms. As the AT makes its way parallel to the east side of the park, you see the High Point Monument in the distance.

Peters Valley Craft Center and Store. 19 Kuhn Rd., Layton; (973) 948-5200; www .pvcrafts.org. This nonprofit education center promotes the enriching role of fine craft creation and exploration. Located west of Stokes State Forest, Peters Valley offers workshops lasting from 2 to 5 days in blacksmithing, ceramics, fibers, fine metals, photography, and wood; also printmaking, books and paper, drawing, and glass art. On the second floor, the Sally D. Francisco Gallery carries American-made fine crafts. The center hosts an annual craft fair in September, a children's creativity camp, and artist residencies.

The Stanhope House. 45 Main St., Stanhope; (973) 347-7777; www.stanhopehousenj .com. This vintage blues venue brags about being "the last great American roadhouse." With shows on the Roadhouse Stage and in the Crossfire Lounge, you can get a taste of almost any genre of music: jazz, rock, reggae, blues—you name it, plus singer-songwriter showcases, NFL tailgate parties, and countless special events. The building dates to 1794 and has been promiscuous in its uses—a home, "a rooming house," a post office, general store, tavern, and stagecoach depot. In its heyday as a blues club, well-knowns in the house included Muddy Waters, Stevie Ray Vaughn, Willie Dixon, and John Lee Hooker. Hours are noon to 2 a.m., Wed through Sun. Many shows involve cover charges, but plenty do not. There are "comfort food" and spirits, but music is the draw. See the entertainment schedule on the website.

where to shop

Candy Apple Shoppe. 967 Route 517, Glenwood; (973) 764-3735; www.applevalleyinn .com. Located at the Apple Valley Inn (described below), the shop carries unique gifts and treats.

Christine's Unique Boutique. 430 Route 23 North, Franklin; (973) 209-7212. The owner specializes in apparel for women and girls who love any excuse for a new outfit at a price that won't break the bank; open from 11:30 a.m. to 7 p.m. Tues through Sat, and until 6 p.m. on Sun.

Old Lafayette Village. Route 15 and Route 94, Lafayette; (973) 383-8323; www.lafayette villageshops.com. This dog-friendly enclave of specialty shops and outlets is a country-style treat. Browse for antiques, gifts, and collectibles, and check out the printed word at the Olde Village Book Cellar.

Tri-State Mall. 10 Route 23. T.J. Maxx is one of the anchors here, plus a ShopRite super-market, pizza places, a liquor store, and deli. The center is south of the junction with Route 84.

Webb's News & Records. 270 Route 23; Franklin; (973) 827-5020. The newsstand has a good selection of newspapers and magazines. It's easy to find and you are welcome to browse.

Westfall Winery. 141 Clove Rd., Montague; (973) 293-3428; www.westfallwinery.com. Red and white wines are sold here—including some award winners. You can sample and purchase country wines here, too. "Spanish Passion" uses the owner's recipe for Sangria. Other wines made from Jersey fresh fruit include apple cinnamon, peach chardonnay, blueberry wine, and cranberry wine. You can picnic on the grounds in a modern pavilion, even using Westfall's barbecue grills. There are winery tours and tastings. Westfall Farm is in its third century, having been in one family for 166 years—from 1774, when Simon Westfall bought the land from the Earl of Perth, until Charles G. Mortimer bought it in 1940. It became a major agri-business, dealing in produce, dairy, and timber. Later members of the Mortimer family converted the dairy business to a horse farm, moving the Holsteins out and welcoming blue-ribbon-winning Morgans. Love was in the air when Loren Mortimer met his future wife, Georgene, at college. They combined their passion for fine wine, his role running Westfall Farm, and her doctorate in environmental science. They taught themselves winemaking and launched the vineyard in 2000.

where to eat

Andre's Restaurant & Wine Boutique. 188 Spring St., Newton; (973) 300-4192; www .andresrestaurant.com. Open since 1998 and drawing diners from New York City and nearby Jersey counties, the restaurant is owned and operated by Chef Andre de Waal and his wife, Tracey. The intimate dining area and bar are an inviting space to enjoy Andre's wonderful and unpretentious interpretations. He favors local produce and shops diligently for the best meats and seafood, and the results are fine flavor and great value. While dining, you are surrounded by rotating exhibits of fine art and photography strategically placed on brick walls. A popular appetizer is house-cured salmon with potato pancake and Andre's secret horseradish sauce—which he has bottled for you, just in case. The menu changes twice a month, and you can specify vegan, vegetarian, or gluten-free. You will enjoy the ele-gant presentations, which rely on the integrity of ingredients. Choose between an a la carte price, which includes a house salad with your entree, and the price for a five-course meal. Not every restaurant offers duck, and Andre's version of pan-roasted duck breast is served with farro and raspberries. Andre plays around with inventive cocktails for each season. His French martini is Grey Goose vodka, Chambord, and pineapple juice, served up. $$.

The Elias Cole Restaurant. 1176 Route 23, Sussex; (973) 875-3550. Nancy Lain and her late husband, Alden, bought this place in the late 1970s, and she still runs it. The 100-seat establishment serves breakfast, lunch, and dinner seven days a week. Aside from not taking any credit cards, the Elias Cole is popular with locals and visitors alike. Some nicknamed it "the pie run," because they stop for homemade pies on the way to High Point. Bread is made on the premises. The menu is all-American, from char-grilled burgers and sandwiches to fried shrimp, chicken, and fish 'n' chips—and there are daily "blackboard" specials. Three partners who built the restaurant in 1965 drew names out of a hat; The Elias Cole won. $.

Granny's Pancake House & Grill. 181 Route 23 South, Hamburg; (973) 827-2390. Granny's is a great family-style spot where you can order breakfast all day: fluffy omelettes, yummy French toast, and fresh fruit. The decor is sort of retro-diner; you could film a movie set in a diner and not change a thing. $.

where to stay

Apple Valley Inn. 967 Route 517, Glenwood; (973) 764-3735; www.applevalleyinn.com. This property in the Pochuck Valley is located in a Colonial-style manor that dates to 1831. The three-story building has wraparound porches and an appealing stretch of gardens. The inn is convenient to towns in Sussex County, as well as Orange County, NY—just a mile from the Appalachian Trail and a few minutes from area ski resorts. Six air-conditioned guest rooms have private baths, TVs, DVD players, and hundreds of movies in its library. $$.

we double-dog dare you

Comb Sussex County and find it, if you can: the 50-foot Silver Spray Falls, which may be the state's prettiest, free-falling water feature. It's worth locating, if you persist, by following an unmarked trail leading from a gravel road south of Laytonsville. Go about 0.5 mile south of Buttermilk Falls; park at what used to be Silver Spray Farm. Walk north on Mountain Road for several hundred feet. Go past a house, turn east, and head for the creek. Once there, you'll wonder what took you so long, as the falls scamper over the Kittatinny's crimson rocks through a valley of hemlock and mountain laurel. Bring a camera, bring lunch, and bring someone to share it with.

The Appalachian at Mountain Creek. 200 Route 94; Vernon; (973) 827-5996; www .mountaincreek.com. Designed with a mountain lodge aesthetic, the Appalachian is one of numerous lodgings at the combined resorts of Mountain Creek/Crystal Springs. The hotel has a four-season pool, hot tubs, a fitness center, and underground parking. $$.

Black Creek Sanctuary. Mountain Creek Resort, Vernon; (973) 827-5996; www.mountain creek.com. This lodging alternative appeals to families, with a gated town-home layout. $$.

Grand Cascades Lodge. 3 Wild Turkey Way, Hardyston; (973) 827-5996; www.crystal golfresort.com. This luxury hotel is tall on Adirondack design and long on luxury. Wooden beams and stonework reflect natural surroundings, within pampered zones inside and out. The Biosphere Pool Complex is a unique, spectacular year-round amenity. The heated indoor freeform swimming pool is flanked by tropical plants, boulders, and waterfalls. Special lighting effects give it an exotic lagoon feel. A Foiltec roof controls the climate, and a retractable segment gives an outdoor feel. While you lounge in the pool, take in mountain views. There's an underground aquarium, a 140-foot water slide, a grotto-like Jacuzzi, and a steam room and sauna styled like a cave. $$$.

The Whistling Swan Inn. 110 Main St., Stanhope; (973) 347-6369; www.whistlingswaninn .com. Daniel Best, a justice of the peace, built this house for his wife, Sarah, in 1905. It was home to several families before it became a bed-and-breakfast in 1985. The atmosphere is a lovely, vintage country home with comfortable rooms and a yummy breakfast. You can join other guests at the dining room table or eat in solitude on the veranda. There are rocking chairs, a hammock, gardens, and a fireplace in the parlor. There are nine guest rooms, some with private baths and some with showers. $$.

worth more time

Lake Hopatcong. I-80 exit 28, Sussex County; www.lakehopatcong.com. Partly in Morris County, the largest freshwater lake in New Jersey is a unique destination. It takes up about 4 square miles in the mountains north of Netcong and its natural outlet is the Musconetcong River. It is popular in the summer for swimming and water sports. Fishing goes on year-round. There are marinas, and you can get to restaurants, bars, and nightclubs directly by boat. Hopatcong State Park lies at one end. Nearby is The Lake Hopatcong Historical Museum.

Sugar Loaf Village. 1371 County Road 13, Sugar Loaf, NY; (845) 469-9181; www.sugar loafny.com. Located north of Vernon, NJ, near Warwick, NY, this artisan village has unusual shops, galleries, and restaurants.

day trip 02

the skylands

>>> **conservation before it was cool:**
milford, pa

Why Milford, PA, you ask?

It is quintessentially quaint, a decided gem of the Delaware River Valley, and only 90 minutes from Manhattan. Milford was called "the prettiest county seat in America" by *Atlantic Magazine;* and according to *Frommer's Budget Travel,* Milford, PA, was No. 2 on its 2007 list of the "Ten Coolest Small Towns in America."

Note: The Pennsylvania town in this chapter is not to be confused with Milford, NJ, or West Milford, NJ.

Here, you will see a plaque that proclaims 1792 as the moment in history when Milford became the parent of the American Conservation Movement. The township was laid out by John Biddis, whose father was born in Wales. Judge Biddis designed the township to resemble Philadelphia.

Appealing retailers abound, and many are housed in intriguing historic buildings. Be certain to visit The Upper Mill, Forest Hall, The Old Lumberyard, and Broad Alley.

Milford is a town determined not to be led astray, and it invites you to shop, dine, stay over, and delve into its treasures—wishing all the while that your ancestors had left you a land grant.

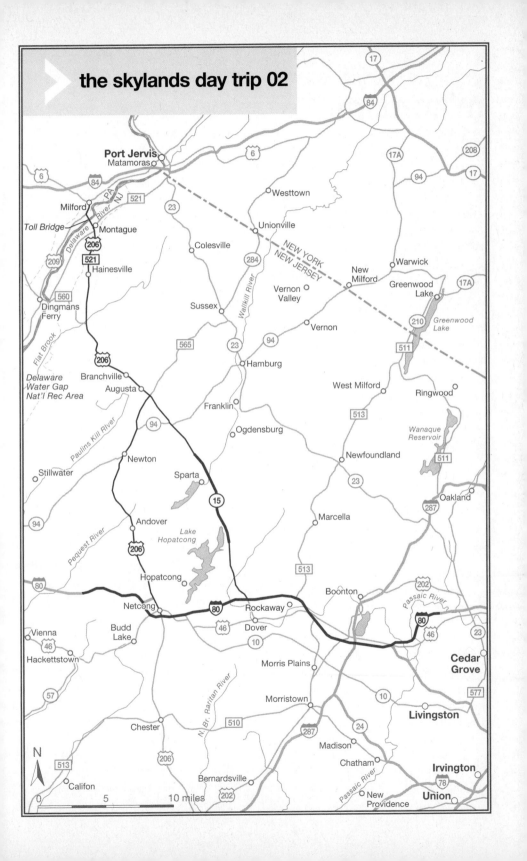

the skylands day trip 02

milford, pa

getting there

From northern New Jersey, go west on I-80 to exit 34; go north on NJ 15; after Ross Corner, you will be on US 206; continue north past Montague and cross the Delaware River on a toll bridge. Bear right into Milford.

where to go

Grey Towers National Historic Landmark. 151 Grey Towers Dr., Milford; (570) 296-9630; www.fs.fed.us/na/gt. Grey Towers was the ancestral home of Gifford Pinchot, conservationist and two-term governor of Pennsylvania. He also was the first chief of the US Forest Service, property manager since 1963. James Pinchot, Gifford's father, built the 19,000-square-foot French chateau-style mansion in 1886 of local fieldstone. You may tour some first-floor rooms and gardens. In the Hall are Italian Renaissance-Revival oak chests and cabinets made around 1800 and imported from England. The walls hold antlered hunting trophies. A saddle sits on one arm of the sofa flanked by a piano. In the library are books owned by James and his wife, Mary. The mansion is filled with antiquities, fine art, and fascinating details such as trompe l'oeil "frames" for canvases. Gifford's wife, Cornelia Bryce Pinchot, added many features after 1914. One-hour tours are offered from 11 a.m. to 4 p.m. from May through Oct. Check the website for maintenance schedules. It is a steep walk of 600 feet from the parking lot to the mansion, with steps involved.

The Columns Museum. 608 Broad St., Milford; (570) 296-8126; www.delawareriverhighlands.com. Built in 1904, The Columns is a 24-room Neo-Greek Revival–style mansion. It is now a museum with seasonal exhibits and permanent artifacts. The most famous fabric on the premises is "the bloody Lincoln Flag," which cushioned the head of the dying president. As the tour guides explain the scene of April 14, 1865, Ford Theater stage manager Thomas Gourlay rushed to Lincoln's side and pulled down bunting from an overhead beam. Backstage was Gourlay's daughter, Jeannie, who was in that evening's play, *Our American Cousin.* Gourlay gave the flag to Jeannie, who later moved to Milford and willed it to the museum. On display is a custom gown from her Ford Theater dressing room—now called "the dress never worn for a song never sung." The Pike County Historical Society runs the museum, displaying Civil War artifacts, historic farm tools and firearms, Native American artifacts, the Hiawatha stagecoach, vintage gowns and uniforms, photos, period letters, and musical instruments. See the museum from Apr through Nov, from 1 to 4 p.m. on Wed, Sat, and Sun. Tickets are $3 for adults.

Forest Hall. 206 Broad St., Milford. Hunt & Hunt designed the French Normandy–style building. James Pinchot built it in 1907, intending the first floor for commercial shops and the upper floor for classrooms for Yale University's School of Forestry. Situated at the corner of Harford Street, it now houses galleries and antiques shops.

Foster Hill Farm. Seventh Street (Forest Hill Road), Milford; (570) 296-6249; www.snyder qualityllamas.com. If you hope to see a llama in your lifetime, locate Dick Snyder's 70-acre spread for a delightful and unusual experience. A former executive, Snyder retired, bought a former dairy operation, and read up on breeding llamas. He wins ribbons in llama contests and coordinates the sale of the animals' sheared fiber. Dozens of llamas roam freely in pastures. There are flower gardens, a vegetable garden, and an orchard with peach, pear, apricot, cherry, and apple trees. A birch glen masks a pond stocked with koi; a turtle and frogs live there, too, and the hideout attracts many species of birds.

where to shop

Blue Sky Red Earth Tribal Arts. 401 W. Harford St., Milford; (570) 409-1826. The Indian nations of America and Canada have a lot of creativity to show you, and you will find a lot of it here: beading, quillwork, clothing, drums, and silver jewelry.

Books & Prints on Pear Alley. 220 Broad St., Milford; (570) 296-4777; www.booksand bookbinding.com. Located in Milford's historic Forest Hall building, the store sells books and art. The selection is geared for both casual readers and serious collectors. In the print room, you will find 19th-century original art, etchings, and engravings. The store also offers custom framing and book repairs on the premises. Hours are 10 a.m. to 5 p.m. daily, noon to 4 p.m. on Sun.

Forest Hall Antiques. 214 Broad St., Milford; (570) 296-4299; www.foresthallantiques .com. From what you see here, you will be tempted to book a flight to Europe or Asia. No need. The shop carries art that is uniquely American, European, and Chinese: furnishings, paintings, porcelain, pewter, and vintage clothing.

The Healthy Skin Shop. 115 Seventh St., Milford; (570) 296-1100; www.healthyskinshop .com. If you love a good soak in cream, lotion, mineral salts, vitamin, and herbal essences, this is for you. Sample the mineral makeup.

Jill Deal. 200 Broad St., Milford; (570) 409-9276. This is the retailer who buys and sells the llama fiber from Foster Hill Farm (described above). It's a cute shop with anything you'd need for knitting, crocheting—or spinning yarns.

Mill Run Booksellers. 150 Water St., Milford; (570) 296-2665. Located in The Upper Mill, the store dates to the 1990s. Hours are 10 a.m. to 5:30 p.m. daily, and from 10:30 a.m. to 5 p.m. on Sun.

Old Lumberyard Antiques. 113 Seventh St., Milford; (570) 409-8636; www.oldlumber yardantiquesllc.com. This facility is spread over two buildings, with 10,000 square feet and

whatever floats your boat

Grey Towers has intriguing spaces, both indoors and out. One extraordinary gem is "The Finger Bowl," a dining table under a wisteria-covered pergola. The stone base is designed like a hollowed-out boat hull filled with water. If you had been among the 18 guests with a plate on the rim, you'd pass the meat and potatoes on top of the water in wooden bowls and balsa rafts. Underneath were hollow glass balls to keep the menu moving along. Were there casualties? Some say a turkey took a dive. But children loved dessert, after which they could play at the table with toy sailboats.

dozens of dealers who carry 19th- and 20th-century collectibles, jewelry, furnishings, art, pottery, glass, and linens. It is located on the second floor of the complex.

Patina Interiors. 320 Broad St., Milford; (570) 296-1128. If you enjoy an upscale style of country living, browse here for vintage and antique accessories, lighting, and rugs. The shop is open year-round and you may find the occasional contemporary item on its way to becoming vintage.

Trading Closets. 113 Route 6, Milford; (570) 409-8178. This upscale consignment boutique carries bunches of things you need or want for a nod to the home front.

Upriver Home. 202 Broad St., Milford; (570) 296-2026; www.upriverhome.com. You will enjoy this store's concept—a mind-set, really—of injecting creativity into every aspect of the home, whether primary residence or vacation hang. Books include *The Produce Bible,* plus titles on bird-feeding, baking, and home decor. One fascinating tome, *Mug Shots,* shows the countenances of the famous and infamous, from Elvis to Mata Hari. Upriver Home carries decorative accessories, bath products, tableware, children's gifts, pet items, and garden stuff.

where to eat

Jorgenson's at The Dimmick Inn. 101 E. Harford St., Milford; (570) 296-4021; www .dimmickinn.com. Steaks are serious business here—filet mignon, New York strip, flat iron, and T-bone—and can be topped with a Gorgonzola crust, frizzled onions, Jack Daniels sauce, or a demi-glace. The menu includes lamb chops, pork chops, seafood, and sandwiches. Our pasta favorite is the Pappardelle Fresca, a house specialty. Inquire about staying at the historic inn as well. Lunch and dinner. $$.

The Muir House. 102 State Route 2001, Milford; (570) 293-6373; www.muirhouse.com. Eat, drink, and be merry here. If you want to stay, rooms are available by the month. The restaurant serves dinner Wed through Sun, and the menu is eclectic. $$.

Tom Quick Inn. 411 Broad St., Milford; (570) 296-6700; www.tomquickinn.com. Stay here or come for a meal, where the slogan is "food we can be proud of." The restaurant is housed in a Victorian home built in 1882 in the center of the historic district. Lunch and dinner selections are down-home, all-American, and the menu will think for you. $.

Waterwheel Cafe, Bakery and Bar. 150 Water St., Milford; (570) 296-2383; www.water wheelcafe.com. Housed in The Upper Mill, the restaurant serves breakfast, lunch, and dinner. The menu is eclectic, with plenty of American choices and several Vietnamese dishes. $$.

where to stay

The Black Walnut Inn & Stables. 179 Firetower Rd., Milford; (570) 296-6322; www.the blackwalnutinn.com. Rustic and charming, this stone Tudor-style inn in the mountains sits on 162 acres of woodlands and a 3-acre spring-fed lake for swimming, fishing, or canoeing. The Emery family built the main house in 1897. Stewart Schneider bought it in 1982, renovated the rooms, and converted it to a bed-and-breakfast. His daughter, Robin, who grew up here, runs the inn with her husband, William Jara. Throughout the woods, you will spot some original stone field dividers, dimpled with berry vines, surrounded by apple and wild cherry trees. From the rear deck overlooking the lake is a forest of oak, maple, and black walnut trees—which attract bald eagles, black bears, and other wildlife. You may bring along your horse, as the estate's scenic trails beckon, or ride one of their mounts. The main house has a dining room, where you enjoy a complimentary breakfast. There are 12 guest rooms with either private, semiprivate, or shared baths; plus one suite and one cabin, which are pet-friendly. $$.

Hotel Fauchère. 401 Broad St., Milford; (570) 409-1212; www.hotelfauchere.com. Open in 1880, this Italianate villa replaced an earlier lodging built by Swiss chef Louis Fauchère. His wife, Rosalie Perrochet, lived in Milford, and her family owned the original hotel. Fauchère worked at Delmonico's in New York City, and ran his summer lodge in Milford—attracting the "city" clientele. Among his guests: the Delmonicos, who stayed in a nearby cottage. Over the next century, the hotel hosted three US presidents (two Roosevelts and JFK), and many stage and screen stars, artists, and writers. Henry Ford and Andrew Carnegie knew the hotel well. Today, after stem-to-stern renovation, the villa is a 16-room luxury hotel with marble baths and Frette linens, fine dining in the Delmonico Room, and a bistro named Bar Louis. Choose from premium, deluxe, and superior rooms. $$$.

day trip 03

the skylands

do you, by chance, speak canoe?:
delaware water gap national recreation area (nj & pa)

If you like it wet, you'll love this Gap, where the star of the show is the middle Delaware River—at a point where northern New Jersey holds hands with Pennsylvania.

What exactly is the gap? It is a geological marvel created by the river making a gash through ridges of the Appalachian Mountains. At the gap itself, the peaks are Mt. Tammany in New Jersey and Mt. Minsi in Pennsylvania. Delaware Water Gap, PA, is a town a bit southwest of the gap. And the Delaware Water Gap National Recreation Area is an absolute blast on both sides of the river—extending for about 40 miles from the Worthington State Forest area in New Jersey north to the outskirts of Milford, PA.

Long ago, the Gap was called a "Wonder of the World," attracting sightseers from New York City and Philadelphia. They still come from all over, for the scenery and activities that shrug off state boundaries.

Take the plunge with a kayak, canoe, or raft. Swim, snorkel, wade, splash, or fly fish. If your get-up-and-go did not yet depart, hike along more than 27 miles of the Appalachian Trail; maybe check out cross-country skiing, rock climbing, biking, or horseback riding.

Yes, you could just stare in serenity at the cascading waterfalls, scenic cliffs, and wilderness; and linger to take in historic sites, art galleries, cultural activities, and picnic havens. Then, you could count your blessings.

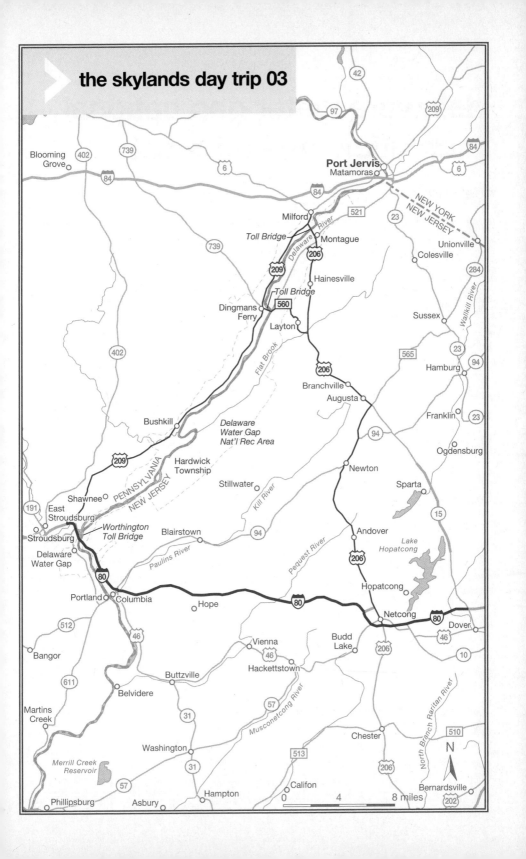

the skylands day trip 03

delaware water gap national recreation area (nj & pa)

getting there

From the Newark area, the trip is about 55 miles; take the Garden State Parkway to I-280 north, and exit west onto I-80. Take exit 1, the last exit on the New Jersey side; turn left at the stop sign (Old Mine Road) and bear right for about 0.5 mile. Turn right into the parking lot for the Kittatinny Visitor Center. You also may stay on I-80 west across the river to PA exit 310; stay to the far right at the toll booth and follow signs to PA 611 south; at the traffic light at the end of a circular ramp, continue straight across the intersection onto River Road; go 2.5 miles through Shawnee-on-Delaware, PA, and stay to the right; continue 6.7 miles on River Road to Delaware Water Gap park headquarters on the right.

Note: River Road is scenic but narrow, a two-lane passage parallel to the river; fraught with hilly, hairpin curves, yet beautiful and wooded. In some areas, 15 to 20 mph is necessary and 30 is the maximum speed limit. US 209 is a more conventional alternative, also two lanes, wooded on both sides, with guardrails and no shoulders. You have only 3 bridges that cross the Delaware River within the park, and there is a small toll (75 cents or $1 each way). From south to north, they are I-80 at the Gap; 28 miles north at Route 560 to Dingmans Ferry (at PA 739); and US 206, at the bridge from Montague, NJ, to Milford, PA.

where to go

Kittatinny Point Visitor Center. Old Mine Road, Hardwick Township, NJ; (908) 496-4458; www.nps.gov/dewa; and www.kittatinny.com. This is the New Jersey headquarters for the Delaware Water Gap National Recreation Area. The staff has park maps, brochures, children's materials, annual park passes, a bookstore, restrooms, outdoor facilities, drinking water, phones, a picnic area, and a canoe launch. Here, you will learn that the best place to view the actual water gap is at one of three overlooks on PA Route 611. The national recreation area covers about 70,000 acres, largely wilderness, spread on both sides of a 40-mile stretch of the river. It is popular for hiking, biking, canoeing, camping, cross-country skiing, horseback riding, and fishing. You can drive through the park, too, to experience the scenery at your own pace.

Delaware Water Gap National Park. River Road, Bushkill, PA; (570) 828-2253; www.nps.gov/dewa. This is about 14 miles north of I-80. If you did not stop at Kittatinny Visitor Center, stop at park headquarters to get an overview of the facilities, trail maps, and directions to specific points of interest.

fiercely fortified

It's hard not to see this setting without thinking of Daniel Day-Lewis and Madeleine Stowe in Last of the Mohicans. *The 1750s were trying times, both for locals born in the region, European settlers, and the tribes who hunted there and made seasonal camps. The border between New Jersey and Pennsylvania, in the heart of what is now the Delaware Water Gap recreation area, was the colonial frontier. During the French & Indian War, the settlements relied on forts in the area for protection. Seven such sites are scattered throughout the national park.*

George W. Childs Recreation Area. Silver Lake Road, Dingmans Ferry, PA. This former state park is now part of the Delaware Water Gap National Recreation Area. It was named for newspaper publisher George William Childs, whose widow deeded the land to Pennsylvania in 1912. You will find beauty in the extreme here, with cascading waterfalls and a path through hemlock groves that is navigable even for those with mobility issues.

Dingmans Falls Visitor Center. 224 Dingmans Falls Rd., Dingmans Ferry, PA; (570) 828-2253; www.discoverpikepa.com. The visitor center and Dingmans Falls are at the end of a 1-mile approach road off Johnny Bee Road, which intersects PA Route 209 near milepost 14, just south of the traffic light at Routes 209 and 739 in Dingmans Ferry, PA. The center is open daily in the summer and weekends in the fall.

Dingmans Creek Trail. Just south of the light at Johnny Bee Road, the trail goes for 3 miles and passes Dingmans Falls, a 130-foot plunge down sandstone cliffs. If you happen to visit during the spring runoff, you can't reach the end of the boardwalk without being sprayed by the falls. The trail also passes by Silverthread Falls, a slender fluid shaft that slices its way through the eyes of narrow sandstone "needles" down to layers of the lower Pocono Plateau.

Dingmans Ferry Boat Access. Just south of the Route 560/Route 739 bridge, Dingmans Ferry, PA; (800) 487-2628; www.adventuresport.com. This is one of the most popular boat-launch areas on the pristine river where you may launch a canoe, kayak, or raft. Visitors may find it convenient to contact a group such as Adventure Sport, which rents boats, life jackets, and paddles. Their rates include shuttle service, maps, and advice. Recently, signs have been posted to warn visitors that floods had caused changes in currents and steep drop-offs.

where to shop

The Icehouse Antiques Shop. River Road, Shawnee-on-Delaware, PA; (570) 420-4553; www.gatehousecountryinn.com. The shop is located in a cylindrical former icehouse built in 1906 on the grounds of The Gatehouse Country Inn described below. Browse here for antiques and collectibles.

Stroud Mall. 454 Stroud Mall, Stroudsburg, PA; (570) 424-2770; www.stroud-mall.com. Located west of the Delaware River Bridge off I-80, take exit 306 (Dreher Avenue) and follow signs to the mall. Anchors include Sears, Bon-Ton, and JCPenney, plus dozens of traditional mall tenants in all categories and a new cinema.

where to eat

The Gem and Keystone. River Road, Shawnee-on-Delaware, PA; (570) 424-0990; www .gemandkeystone.com. The tavern serves seasonal cuisine, much of it locally sourced, and handcrafted beer brewed on the premises. There is light pub fare, steaks, ribs, seafood, burgers and panini, salads, and plenty of choices. Lunch and dinner daily. $$.

The Layton Country Store and Cafe. 150 Route 560, Layton; (973) 948-0045. Anglers can buy bait here. This ancient depot changed management in 2011. You can count on breakfast and lunch every day and dinner five nights a week. The menu is American, and you may bring your own jug. The restaurant also carries prepared dinners for take-out. $.

war & ore no more

Old Mine Road, which begins at the Kittatinny Point Visitor Center, parallels the middle Delaware River through Warren and Sussex Counties in New Jersey before it steps across the state line into New York. It is one of the constants of the vast national recreation area and one of the oldest commercial roads in the Northeast. Local lore suggests that the Dutch took this route to carry copper ore in the mid-1600s. Certainly, regiments marched it during the Revolutionary War. But today, Old Mine Road is all about play—as access for outdoor leisure and recreational pursuits: watching birds and wildlife, hiking, cross-country skiing, bicycling, swimming, boating, camping, and picnics.

bed, breakfast & background

The current owners of The Gatehouse Country Inn took over in 2001. For almost four decades, it was the home of musician and band leader Fred Waring, who spent three years completing an elaborate restoration of the property. Waring bought it from C.C. Worthington, a rich New Yorker who built the gatehouse as a support structure for his country home, Fort Depuy, in 1906. The main house was called Fort Depuy when it became a garrison in 1755 during the French & Indian War. Namesake Nicholas Depuy was an early white settler who came to the Delaware River in 1727.

where to stay

Fernwood Hotel & Resort. Route 209 at River Road, Bushkill, PA; (888) 337-6966; www .fernwoodhotel.com. Once you arrive at this Pocono Mountain compound, you can relax without having to leave the resort to dine, play, or be entertained. There is an 18-hole golf course, horseback riding, indoor and outdoor swimming pools, a game zone, spa, and fitness center. Nearby, you can ride in a hot-air balloon, go sky-diving or take a sightseeing flight. You are near Bushkill Falls—the Niagara of Pennsylvania—popular for guided walks and bike tours of the surrounding area. Choose among guest rooms, suites, and villas with one or two bedrooms. $$.

The Gatehouse Country Inn. River Road, Shawnee-on-Delaware, PA; (570) 420-4553; www.gatehousecountryinn.com. This bed-and-breakfast has a handful of guest rooms with private baths and either queen- or king-size beds. There are two suites, including the 1,000-square-foot Loft above the great room. Rooms are individually decorated with antiques, Oriental rugs, and local accessories. The inn is near the Shawnee Golf Resort, where you can ski and enjoy other activities. See the inn's website for more area landings. $$.

day trip 04

the skylands

taking a chance on loving it:
mount pocono, pa; jim thorpe, pa

A bit west of northern New Jersey's border with Pennsylvania is the "gateway to the Poconos," often called "the Switzerland of America" for its scenery and Victorian-era architectural treasures. Still holding with a modest population of 4,000 folks, the town now called Jim Thorpe, PA, was founded in 1818 by Josiah White, head of the Lehigh Coal and Navigation Company.

In addition to gorgeous mountains and valley terrain, whitewater rafting on the Lehigh River and other outdoor adventures, Jim Thorpe has a charming historic downtown with restaurants, shops, galleries, and venues. It has 8 buildings on the National Register of Historic Places, and architecture in a feast of styles: Federalist, Greek Revival, Second Empire, Queen Anne, Romanesque Revival, and Richardsonian Romanesque.

From antiques to paintball, live music and art, wineries and history, Jim Thorpe confirms that Victorian is indeed a hip trip-capture.

In the Poconos, you will revel in the gamut of satisfying pastimes: cultural attractions, golf, skiing, nature trails, and historic sites—even a self-contained casino resort. And the area is readily accessible from any point in central and northern New Jersey.

mount pocono, pa

This petite borough in the Pocono Mountains has an elevation of almost 2,000 feet above sea level. It is bulging with outdoor recreation and indoor entertainment choices for all ages—whether solo, a twosome, or a family.

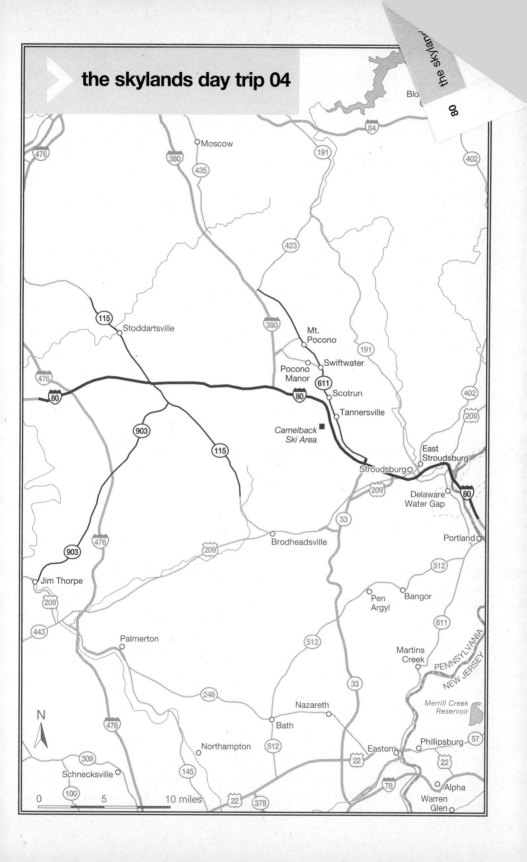

Moscow

476

380

435

191

84

402

Blo

80

the skyland

423

115

Stoddartsville

380

Mt.
Pocono

191

476

80

Pocono
Manor

Swiftwater

611

80

Scotrun

402

903

Tannersville

Camelback
Ski Area

115

East
Stroudsburg

Stroudsburg

209

80

Delaware
Water Gap

476

903

209

33

Brodheadsville

Portland

512

Jim Thorpe

209

Pen
Argyl

Bangor

611

443

Palmerton

512

Martins
Creek

PENNSYLVANIA

248

NEW JERSEY

33

Merrill Creek
Reservoir

N

Nazareth

476

Bath

Phillipsburg

57

309

Northampton

512

Easton

22

22

145

22

Schnecksville

100

0   5   10 miles

22

378

78

Alpha

Warren
Glen

getting there

The area is about an hour and a half from Newark. Take the Garden State Parkway to I-280 north, exit 47 onto I-80 west; take exit 298 (PA 611 north) toward Scotrun, PA; and turn left onto PA 611 for Mount Pocono.

where to go

Camelback Mountain Resort. 1 Camelback Rd., Tannersville, PA; (570) 629-1661; www .skicamelback.com. This resort is a perennial favorite when you want a family-focused attraction. Choose your skiing level among 34 trails—can you say Dromedary?—or take up snow-tubing and other flaky pastimes. New in 2011 was a Magic Carpet Lift. Also new is a summer destination, the Camelbeach Waterpark. See the website for a map of ski trails, parking, and amenities.

Great Wolf Lodge. 1 Great Wolf Dr., Scotrun, PA; (570) 688-9899; www.greatwolf.com. This family-oriented resort is part hotel and spa and part amusement park. It is one of a dozen or so self-contained Great Wolf operations around the country, with restaurants, shops, and activities. Suites are laid out for families; some even have a "tent" or "log cabin" for children's sleeping quarters. The water park is on a level you'd expect at a large amuse-ment park such as Kings Dominion or Disney. $$.

Mountain Laurel Pocono Mountains Performing Arts Center. 1 Bushkill Falls Rd., Tamiment, PA; (570) 251-1512; www.mtlaurelpac.com. This amphitheater reopened in 2011 after a four-year hiatus. There are 2,500 fixed seats under cover and open-air lawn seating. A variety of music acts performed that season, including ZZ Top (no extra charge for their beards), and da joisey boys, Frankie Valli and the Four Seasons. The venue brought in some Detroit action with a display of hot rods and street rods and a classic and antique-car show. These special events were held prior to the concerts, and included carnival games and food vendors.

Mount Airy Casino Resort. 44 Woodland Rd., Mount Pocono, PA; (877) 682-4791; www.mountairycasino.com. Concurrent with the completion of a half-billion-dollar retooling from A to Z, this transformed mountain lodge got state permission for casino gaming and launched in 2010. It also became the first casino resort in Pennsylvania to receive a AAA Four Diamond Rating. The casino is an intimate size, with more than 70 tables for black-jack, roulette, craps, baccarat, and poker; more than 2,400 slot machines; and a separate floor for nonsmokers. The resort features an 18-hole golf course—more than 6,000 scenic yards of challenging terrain, rolling wooded fairways, and plenty of water hazards. There are nightclubs, five restaurants, outdoor activities, and 188 renovated guest rooms and suites. Mount Airy's Spa and Salon offers traditional services such as facials, skin treatments, and massages. The resort is especially popular the week of New Year's—when it often is sold out. In 2011 the resort hosted a prestigious Italian Cars event, The Concorso d'Eleganza at Le Belle Macchine d'Italia. Participating marques represented Alfa Romeo, Bizzarrini, DeTomaso, Ferrari, Fiat, Iso, Lamborghini, Lancia, Maserati, Motorcycles, and an Open Class. There are two fine-dining restaurants inside the resort—Le Sorelle Cucina, upscale Italian, and Red Steakhouse—plus a busy Sunday brunch, buffet-style, and other informal eateries. $$–$$$.

Casino Theatre Entertainment Center. 110 Pocono Blvd. (Route 611), Mount Pocono, PA; (570) 839-7831; www.casinotheatre.net. This family-oriented fun hub combines a movie house with a restaurant, ice cream shop, mini-golf and game arcade, and retro gift shop. The menu in The Village Malt Shoppe has sandwiches, burgers, sliders, wraps, panini, soups, salads, and sides. $.

where to shop

The Crossings. 1000 Route 611, Tannersville, PA; (570) 629-4650; www.premiumoutlets .com. Take I-80 to exit 299 for this outlet mall with 100 stores. Several eateries are open in the complex, which is near all the major resorts in the Poconos.

where to eat

Desaki Restaurant. Route 611, Swiftwater, PA; (570) 839-2500; www.desakirestaurant .com. From I-80 west, take exit 298 (PA 611 North) toward Scotrun; turn left onto Route 611. Desaki is about 2 miles north on the left. Here, your dinner is part hibachi, part theater, as the chefs perform some swift-blade action and pyrotechnic displays. The menu includes sushi items, including specialty rolls. The Desaki is shrimp tempura topped with yellowtail, spicy tuna, caviar, and crunchies, and glazed with eel sauce and spicy mayo. There are entree combos and a children's menu. The restaurant and bar are open Tues through Sat, 4 to 10 p.m., and Sun, noon to 10 p.m. Desaki becomes a dance club on weekends, from 9:30 p.m. to 2 a.m. $$.

Hickory Valley Farm Restaurant. Swiftwater, PA; (570) 839-6492; www.hickoryvalley farm.com. This once was a store that specialized in Pennsylvania Dutch cured ham, bacon, turkey, and sausage that came from a nearby farm. Continuing the tradition of "ham and eggs in a pan" since 1949, the restaurant serves breakfast and lunch daily, from 7 a.m. to 3 p.m. $.

where to stay

The Inn at Pocono Manor. 1 Manor Dr., Pocono Manor, PA; (800) 233-8150; www .poconomanor.com. This historic property has preserved its 1902 architectural aesthetics while updating the 237 guest rooms and suites with comfortable, luxurious amenities. The Laurel Spa has 20 treatment rooms for massages, facials, steam, body wraps, hydro-therapy, and numerous other services. There are two 18-hole golf courses, a sports center, horseback riding, dogsledding, and numerous outdoor pursuits. The inn's restaurant, The Exchange, serves dinner nightly and has an international wine list to complement its Continental-American menu. The Old Lamplighter Lounge opens at 11:30 a.m. and has a pub menu. $$.

jim thorpe, pa

No one would dare to mock this chunk . . . yet until the 1950s, the name on the map was Mauch Chunk (pronounced "mock-chunk"), a Lenape tribal name for "bear mountain." Locals hoping to reinvent their tourism profile chose the name "Jim Thorpe" after the legendary Olympic athlete, who had gone to school in Pennsy.

getting there

The town is about 2 hours from Newark, via the Garden State Parkway, I-280 north, and I-80 west into Pennsylvania; take the Blakeslee exit 284 and turn left onto PA 115 south for about 3 miles; turn right onto PA 903 south for about 18 miles; cross the bridge and turn left into the historic district.

where to go

Pocono Mountain Visitors Bureau. Route 209, Jim Thorpe; (570) 325-3673; www.800poconos.com. Get your bearings here and sort among myriad activities depending on the season you visit.

Lehigh Gorge Scenic Railway. 1 Susquehanna St., Jim Thorpe; (570) 325-8485; www.lgsry.com. Coach, open-air car, or caboose? Choose your connection for a 16-mile, narrated train ride from Jim Thorpe to Old Penn Haven. The trip winds along the river, curving around hills, for about 1 hour. When the train leaves the station, you leave restrooms behind. The coach is not air-conditioned, so ask about seats in the open-air car. Coach tickets are $12 for adults; open-air and caboose tickets are $18. Ask about special events, such as the 50-mile Dutch Treat ride to White Haven. The rail trip offers an excellent overview of the surrounding Lehigh Gorge State Park.

Asa Packer Mansion. Packer Hill, Jim Thorpe; (570) 325-3229; www.asapackermansion.com. Born in Connecticut, Packer went from hired hand to railroad magnate by taking a chance on the future of railroads. He bought a controlling interest in an incomplete line: the Delaware, Lehigh, Schuylkill and Susquehanna—a move that would place him among the most accomplished men in the Commonwealth. Packer and his wife were in their 50s when they built this 3-story, 18-room Italianate mansion. A red-ribbed tin roof with a cupola covers a cast-iron frame. Several of Packer's children died young. His daughter, Mary Hannah Packer Cummings, left the house and its furnishings to the borough when she died in

1912. It sat vacant until 1956, when it reopened as a museum. The interiors exist as they did during a half-century as the Packers' home. Museum hours are 11 a.m. to 4 p.m., on weekends in Apr and May, and seven days a week from Memorial Day through October 31. Admission is $8 for adults, $7 for seniors, and $5 for children.

Mauch Chunk Historical Society. 16 W. Broadway, Jim Thorpe; (610) 457-0370; www .mauchchunkhistory.com. Every season deserves a look, and Jim Thorpe historians are happy to oblige. Call to reserve a fall foliage weekend tour, or perhaps an entertaining guided tour of Old Mauch Chunk, weekends from May through November. In late September, reserve the Jim Thorpe Victorian House Tour, a self-guided look at 19 buildings. The cost is $10 for adults, $5 for children.

Mauch Chunk Opera House. 14 W. Broadway, Jim Thorpe; (570) 325-0249; www .mauchchunkoperahouse.com. American Vaudeville theaters are a blast from the past, and this one is among the rare originals in operation since 1882. National artists love the venue for its stellar acoustics and intimate atmosphere. The year-round schedule ranges from a Chopin program on an 1890 Chickering 9-foot grand piano, to Bill Miller, Tuck and Patti, Gallagher, The Wailin' Jennys, The Manhattan Lyric Opera, and The Slambovian Circus.

a spirited storefront

Why settle for selling votives and tapers when your haunted basement is moaning, for crying out loud? Hence, Linda Schlier, a veteran candlemaker, added a new element to her shop, which she operates in a 2-story brownstone at Route 611 and Route 314 North in Swiftwater, PA. The house was built in 1897 as a mountain retreat for Hoboken, NJ, physician Dr. William Redwood Fisher. His associate was Dr. Richard Slee of the Pocono Biological Laboratories. Fisher died in the home in 1926, when an antiques dealer took over the site. Fast-forward several decades, when Linda's husband, Jim, bought the property for his wife's creative candle business. And that would have been that—except she and her employees talked about hearing anguished cries coming from the basement and read stories about the good doc and his partner conducting experiments on monkeys. And that would have been that—until Linda called in an "expert" on paranormal whatnot. After the suits wrote their report, Animal Planet called to film an episode of The Haunted, and Linda really had no choice but to reinvent herself. Now, when you approach The Candle Shoppe of the Poconos—and you really can't miss it—you will see the classy brownstone with boulder-size sculptures of skeletons and other spooky props in the yard.

Popular at Christmas time are the Bach and Handel Chorale concerts. With only 400 seats, you need to be in one of them.

where to shop

Marianne Monteleone. 97 Broadway, Jim Thorpe; (570) 325-3540; www.shopmm.com. The designer displays her unique jackets and coats, plus jewelry and accessories.

Shabby foo foo. 25 Broadway, Jim Thorpe; (570) 325-8858; www.prettyshabby.com. Kellie and Carol are a mother-daughter team who run this unusual storefront as well as their online emporium, Pretty Shabby. Charming, feminine items for the boudoir, bath, and home are all around you, plus decorative accessories for any room. Ah, yes—lace runners and doilies.

where to eat

The Albright Mansion. 66 Broadway, Jim Thorpe; (570) 325-4440; www.albrightmansion .com. Sited in a Civil War–era home, the restaurant serves lunch, dinner, and a proper English tea, courtesy of the British proprietor, Meriel Springer. Breakfast items are abundant, from Meriel's crepes to Eggs In Bed—eggs on a bed of sautéed onions, with bacon bits on top. Dubbed the Campaign Sandwich in 2012 but popular any year: scrambled eggs, cheese, and ham on an English muffin. There is a wine list, or you may bring your own bottle, for a corkage fee. $$.

Broadway Grille & Pub. 24 Broadway, Jim Thorpe (inside The Inn at Jim Thorpe); (570) 732-4343; www.broadwaygrillepub.com. The restaurant serves breakfast, lunch, and dinner every day. The menu is American with some far-off influences—steaks, seafood, burgers, sandwiches, pasta, salads, and more. $$.

Flow. 268 W. Broadway, Jim Thorpe; (570) 325-8200; www.thecccp.org. This restaurant and gallery are what happens when an artist and a writer collaborate to feed both you and your soul. Victor Stabin and Joan Morykin are the creative team. The dining room, housed in a rebuilt stone factory, reveals an underground stream. Their building dates to circa 1850, when a wire mill on the premises produced braided cable for the Brooklyn Bridge. After tours as a silk mill, dressmaking factory, and a toy factory, The Stabin Morykin Building is a post-Industrial bastion of hospitality and culture. There is bar service and farm-to-table fare. Or take in an art class or workshop. Check out the website for special events. $$.

Macaluso's at The Lantern Inn. 1257 E. Catawissa St., Nesqahoning; (570) 669-9433. Two sisters run this operation, and they put out some delectable Italian and Continental cuisine. The chicken Lucia is definitely unusual, in a good way, and there was a lot to love about the shrimp entree and rack of lamb. The location is about 3 miles from Jim Thorpe via Route 209. Lunch and dinner. $$.

depending on gravity

The Lehigh Coal and Navigation Company began to build the Mauch Chunk Railroad on an existing road in 1827, and the line opened later that year. It carried anthracite from the company's mines at Summit Hill to its coal chutes on the Lehigh River, a ride of half an hour—compared with 4 hours by mule. The scenic downhill trek was quite a rush, and its reputation grew. Soon, tourists began asking to ride along. Coal became a morning run, with passengers buying up the afternoon slots. After a while, tourism won out and the downhill railroad was a catalyst for the roller coaster. Thomas Edison, the Menlo Park "wizard" who invented the phonograph and the first underground electrical system at his laboratory in New Jersey, was fascinated with the Lehigh railroad; so was President Ulysses S. Grant. In 1874 the Central Railroad of New Jersey bought the line and leased it to two brothers, Theodore and H. L. Mumford, who ran it as a tourist attraction. Less than 6 months before the stock market crash of 1929, CRNJ sold the line. The Mauch Chunk Switchback Railway Company was on track with freight runs until 1932. Roller coaster ridership continued until 1938. The line became a casualty of the Great Depression and was sold for scrap.

Molly Maguires Pub & Steakhouse. 5 Hazard Way, Jim Thorpe; (570) 325-4563. The establishment is on the ground floor of the historic Hotel Switzerland, built in 1830 and the oldest commercial structure in town. Home of the 24-ounce steak and named for the infamous trial of four men hanged for murder. There is a 2,400-square-foot outdoor deck. Hours are 11 a.m. to 10 p.m. $$.

where to stay

Harry Packer Mansion. 19 Packer Ave., Jim Thorpe; (570) 325-8566; www.murder mansion.com. The rose-colored Second Empire mansion is next door to the one built by Harry's parents (described above). The Harry Packer Mansion is a bed-and-breakfast. It has a steep-pitched mansard-style roof, with unique rooflines and complex elements. Ornate porches are of carved bluestone. There is a 2-night minimum for weekends. Rates for "Murder Mystery Weekends" are for the whole weekend and include breakfast and dinner. $$$.

The Inn at Jim Thorpe. 24 Broadway, Jim Thorpe; (570) 325-2599; www.innjt.com. This New Orleans–style redbrick structure with wrought-iron balconies dates to 1849, yet the guest accommodations are up to the minute. Consider a room with a fireplace or whirlpool. It was built to replace The White Swan Hotel, which perished in a fire. It had later incarnations as the New American Hotel before being renamed The Inn at Jim Thorpe in the late

a prescient prenup

Mary Hannah Packer was more fortunate than her six siblings. Her parents, Sarah and Asa Packer, lost three daughters before the age of 3. Another daughter died during their lifetime. Asa died in 1879, and his wife died in 1882. Their heir, son Robert, died a year later. Mary's younger brother Harry, the next beneficiary, died a year after that. Victorian-era laws prevented Mary from inheriting the family fortune because she was single. So Mary wed Charles Cummings, a railroad engineer, in a convenient arrangement. In the event of a divorce, he would get $100,000 in Lehigh Valley Railroad stock and a house in Florida. A year later, she was a divorced, very wealthy heiress who commenced a lifestyle of world travels and philanthropy. Visitors to the Asa Packer Mansion will see her 1905 Model D Grand Welte Cottage Orchestrion, said to be the only working Model D left in this country.

1980s. Also ask about a companion property, 55 Broadway, across the street, which has guest rooms and apartments. $$.

Mary's Guesthouse. 39 W. Broadway, Jim Thorpe; (570) 325-5354; www.marysjimthorpe .com. Unlike a bed-and-breakfast, this guesthouse has a few guest rooms, a few bathrooms, and a kitchen, dining room, living room, and patio for your use. The proprietor prefers cash; there is a 2.5 percent charge for credit cards. Bring your own toiletries. $.

day trip 05

the skylands

>>> **love for the links & their legends:**
far hills & bernardsville, nj

No need to play or love golf to enjoy this engaging day trip—which gives a nod to some Americana that novices will appreciate. You gotta love a 10-year-old caddy loping along with a golf bag bigger than he is—tending to a 20-year-old working-class stiff beating the knickers off the pretty boys hogging the headlines.

America got into the game in 1913, thanks to Francis DeSales Ouimet, a first-generation American, and his kiddie-caddy, Eddy Lowery. Ouimet, an upstart from Brookline, MA, won the 1913 US Open, wresting the tournament from the more famous, hoy-polloy Brits. The saga is romanticized in the 2005 film, *The Greatest Game Ever Played,* starring Shia LaBeouf as Ouimet.

Far Hills is part of Bernards Township and is home to the headquarters of the US Golf Association and its museum. Here, you will find an inviting valentine to all the heroes and heroines who have raced pulses and raised trophies during its 117-year history.

In the vicinity are the boroughs of Bedminster, Bernardsville, and Peapack-Gladstone, where a 19th-century country estate got another lease on life in the form of a public park on the North Branch of the Raritan River. On a leased portion of the original woodlands, development is well under way on a visionary hotel/restaurant/spa complex.

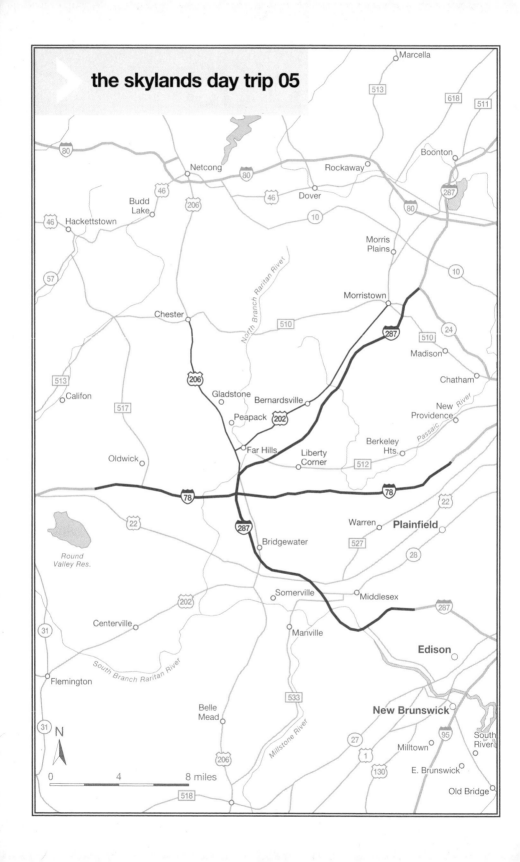

the skylands day trip 05

far hills & bernardsville, nj

getting there

From the Gateway Region, take I-78 to exit 29 and head north on I-287; take exit 26 (Mt. Airy Road) and turn left. The USGA museum is about a 30-minute car ride from Newark; on Mt. Airy Road, proceed to the first traffic light, about 1.4 miles; turn right onto Lyons Road and go 0.6 mile; turn right onto Liberty Corner Road; go 1.8 miles to the facility on your left. Scenery throughout the Somerset Hills is enchanting—as are the many examples of distinguished architecture among the surviving country estates that were built in its "Mountain Colony" in the late 19th century and early 20th century. Nature is a magnificent backdrop for the residential grandeur created for the era's landed gentry.

In Bernardsville, note the rewards of historic preservation among the shops and boutiques housed in restored vintage buildings.

where to go

Arnold Palmer Center for Golf History. 77 Liberty Corner Rd., Far Hills; (908) 234-2300; www.usgamuseum.com. The US Golf Association's stately headquarters has long housed a museum. But in 2008, the group completed a 3-year expansion and opened what amounts to a game-changer in the way fans and history buffs can bask in the sport. Entering the new wing, visitors will delight in James David Chase's engaging portrait of Palmer. *Gratitude,* a black-and-white work in pen and ink, uses 22,000 of Palmer's words about golf to convey the sports legend's facial features. Chase spent 14 years creating the work. In the

timeline through the tube

An exhibit at the Arnold Palmer Center for Golf History features a stack of vintage television sets that provide a fascinating chronology of world events through the lens of golf matches. "Rabbit ears" and all, showing black-and-white "snow," then moving into color images as time marched on, the exhibit at Far Hills gives you decade-by-decade snapshots: the Dawn of American Golf, the Golden Age, the Great Depression, World War II, the Comeback Age, the Age of the Superpowers, and the Global Game. There are highlights such as the "revolution," when Jack Nicklaus unseated Arnold Palmer; the fall of the Berlin Wall; the moments when foreign competition upped the ante in America; and concurrent events that shaped the world and the game.

Hall of Champions are authentic trophies. Among the vintage photos is Francis Ouimet, the first American golf hero. Exhibits cover the various "ages" of golf from the 19th century to today. In addition to the Palmer den are salons appointed for Bobby Jones and Ben Hogan. There is a library, test center, and putting green. The museum is open Tues through Sun, 10 a.m. to 5 p.m.; the research center is open weekdays. Admission is $7 for adults, $5 for seniors, and $3.50 for children younger than 12.

The Leonard J. Buck Garden. 11 Layton Rd., Far Hills; (908) 234-2677; www.somerset countyparks.org. This 33-acre site is considered a premier rock garden in the eastern United States, reflecting the maturity of work based on a master plan begun in the 1930s. A series of alpine gardens are situated in a wooded glacial-stream valley that originated in the Moggy Hollow Natural Area, a National Natural Landmark next door. Geologist Leonard Buck began the garden as part of his estate. His widow, Helen, donated it to the county in the 1970s. The concept created by landscape architect Zenon Schreiber was a naturalistic garden that maximized rock outcroppings shaped by ancient waterfalls. Plants on the site include exotic varieties, and wildflowers and abundant ferns rim its trails. Azaleas

overflowing royals

About 1,000 acres of woodlands surround 2 miles of the North Branch of the Raritan River. The property once belonged to lawyer-yachtsman Walter Graeme Ladd and his wife, philanthropist and shipping heiress Kate Macy Ladd. The estate's name, "Natirar," is an anagram for Raritan. In 1912 work was completed on their 40-room, brick Tudor-style manor on a hill, featuring limestone trim, a turreted slate roof, extensive oak paneling, and molded plaster ceilings. Mrs. Ladd also created a convalescent home on the grounds for "deserving gentlewomen." Half a century after Walter Ladd's death—in accordance with the provisions of his will—Natirar was sold to King Hassan II of Morocco. Occasionally, the king visited his children, who lived there while attending classes at Princeton. The county bought the property in 2003 from the king's heir, Mohammed VI, and made 404 acres into a public park. That left 90 acres available for lease. The tenants are aviation billionaire Sir Richard Branson and New Jersey developer Robert Wojtowicz, who are redeveloping the Ladd mansion into The Virgin Spa at Natirar, a 76-room luxury hotel and private club, an upscale farm-table restaurant, and the ultimate spa retreat. A century-old carriage house was converted to Ninety Acres restaurant, organic farm, and culinary showcase in 2010. Phase II brought a club members' fitness center, tennis courts, swimming pools, a temporary spa, and guest cottages. Phase III is underway and will complete the hotel and spa.

and rhododendrons offer a burst of color in late spring, and the rest of the year is a much-anticipated botanical surprise. You may enjoy a picnic on a deck next to the visitor center, which was created from a renovated carriage house. Hours are 10 a.m. to 4 p.m. Mon through Fri, 10 a.m. to 5 p.m. Sat, and noon to 5 p.m. Sun. The garden is closed on major holidays and weekends from Dec through Mar. Donations are requested; no smoking is a mandate.

Natirar Park. 2 Peapack Rd., Peapack; (908) 781-2560; www.somersetcountyparks.org. This unique public space straddles multiple boroughs and townships—Peapack, Gladstone, Far Hills, and Bedminster. Its colorful history is surpassed only by the grandeur of more than 400 acres of woodlands surrounding the North Branch of the Raritan River. The park includes miles of walking trails, extensive meadows and historic farm buildings, and outbuildings that date to the 19th century and earlier. A designated fishing area follows the river and Peapack Brook. The park is open daily from dawn to dusk for walking, jogging, horseback riding, and mountain biking.

The F. P. Olcott Building. 24 Olcott Ave., Bernardsville. Designed by New Jersey native and legendary New York architect Henry Janeway Hardenbergh, this Tudor-Revival edifice was commissioned by Frederick P. Olcott, a banker who owned a summer home in Bernardsville's affluent Mountain Colony. He donated the land and paid for construction of a high school. The building today houses the administrative offices for the county school district. The architect—best known for The Plaza Hotel and the Dakota Building in New York—selected Waterloo granite and red-clay roof tiles for the Olcott site. From Far Hills, turn north onto Route 202 to Olcott Square and Olcott Avenue.

English Farm. 3625 Valley Rd., Liberty Corner; (908) 647-3420; www.englishfarm.org. This property has been family-owned for eight generations, and was the site of French General Rochambeau's encampment on the way to the Battle of Yorktown. There is a working farm, a farm market, and barnyard animals. English Farm is open from July 1 through October 31, and you can buy eggs and seasonal vegetables, including tomatoes, corn, squash, and peppers. The market is closed Tues and Wed. The farm also sells herbs and plants from nearby Harrison Brook Farm and peaches and apples from Ripple Hill Farm. In the fall, there are hayrides and pumpkin picking.

Scherman Hoffman Wildlife Sanctuary. 11 Hardscrabble Rd., Bernardsville; (908) 766-5787; www.njaudubon.org. The center's Wayrick Wildlife Gallery has a rotating schedule of art and photography exhibits that showcase natural subjects. The Nature Store carries binoculars, books, birding accessories, and natural gift items. You will find a year-round schedule for adult, children, and scout programs, as well as those geared for teachers, on the website. You may hike along 3 miles of trails through forests and meadows near the headwaters of the Passaic River. The sanctuary's neighbor is the Morristown National

sight-unseen visionary

Evander Schley, a land developer in New York, bought large tracts of farmland in the Somerset Hills in the 1880s—some of it without even a peek at the turf. Given that rail service had arrived a decade or so earlier, Schley realized the area would draw city dwellers eager for a day or longer in the country. In 1887 his brother, Grant Schley, and wife, Elizabeth, arrived in a carriage—prompting Elizabeth's comment on the vista of "far hills." The diminutive village in the vicinity of Schley Mountain has retained its heritage of 10-acre minimum tracts. Several boldface names live here, including Forbes editor-in-chief and former politician Steve Forbes, and former New Jersey Gov. Christine Todd Whitman, whose maternal grandfather was Reeve Schley, a cousin of Evander's nephew.

Historic Park, which is described in The Skylands Day Trip to Morristown. The center is open Tues through Sat, 9 a.m. to 5 p.m.; Sun, noon to 5 p.m.; closed Mon and holidays.

where to shop

The Bookworm. 99 Claremont Rd., Bernardsville; (908) 766-4599; www.bookworm bernardsville.com. More than an independent bookstore lurks behind this door. At The Bookworm, you can buy greeting cards, motion-journals, stationery, fun bookmarks, and page-tabs. Browse the website for what's new, the books that showcase the culture and history of Somerset County, and books for children. The shop is open 9:30 to 5:30 weekdays and 10 to 5 on Sat. Check the website for favorites and author signings.

Diehl's Jewelers. 24 Olcott Square 9 (Route 202), Bernardsville; (908) 766-0509; www .diehlsjewelers.com. Kris Schmid, grandson of the founders and a master gemologist and jewelry designer, runs the operation. It was founded in 1946, at a time when you had to buy an existing business to open a new one. So Eleanor Diehl and her watchmaker husband, Robert, bought a dry-cleaning establishment and operated dual businesses for decades. Now located just a few doors from the original address, Diehl's also sells Debbie Brooks handbags, Mokume-Gane designs, Gallatea Pearls, Eyris Blue Pearls, and other unusual gifts.

The Streets of Chester. 270 Route 206, Chester; (203) 962-5526. This upscale, open-air shopping center opened in 2006. Tenants include Ann Taylor, Coach, J. Crew, Banana Republic, and Chico's.

where to eat

Ninety Acres. 2 Main St., Peapack-Gladstone; (908) 901-9400; www.natirar.com. This unusual destination is on the grounds of the 494-acre Natirar Estate, which is described above. The restaurant is open for dinner Tues through Sun, and reservations are recommended. The menu is "American inspired"—heavy on regional ingredients, especially produce from its backyard organic farm. Dine a la carte inside or on the patio by the farm, sit by the kitchen and eat what someone puts in front of you, or congregate in the Cognac Room for tapas-style samples. The wine cellar is robust, and the prices are in line with the royal surroundings. $$$.

Sublime. 12 Lackawanna St., Gladstone; (908) 781-1888; www.sublimenj.com. Opened in 2009 by Chef Scott Howlett, this upscale-casual restaurant/bar is near the Gladstone Train Station. His menu reflects his experiences cooking Asian, Latin, and fusion dishes. The portions are generous, as is the inventive seasoning. Friends love the seared scallops; others, the filet mignon; and the Thai sauce on PEI mussels is an odyssey all its own. Sublime has indoor seating for 90, plus tables on the patio and full bar service and wines by the bottle or glass. It is open for dinner Tues through Sun. $$.

where to stay

The Bernards Inn. 27 Mine Brook Rd., Bernardsville; (908) 766-0002; www.bernardsinn .com. This historic property reflects the era it was built, 1907, and the compatible styles of renovated American country inn and European boutique lodging. There are 20 guest rooms/ suites. Occasionally during the summer, pet owners may bring their little darlings to the inn for a meal on the terrace. $$$.

Somerset Hills Hotel. 200 Liberty Corner Rd., Warren; (908) 660-4506; www.thesomerset hillshotel.com. Choose among guest rooms, efficiencies, suites with whirlpool tubs, and bigger suites. Amenities include a fitness center and swimming pool. The hotel gives you a lot for the money and offers some off-season specials to soften the blow. $$.

day trip 06

the skylands

veggie valhalla:
montville, nj

New Jersey loves Montville, and so does "Money."

In 2011, CNN Money named this Morris County township the 17th best place to live in the United States.

Montville is only 35 minutes from Newark and not much farther into Manhattan. It also is a convenient sojourn from anywhere in The Skylands.

Settled by Dutch farmers from New Amsterdam in the early 1700s, the lands were coveted for their fertile soil. Can you say Jersey tomatoes and not be grateful? Apple orchards, cornfields, and berry shrubs are plentiful—and many farms allow you to pick your own.

By the 1740s, the growing settlement merited its first road, now called Route 202. It linked farms with tanneries and various mills. Given specific boundaries in 1800, the town's name came from the local Mandeville Inn, which the Dutch pronounced Mondeveil. The spelling later was altered to Montville.

In 1828 the Morris Canal was completed here, boosting commercial navigation. Two smaller villages arose nearby: Pine Brook to the south, a fertile agricultural area; and Towaco on the Morris Canal.

The Ramapo River runs into Montville, and the Passaic River passes on its border. In the vicinity are Caldwell, the birthplace of President Grover Cleveland; Little Falls, a repository of baseball lore; Whippany, stoked on trains; and Wayne, a site for Revolutionary provenance.

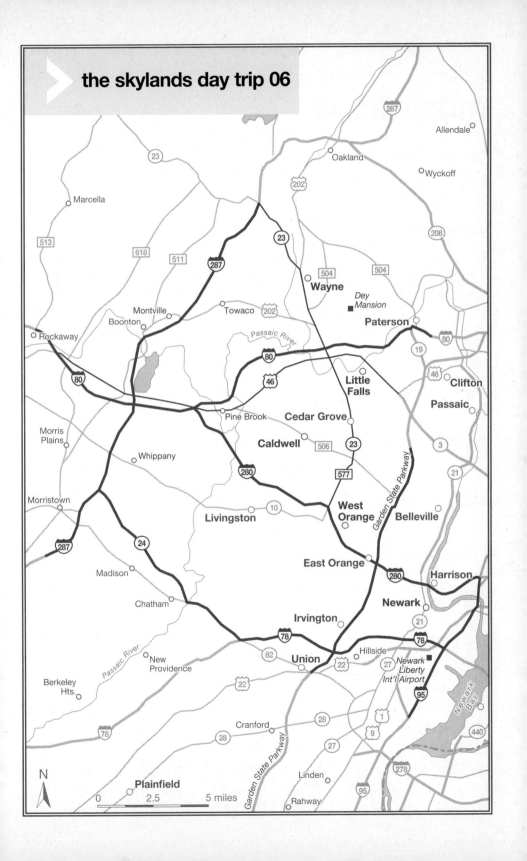

montville, nj

getting there

From the Newark area, take I-280 north to I-80 west; go a few miles and get on I-287 north to exit 47 (US 202). Montville is about half an hour from Newark.

where to go

Bader Farm. 290 Changebridge Rd., Montville; (973) 227-0294; www.baderfarm.com. Five generations of Baders have operated this farm since 1892, and today's proprietors include Ivan and Jean Bader and their sons Sean and Ian. Stop by their store for fresh fruits and vegetables and the luxury of meeting a family proud of its devotion to the land. Around Thanksgiving, you can buy holiday wreaths, seasoned firewood, and bountiful poinsettias; in spring, Easter plants, rose bushes, tulips, and daffodils. Butternut and other squashes, broccoli and cabbage abound in the fall, along with pumpkin city. During August and September, visit the source for cucumbers, green beans, zucchini, Jersey tomatoes, peppers, sweet corn, and eggplant. Pick your own, if you insist, and take time to peruse Bader's jams, jellies, and local honey.

Towaco Station. 632 Main Rd. (Route 202), Towaco; www.njtransit.com. The New Jersey Transit station, which dates to 1910, is in the Towaco section of Montville. It is part of the Montclair-Boonton Line, with stops at Montclair State and New York's Penn Station.

Whippany Railway Museum. 1 Railroad Plaza, Whippany; (973) 887-8177; www.whip panyrailwaymuseum.net. Train buffs, this one is all about you, and about "ties" to the state's spiked-tracks-and-steam-locomotive history. Exhibits rotate, highlighting various railroad lines. The stone Whippany passenger depot is an exterior landmark, and you will see countless examples of oldie "iron horses." One special excursion is a ride on the restored Jersey Coast Club Car, built in 1927. The museum closes in the winter, with the exception of five days for the Santa Claus Special, a 10-mile ride to Roseland and back. If you go to the museum from Montville, you can ride through a quaint small town along the way, Lake Hiawatha. Take Changebridge Road onto River Road in Montville; turn left onto Beverwyck Road, which winds through Lake Hiawatha and brings you into Whippany.

Yogi Berra Museum & Learning Center. 8 Quarry Rd., Little Falls; (973) 655-2378; www .yogiberramuseum.org. This facility dedicated to baseball glory is located on the campus of Montclair State University. The best part here is, you don't have to chew tobacco, or spit on the mound, to feel nostalgia for the game.

Dey Mansion. 199 Totowa Rd., Wayne; (973) 696-1776; www.rt3.com. It isn't every day that you can tour a structure built in the mid-18th century, and one that had a pivotal role as one of General Washington's wartime headquarters. It was begun in the 1740s by Dirck Dey, a Dutch-born planter whose grandfather had settled in the "colonies" in 1641. Dey bought 600 acres of land in Preakness Valley. By 1764, he passed the property to his son, Theunis Dey. A colonel in the militia during the Revolution, he met Washington and offered his home for a headquarters. Washington accepted Dey's hospitality twice, for months at a time.

Essex County Turtle Back Zoo. 560 Northfield Ave., West Orange; (973) 731-5800; www.turtlebackzoo.com. There are more than 500 animals here representing hundreds of species. Focusing on wildlife native to New Jersey, the collection includes cougars, bison, eagles, and wolves; plus elk, llamas, white-tailed deer, otters, owls, and sea lions. There are domestic animals that kids may feed. Attractions include a pony ride and train ride. See the website for the year-round calendar of events. Open daily.

where to shop

Barry's Montville Pharmacy. 185 Changebridge Rd., Montville; (973) 335-6688. A pharmacist owns this petite jewel box and sells gems—and jewel boxes—on the side. Yes, the pharmacist dispenses prescriptions, and the shelves hold plenty of over-the-counter essentials and sundries. But the bulk of display space is devoted to a browser's haven— Vera Bradley handbags, totes, wallets, and lanyards; tableware; stationery; novelty wear such as Sugarless bandeaus and Malibu Sugar tank tops and camis. There is a nice candy selection with tons of Godiva, plus Melissa & Doug toys, Alex toys, Yankee candles, and the Crabtree & Evelyn line.

Bliss Salon. 628 Main Rd. (Route 202), Towaco; (973) 402-8100. Day-spa owner Donna Benelli keeps plenty of goodies here for you to browse while waiting for a new hairdo, facial, manicure, or massage. Conveniently located across the road from the Towaco Station, the salon carries professional hair and skin-care products you won't find elsewhere, plus handbags, scarfs, belts, and jewelry.

Condursos Garden Center. 96 River Rd., Montville; (973) 263-8814; www.condursos .com. Open since 1929, this is a serious outpost for gardeners, would-be green thumbs, or anyone who loves the cultivated outdoors. You can also buy flowers and candy, browse the dual-wick Village Candle selection, choose a gift for someone's patio, and select birdhouses and garden accessories.

Conturso's Market. 446 Main Rd. (Route 202), Towaco; (973) 588-7888; www.contursos market.com. A former chef and his wife operate this specialty food market and catering operation. You can buy artisan breads, soups, sauces, pasta, pizza, and sandwiches; there is an espresso bar. You can order prepared meals ahead to be picked up, or Conturso's will deliver.

MJM Designer Shoes. 44 US Route 46, Pine Brook; (973) 276-1164; www.mjmdesigner shoes.com. This outlet location in the southern portion of Montville carries brands such as Adidas, Timberland, Skechers, Guess, Kenneth Cole Reaction, and Steve Madden. Open seven days.

Willowbrook Mall. 1400 Willowbrook Mall, Wayne; (973) 785-1655; www.willowbrook-mall.com. Conveniently located at the convergence of Route 46, Route 23, and I-80, the mall's anchors include Lord & Taylor, Bloomingdale's, and Macy's.

where to eat

Calandra's Italian Village. 234 Bloomfield Ave., Caldwell; (973) 226-8889; www.calan drasitalianvillage.com. This multitasking operation combines a full-service dining room, a taverna, an Italian bakery, a gelateria, espresso bar, deli market, and wine store. And that is just under one roof. The patriarch of this company, Luciano Calandra, grew his empire from humble beginnings at a small bakery in Newark. His sons run the operation, which includes other bakeries in Newark and another restaurant and bakery in Fairfield. You also will see Calandra's baked goods in Jersey supermarkets. The food is good, the decor appealing, and it has a convenient bambini menu. $$.

The Columbia Inn. 29 Main Rd. (Route 202), Montville; (973) 263-1300; www.thecolumbia inn.com. This quaint structure dates to the 1870s and once housed Montville's town hall. It also was an inn convenient to the Morris Canal. The current owners bought the building in the late 1990s, restored it, and converted the inn into an Italian restaurant. It is much in demand for fine dining and Sunday brunch—and Zagat praises its "honest, reliable cooking . . . " and imaginative specials. The brick oven produces delectable thin-crust pizza, and there is full bar service. Open for lunch Tues through Fri; dinner Tues through Sun. $$.

The Montville Inn. 167 Main Rd. (Route 202), Montville; (973) 541-1234; www.montvilleinn .com. Located at the intersection of Main and River Roads, the inn is located at the site of the pre-Revolutionary War Mandeville Inn. After a complete makeover, which preserved the integrity of its Colonial exterior, the inn is a comfort zone for fine dining, tavern fare, or a casual bite outside in an Adirondack chair. There is a fieldstone fireplace in the dining room and a cozy, clubby full bar. It's not every day you can order fried deviled eggs, but the inn is happy to oblige. There are inventive salads, pastas, thin-crust pizza, sandwiches, panini, chicken Savoy—a regional standard—and steaks. For dessert, try the fried apple and ice-cream sandwich with an espresso martini. Open for lunch Tues through Fri and dinner Tues through Sun. Making a reservation is quicker than a phone call, with the inn's online system. $$.

Tiffany's. 73 Route 46 West, Pine Brook; (973) 227-2112; www.tiffanysrestaurant.com. When co-owner Tony "The Goose" Siraguso bought an interest in the restaurant company, an already popular rib house gained a big boost in the sports-bar category. "Tiff's" was founded by Michael Romanelli, whose son, Michael Jr., is the chef. Be sure to sample "Grandma's Meatballs," served with garlic toast, fresh shaved Parmesan, and fresh basil. Baby back ribs are the specialty, but you have plenty of other choices: steaks, seafood, salads, Asian dishes, chicken, a children's menu, and "Sunday Pasta" every day. Open daily for lunch and dinner. $$.

worth more time

Wild West City. Lackawanna Drive, Netcong; (973) 347-8900; www.wildwestcity.com. This attraction dates to 1956 and bills itself as "the best of the West in the heart of the East." Only 35 miles from Newark, it is located off I-80 exit 25 and Route 206 North. Taking a page from 1880s Dodge City, Kansas, this is a Western heritage theme park featuring live-action shows. You can witness a stagecoach "holdup," observe a gunfight at the OK Corral, and learn more about the Sundance Kid, Katie Fisher, and the Forty-Five-Caliber Law.

day trip 07

the skylands

>>> **jockeying for position in a ford:**
morristown, nj

Nature, history, romance, art, and period architecture—can one hope for a more complete afternoon? You will want more than one to fully experience Morristown, which is tradition on the hoof, reflecting three centuries as the center of portent in New Jersey.

From the 1870s through the 1920s, the area around the Somerset Hills was strongly coveted by wealthy New York financiers and industrialists. So many of them bundled large tracts of land for their summer mansions, people started calling the area around Morristown "The Inland Newport."

Formerly the township of New Hanover—renamed to honor Gov. Lewis Morris—Morristown witnessed significance across the board. Called the military capital of the American Revolution, it also was the scene for major innovations during the Industrial Revolution.

It was a village of churches, a courthouse, mills, farms, schools, stores, inns, and taverns—at a time when balance was not an ideal. For the yin, Morristown weathered two winters of our discontent. For the yang, it is also the place where George Washington decided that St. Patrick's Day should be celebrated as a holiday for his Irish troops.

Morristown's quaint downtown could keep you entertained for days, with specialty shops, dozens of restaurants, and numerous nightspots presenting entertainment. For a special treat, bank on the "2012 Mansion in May."

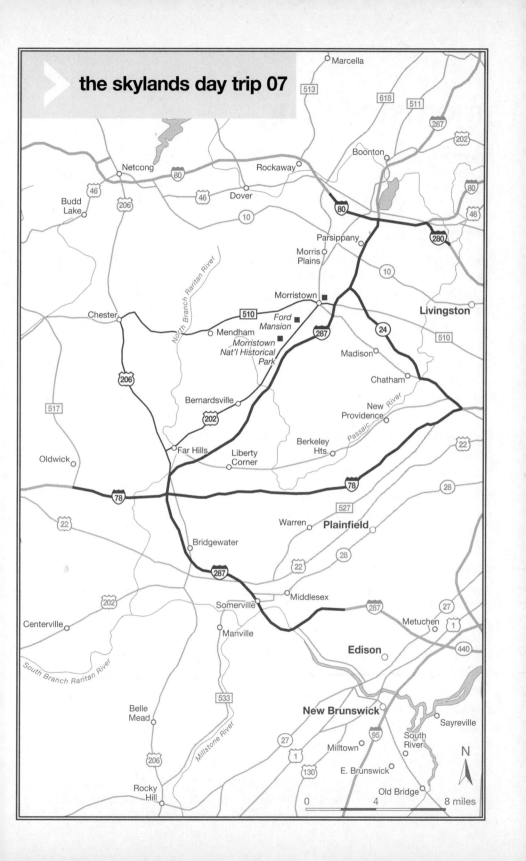

the skylands day trip 07

morristown, nj

getting there

This destination is less than an hour from Newark and about 30 miles from Manhattan. Take I-78 west to NJ 24 north, exit 37; then I-287 south to exit 36.

where to go

Acorn Hall. 68 Morris Ave., Morristown; (973) 267-3465; www.acornhall.org. Acorn Hall was named for one of the largest and oldest red oak trees in New Jersey. Built in 1853, this Italian-style mansion is the epitome of the Victorian-era lifestyle of Morris County. Its first owner was Dr. John P. Schermerhorn. The second was Augustus Crane, who brought his wife, Mary, and their children from New York City. Acorn Hall still reflects the ornate, largely decorative elements of Victorian architecture and its details are considered the most intact and authentic examples in town. You will see many original furnishings, including Schermerhorn's Rococo-Revival parlor set. Original trompe l'oeil effects grace a bedroom. The antique Japanese porcelain was a gift from Commodore Matthew Perry, a relative by marriage. Gifts from locals were "made in Morristown." Gardens designed by the local garden club feature flowers and shrubs typical of a 19th-century landscape. This headquarters of the Morris County Historical Society includes a Victorian Research Library, the only one of its kind in New Jersey. Hours are Mon and Thurs, 10 a.m. to 4 p.m., and Sun, 1 to 4 p.m. Admission is $5 for adults, $4 for seniors, and $2 for students.

The Ford Mansion/Morristown National Historical Park. 30 Washington Place, Morristown; (973) 539-2016, ext. 210; www.nps.gov/morr. The park's centerpiece, a Georgian-style manor home begun in 1772, has much to admire—even if it were not better known as Washington's Headquarters. Jacob Ford Jr., who managed his father's nearby iron mines, lived here with his wife, Theodosia Johnes Ford. Its English silhouette is grand but not pretentious, and the spectacular main doorway is a Palladian gem. In keeping with the period, the layout features wide center halls opening onto modest-size rooms, four to a floor. Ford, a brigadier general in the Continental Army, died in January 1777 while marching his men to Chatham. The rest of that winter, Washington camped in town. In December 1779, Ford's widow invited George and Martha Washington, their staff, and his officers to move into the Ford mansion—which turned the area into the republic's military capital for several more months. On tours here, you will see Washington's living quarters and rooms where he and his officers strategized battle plans. The "dining room" became the living area for Theodosia and her daughter; Jacob Ford's library was converted to a bedroom for three sons. After the war, Ford's son, Gabriel, a justice of the Supreme Court of New Jersey, lived in the mansion, as did his son, Henry A. Ford. In 1872 Henry's will directed the sale of the house at a public auction. The buyers, the Washington Association of New Jersey, gave the mansion to the

United States in 1933, when related sites became the nation's first national historical park. Behind the mansion is the Washington's Headquarters Museum and research library, which contains 22,000 books and 34,000 manuscripts. An arms exhibit has British, French, and American muskets, rifles, swords, and pistols—including a rare breech-loading Ferguson rifle and a silver-hilt sword that Washington carried at his 1789 inauguration as our first president. One permanent display shows how the war years affected civilians when thousands of soldiers arrived in 1777.

Jockey Hollow. Tempe Wick Road, Morristown; (973) 543-4030; www.nps.gov/morr. A few miles south of Morristown, 13,000 troops of the Continental Army spent the coldest winter of the eighteenth century, 1779–80, enduring 28 storms and blizzards. Soldiers hacked timber from the oak, walnut, and chestnut forests, and they built huts and drainage trenches on the hillsides—1,200 huts, 14- by 16-feet each, a dozen men to each hut—with beds of loose straw and meager provisions. It has been said that wintering in Morristown that year was a greater risk than most battles of the war. Today, you can hike miles of trails, with some up-and-down terrain. You will see orchards, a pond, and rebuilt soldier huts. In the visitor center is a movie theater and gift shop. If you are not into hiking, an asphalt road winds through Jockey Hollow.

Wick House/Farm Herb Garden. Morristown National Historical Park, Morristown; www .nps.gov/morr. At Wick House, built in 1750, you will meet "reenactors" who portray period characters. Listen for an anecdote about Temperance Wick, namesake for Tempe Wick Road, who was 22 during the winter of 1780. While riding her horse, she was accosted by mutineers. Fooling them into thinking she might give up her mount, Tempe galloped home and hid the horse in her bedroom. Her father, Henry, moved here from Long Island, buying 1,100 acres and building a Cape Cod–style house—featuring a central chimney, three fireplaces, and the kitchen. Wick grew corn, buckwheat, oats, and rye, and he had a barn and yard full of animals. The authentic herb garden outside Mrs. Wick's kitchen has annuals and perennials. The orchard has heirloom varieties. During winter 1779–80, Major General Arthur St. Clair was based here.

The Cross Estate Gardens. Leddell Road, Bernardsville; www.crossestategardens.org. English-style formal gardens and native gardens make up this property, plus a wisteria-covered pergola and a mountain laurel allée. Flanked by the headwaters of the Passaic River, the Cross Estate was built in 1905 in the Mountain Colony of Bernardsville. It was typical of country manors that the landed gentry built for summer retreats. With a few exceptions, that lifestyle is a memory that you may glimpse here. John A. Bensel named his estate Queen Anne Farm, with a carriage house, a 5-story stone water tower, and a gate house. In 1929 W. Redmond Cross renamed it "Hardscrabble House." His wife, Julia Newbold Cross, expanded the gardens. In 1975 the property was added to the Morristown National Historical Park. The transfer included the mansion and 162 acres. The grounds are open from dawn to dusk. Parking and admission are free.

two thumbs up

Should you want to poke your green thumb into a glove, pat some soil, or pull a pesky weed, you'd be welcome at the Cross Estate Gardens in Bernardsville. Each Wednesday morning, from Apr through Nov, volunteers meet from 9 a.m. to noon to work in the dirt. Maintaining the plants and flowers is a labor of love continued since 1977, when Jean Pope launched a project to rescue the foundering gardens. Two years after the Cross Estate was turned over to the National Park Service, Pope's team cleared paths and walkways, removed unwanted vegetation, pruned the rest, and replaced some casualties. The result is a restored English-style country garden open to the public. These days, Janet DiMauro coordinates the volunteers. To pitch in, put on a glove and call her at (908) 766-1699.

Willowwood Aboretum. 300 Longview Rd., Chester Township; (973) 326-7600; www.morrisparks.net. Have you hugged a tree today? It's easy to do so at this county park, which showcases 130 acres of rolling farm land and thousands of native, exotic, and rare plants. On a self-guided tour, you will see undisturbed forest gems such as oak, maple, willow, magnolia, lilac, cherry, fir, pine, and an unusual specimen of Dawn Redwood almost 100 feet tall; plus blankets of ferns and stands of wildflowers. A residence on the grounds dates to 1792. The lands were bought by brothers Henry and Robert Tubbs in 1908 and their hobby for half a century was collecting and cultivating distinctive plants.

Morris Museum. 6 Normandy Heights Rd., Morristown, NJ 07960; (973) 971-3700; fax (973) 538-0154; www.morrismuseum.org. Among the wealthy to build grand homes in Morris County was Peter Hood Ballantine Frelinghuysen, son of the president of P. Ballantine & Sons Brewery. In the early 1900s, he built a neo-Georgian mansion on his 150-acre estate and named it Twin Oaks. He converted part of the land into the Twin Oaks Dairy Farm. Frelinghuysen's mansion became the Morris Museum, where you can view rotating exhibits and permanent collections. In addition to fine arts, anthropology, geology, decorative arts, history, and natural science, the collections include model trains, dinosaurs, and two American Indian exhibits. The site includes the 312-seat Bickford Theatre, where you can enjoy a year-round schedule of performing arts. The Museum Gift Shop sells books, artwork, and novelties. Hours are Tues through Sat, 10 a.m. to 5 p.m.; Thurs 10 a.m. to 8 p.m.; and Sun from 1 to 5 p.m., excluding major holidays. Admission is $6 for adults, $4 for seniors and children. Admission is free on Thurs, 1 to 8 p.m.

Frelinghuysen Arboretum. 53 E. Hanover Ave., Morristown; (973) 326-7600; www.arboretumfriends.org. The 127-acre formal gardens and nature preserve were part of Whippany

Farm, an estate built in 1891 by George Griswold Frelinghuysen, the son of US Secretary of State Frederick Frelinghuysen. George and his wife, Sarah Ballantine of Newark, built a Colonial-Revival–style mansion and formal gardens. Their heir gave the property to Morris County in 1969. Readers of *New Jersey Monthly* named the place "The Best Public Garden and Arboretum" for 2011. You may take self-guided nature trails, and all the trees and shrubs are labeled. Strolls are free of charge and the site is open daily from 9 a.m. to dusk.

Fosterfields Living Historical Farm. 73 Kahdena Rd., Morristown; (973) 326-7645; www .morrisparks.net. In the mid-1800s, Gen. Joseph Warren Revere, grandson of Paul Revere, bought this farm, built a Gothic-Revival home, and named it The Willows. Charles Foster bought it in 1881 and changed the name to Fosterfields. Caroline Foster lived here for 98 years—having moved here at age 4—and willed it to the county. She stipulated that it remain a working farm using turn-of-the-century methods. It is open Wed and Sat from 10 a.m. to 5 p.m. and Sun from noon to 5 p.m.

Schuyler-Hamilton House. 5 Olyphant Place, Morristown; (973) 267-4039; www.morris .nj.us. During the Revolution, patriots on the move accepted the hospitality of sympathetic town residents. Dr. Jabez Campfield and his wife, Sarah, moved here in 1765. In the pivotal winter of 1779–80, the couple hosted Dr. John Cochran, personal physician to George Washington, and Cochran's wife, Gertrude, whose brother was Gen. Philip Schuyler of Albany, NY. Schuyler's daughter, Elizabeth, visited her aunt in Morristown, and a frequent caller was Col. Alexander Hamilton, Washington's aide-de-camp. This is where Hamilton courted "Betsy" and proposed marriage. In 1923 the local chapter of the Daughters of the American Revolution bought the house. It was renamed to reflect their romance and opened as a museum. You will see furniture and artifacts from the Colonial and Federal periods. The house is open from 2 to 4 p.m. Sun or by appointment.

Macculloch Hall Historical Museum and Gardens. 45 Macculloch Ave., Morristown; (973) 538-2404; www.macullochhall.org. The museum has the largest single collection of original works by Thomas Nast in the United States. They include drawings in pencil and ink, gouache, oil paintings and watercolors, preliminary drawings, doodles, and artist and printer proofs. In keeping with museum founder W. Parsons Todd's affinity for antique porcelain, hundreds of examples of fine French, German, English, and Chinese designs reflect the major houses making them from the 8th century through the mid-19th century. The Presidential Collection includes silver, porcelain, letters, images, documents, and one of only five copies of Washington's first Thanksgiving proclamation. The oldest garden in Morris County won't disappoint, especially if you melt over more than 60 varieties of roses. Two are mystery guests known as Old Macculloch Hall Roses. The wisteria was a gift from Commodore Perry, who visited the family about 1857. Tour on Wed, Thurs, and Sun from 1 to 4 p.m.; the gift shop is open 9 a.m. to 4 p.m. weekdays. To tour the garden, call for an appointment. Admission is $6 for adults and $5 for seniors and children.

craving a castle crawl? save the date

If you relish a peek inside Gilded Age living, you're in for a treat. Glynallyn in Convent Station is the setting for the "Mansion in May Designer Showhouse & Garden," presented to the public by the Women's Association of Morristown Medical Center every other May. Glynallyn is a 66-room Tudor-style manor on 7.5 rolling acres. It was begun in 1914 and at 32,000 square feet, the manor has enough architectural drama to intrigue Shakespeare—including a stage. This castle was the vision of yachtsman George Marshall Allen, heir to the Old Crow Whiskey fortune. He became enamored with Compton Wynyates, the early-16th-century home of Sir William Compton in Warwickshire, England, where King Henry VIII was a frequent houseguest. Modeling his Elizabethan fantasy after Compton Wynyates, Allen looked for land that resembled Warwickshire terrain. He chose a 4-mile tract near the country estates of wealthy New Yorkers. Architect Charles I. Berg stayed in England for several months, studying the house his client coveted and all things Tudor. Glynallyn was built of irregular brick, pitted limestone, and weathered timber. Its elaborate roof line has a forest of 25 chimneys—brick-fluted, twisted, each pattern unlike the others. Its silhouette pulls the eye among turrets, crenellated parapets, gables, gargoyles, balconies, and terraces to carved plaster, stained-glass windows, and a two-story Gothic bay window. Passing through brick pillars topped with gargoyles,

Lewis Morris Park. 270 Mendham Rd. (Route 24), Mendham; (973) 326-7600; www .parks.morris.nj.us. If you're looking for winter adventures, the park is great for cross-country skiing, ice-skating, ice fishing, and hockey time.

Bamboo Brook Outdoor Education Center. Longview Road in Chester Township; (973) 326-7600; www.morrisparks.net. Originally named Merchiston Farm, from 1911 to 1959 it was the home of William and Martha Brookes Hutcheson, one of the first women in the United States trained as a landscape architect. There are 100 acres of fields, woodlands, and a formal garden. Bamboo Brook is one of the many stops on Patriots Path, a network of federal, state, county, and municipal parks in Morris County, designed for hiking, bike riding, horseback riding, and cross-country skiing.

Historic Speedwell. 333 Speedwell Ave., Morristown; (973) 540-0211; www.morrisparks .net. Alfred Vail was not destined to follow his father's innovative lead in mining and iron ore production; nor was he destined for the career he chose in the ministry, although he completed theology studies at New York University. Yet here at Historic Speedwell, you will

along a tree-lined driveway, it's easy to imagine a knight in armor, sword at the ready. Landscape architects Brinley & Holbrook created the elaborate grounds: an Enchanted Garden surrounded by 10-foot hews hedges; wrought-iron gates behind arched cutouts; a fieldstone terrace and brick balustrade; a Gothic cloister with arched windows and wrought-iron door; broad lawns dropping into a ravine with walkways, gardens, and stairs. Oaks stand sentinel at a glen-like area drawing foxes and white-tailed deer. Accentuating the ambiance, a limestone staircase descends to a garden with fountain remnants and water basins. A hall off the foyer has carved oak paneling more than 500 years old, and a fireplace like the original in a cottage built for Anne Hathaway, aka Mrs. Shakespeare. Stained-glass windows reveal crests, saints, and motifs. The Great Hall has a whitewashed timber ceiling two and a half stories high. The library of oak paneling and carved moldings has pocket doors, a fireplace, and hidden shelves. The jewel of the third floor is the "Priest Room," with timbered cathedral ceiling, carved wainscoting, and a 128-square-foot skylight. A stairway secreted behind a panel in the Great Hall descends to a vaulted dungeon with Gothic arches. The space doubled as a stage where actors performed for Allen's guests. Tickets are $30 for adults and $25 for seniors (no children under age 12). Glynallyn is not wheelchair accessible. For tickets and parking information, see www.mansioninmay.org.

learn how each Vail left an indelible legacy that greatly advanced the Industrial Revolution. The surrounding hills were rich in iron ore, which was mined, forged, and manufactured into instruments, machinery, and engine parts. A forge was built here in the 18th century. Stephen Vail acquired an interest in the operation in 1814 and built a homestead. Pig iron produced in local furnaces traveled far, including machinery for the SS *Savannah,* the first steamship to cross the Atlantic. When Alfred Vail visited his alma mater, he happened to see a demonstration of a prototype for the telegraph. Vail offered financial backing to inventor Samuel F. B. Morse, in exchange for part ownership of the patents. While Vail worked at Speedwell to refine instruments for the device, Morse visited and painted portraits of Alfred's parents. In 1838 Vail gave the first successful demonstration of the electromagnetic telegraph at Speedwell. On May 24, 1844, Vail sent the famous message from Baltimore in Morse's custom code: "What hath God wrought." Today, you can see part of Stephen Vail's home, including original furnishings, period antiques, and the Morse portraits, and the building where Alfred Vail refined Morse's invention. In the restored factory is a working waterwheel. Exhibits show the route from a small nail-producing mill to a major manufacturing complex where history was changed on multiple levels. The museum is open to the public Wed through Sat, 10 a.m. to 5 p.m., and Sun, noon to 5 p.m.

where to shop

F. Gerald New Inc. 1107 Mt. Kemble Ave. (Route 202), Morristown; (973) 425-4485; www.fgeraldnew.net. Family-owned, now run by the third generation, this jewelry, home, and accessory emporium was an expansion from the business begun by F. Gerald New. After honing his art at Black Star and Gorham on Fifth Avenue in Manhattan, New opened his first store in East Orange on the day after the Pearl Harbor attack. In 1970 he relocated to Chatham and expanded to Morristown a decade later. The jewelry store reflects New's interest in antique silver and distinctive jewelry. The home store has wares for fine dining and entertaining, baby gifts, handbags, and accessories. Look for the perky yellow house near Wightman's Farms.

Mendham Books. 84 E. Main St., Suite G, Mendham; (973) 543-4949; www.mendham books.com. Not far from Morristown is an independent bookseller, located in the Mendham Village Shopping Center on Route 510 (Route 24 West). You'll find hardcovers, paperbacks, fiction, nonfiction, children's books, cookbooks, and travel books. The website has the schedule for author signings and special events.

Wightman's Farms. 1111 Mt. Kemble Ave. (Route 202), Morristown; (973) 425-9819; www.wightmansfarms.com. This family-owned operation dates to 1922. Farmer Albert Wightman started driving around in a wagon selling apples and vegetables, as his wife, Lae-titia, got a reputation for yummy fruit pies. Now, the family's third generation runs the much expanded show. With a cider mill on the premises, the farm market features Jersey sweet corn and other seasonal vegetables and fruits. You will find charming Christmas wreaths and decorations, gift baskets, and baked goods. If you happen to swoon over the aroma of warm cider and fruit pies just out of the oven, plan to stay awhile. Wightman's also sells fresh milk, butter, farm eggs, and cheeses; ham and bacon cured the old-fashioned way; locally produced honey, fruit preserves, relishes, coffees, teas, sauces, and stone-ground flours; and Vermont maple syrup. If you know a Granny Smith from a Pink Lady, a Cortland from a Stayman Winesap, you'll appreciate a visit during harvesting schedule. Pick some apples, chuck a pumpkin, and sample the homemade doughnuts.

where to eat

GK's Red Dog Tavern. 1 Convent Rd. (Madison Avenue), Morristown; (973) 585-5700; www.gksreddog.com. In a nod to Rod Keller Sr.'s roots, his family has opened a more casual 120-seat restaurant that occupies a spruced-up part of the log cabin. Sharing the same address as Rod's, the tavern is open for lunch and dinner. There is a raw bar, and the menu features baby back ribs, sandwiches, salads, burgers, and a children's menu. $$.

Provesi. 50 South St., Morristown; (973) 993-1944; www.provesinj.com. Traditional Italian cuisine is served here, lunch and dinner. Choose among plentiful antipasti, pasta dishes, brick-oven pies, fish, shellfish, and veal. Provesi is a bring-your-own-wine establishment. $$.

Rod's Steak and Seafood Grille. 1 Convent Rd. (Madison Avenue), Morristown; (973) 539-6666; www.rodssteak.com. This well-appointed establishment reflects a colorful history. Gerard "Rod" Keller opened the original Rod's in West Orange in 1936, serving nickel beer and 75-cent steak sandwiches. He bought a log cabin on Madison Avenue and opened Rod's Ranch House, which grew into Rod's 1890s Ranch House. With further refinements into a sophisticated fine-dining restaurant in 1998, it sustains Rod's vision. The decor reflects his penchant for authentic antiques, with a stained-glass skylight, Victorian chandeliers—even a separate dining room created by joining two Pullman parlor cars. The menu is contemporary American, with prime steaks, seafood, and pasta. Rod's is open for lunch, dinner, and Sunday brunch. $$$.

Tashmoo Restaurant and Bar. 8 Dehart St., Morristown; (973) 998-6133; www.tashmoo bar.com. Casual and comfortable and close to downtown shops, Tashmoo serves lunch and dinner seven days and has occasional live entertainment. The place was named after a lake on Martha's Vineyard, and a map of the island is displayed over the bar. It's popular as a meeting place—hence the American Indian name. If you happen to favor Scotch, there are more than 40 whiskey varieties, as well as beer selections on draft. $.

where to stay

The Madison Hotel. 1 Convent Rd. (Madison Avenue), Morristown; (973) 285-1800; www .themadisonhotel.com. Grand in appearance, gracious in its approach to guest services, and a great value, this Georgian-style hotel opened in 1981 as something of a showcase for the owner's penchant for Victorian antiques. With a clock tower rising above the entrance, the 4-story lodging has 186 guest rooms and suites, a fitness center, indoor heated swimming pool, restaurant, and bar. Parking is complimentary, and the business center is available 24 hours a day. The lobby keeps coffee and tea for your comfort, 24/7. Guest rooms are individually furnished with period furniture, contemporary amenities, Keurig coffee stations, and cordless phones. $$.

the shore

day trip 01

the shore

keen for the kids,
grand for old-times' sake:
keansburg, nj

This longtime "land of plenty" and "Poor Man's Riviera" has always gotten by and gotten along, without getting too far ahead of itself. Families return to the eastern reaches of Raritan Bay for recreation and amusement, as they have for generations.

Known as Waackaack from the 1600s, so named by the Native Americans in the area, the settlement changed its name to Granville a century later. In 1884 US Rep. John Kean lobbied for a post office, and the town renamed itself Keansburg. It remained part of the Middletown & Raritan Borough until 1917.

Two lighthouses marked the area where ships passed on the way toward Lower Bay and the Narrows tidal strait named for Giovanni da Verrazzano. The Point Comfort Light was a simple tower put on top of a frame cottage in the 1850s. The Waackaack Rear Range Light, displayed at the Chicago Exhibition, was 106 feet high, built of iron with a circular staircase.

William Gelhaus created the New Point Comfort Beach Company in 1908, establishing a grid of roads leading to the curved waterfront. After a hotel and dance hall and boardwalk were built, Gelhaus launched the Keansburg Steamboat Company to transport visitors from Jersey City and New York. Cargo vessels also shipped Keansburg produce, fish, and Raritan Bay clams to markets all over the region.

The Gelhaus family still has a large hand in the town's staying power—as they continue to own and operate the star family attraction.

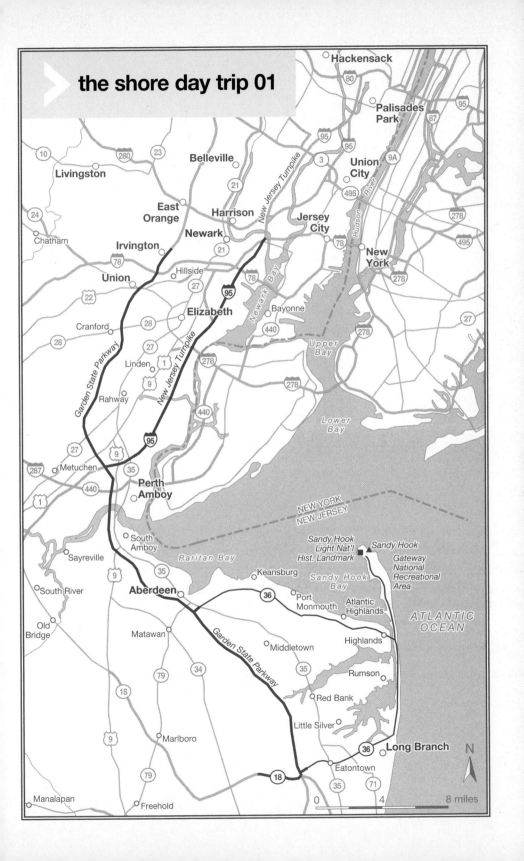

the shore day trip 01

keansburg, nj

getting there

Garden State Parkway to exit 117; head east on NJ 36. Keansburg is about 1 hour from Newark.

where to go

Keansburg Amusement Park and Runaway Rapids. 275 Beachway Ave., Keansburg; (732) 495-1400; www.keansburgamusementpark.com. This small-scale, family-owned amusement park remains old-fashioned by design. Still fun for kids after more than a century, the Jolly Caterpillar is the senior statesman of its original rides. There are vintage bumper cars, a restored 1899 carousel, roller coasters, a go-kart track, dozens of rides, snack stands, and restaurants. It is the oldest amusement park on the Shore, yet *New Jersey Monthly* magazine named Keansburg the state's "best amusement park overall" in 2011. Visitors who return with their children often remark that it is comforting to see the park's current look match up with their childhood memory. The park was built on a curving avenue along the waterfront. In the old days, Keansburg welcomed visitors who arrived by steamer, railroad, buggies, and then cars. It conjures nostalgia for the old-time boardwalk amusement parks—surviving long after many Shore attractions folded. A good splash never goes out of style, and the Runaway Rapids water park was renovated in 2005. At a time when entertaining kids is seldom in a sentence with "cost-effective," Keansburg remains affordable: $18.95 per person when you buy two passes.

Keansburg Fishing Pier. 275 Beachway Ave., Keansburg; (732) 495-8842; www.keansburgfishingpier.com. The 2,500-foot pier is behind the amusement park's picnic pavilion. If this is an impromptu stop, you can rent fishing gear. The pier is open from 7 a.m. to 10 p.m. weekdays and 6 a.m. to 10 p.m. on weekends. Rates are $8 for adults, $5 for children, and $1 just to stroll the pier. The website offers helpful links for water temperatures, tide charts, and fishing regulations.

Keansburg Historical Society Museum. 59 Carr Ave., Keansburg; (732) 471-0408; www.keansburg-historical.org. The society was created in 1995 and opened its museum in 1999. On display are two remarkable ship models built by Jack Campbell, who replicated two vessels from "The Gelhaus Navy," the side-wheeler *Keansburg* and the twin-screw *City of Keansburg*. Local memorabilia is on display, and the hours are 1:30 to 3:30 p.m. Wed and Sun, or by appointment. No charge for admission.

day trip 02

the shore

through the looking glass:
atlantic highlands, nj

Originally called Portland Pointe, Atlantic Highlands is the highest mainland point on the Eastern Seaboard south of Maine—a gem of a brooch on the Bayshore bosom. This petite town has been a popular vacation stay for 130 years. At one time, visitors arrived by steamer to board rail cars.

Victorian homes on the hills overlooking Bayshore Trail have made peace with the notion that one might have to bare an ankle now and then to have a little fun. Downtown, then, to the playhouse, perhaps; or the harbor to book a fishing charter. Think big! Sip some bubbly while waiting to catch the *SeaStreak* for Wall Street.

Then again, howsabout we dawdle at those new-fangled magnifiers on the overlook. Do they, perchance, see all the way to the dudes with no Speedos at Gunnison Beach? Ahem.

atlantic highlands, nj

getting there

Garden State Parkway to exit 117; head east on NJ 36 for about 10 miles until you see a "jug handle" sign for the Scenic Road. Watch for other "jug handles" for First Avenue.

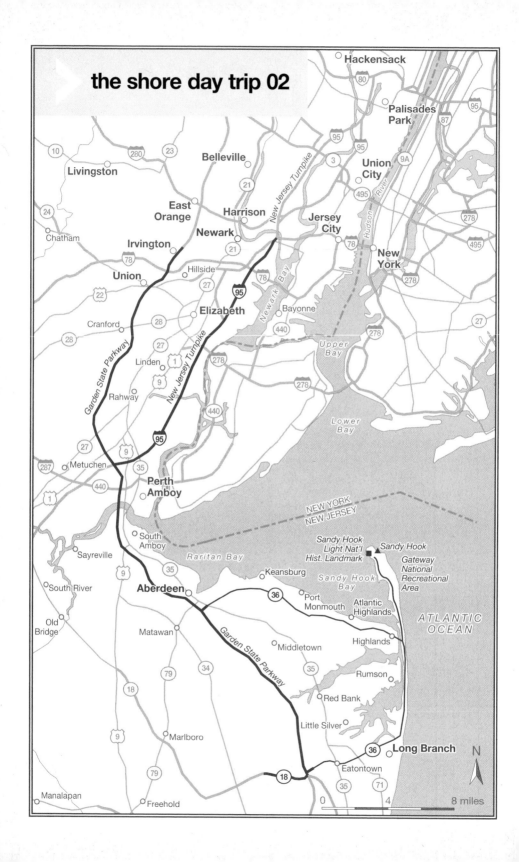

the shore day trip 02

where to go

Mount Mitchell Scenic Overlook. 460 Ocean Blvd., Atlantic Highlands; (732) 872-0336; www.monmouthcountyparks.com. This county park is high cotton, indeed, by coastal standards, at 266 feet above sea level. There are coin-operated vista magnifiers in two locations. On a clear day, they show the Sandy Hook peninsula, the Verrazano-Narrows Bridge, and the Manhattan skyline. The park also is home to the Monmouth County 9/11 Memorial, which honors local residents who died in the 2001 terrorist attacks. The 12-acre site includes the 1980 Hostage Memorial, which pays tribute to 52 Americans held hostage in Iran. The park is open daily from 8 a.m. to dusk, free of charge.

The First Avenue Playhouse. 123 First Ave., Atlantic Highlands; (732) 291-7552; www .firstavenueplayhouse.com. This community theater has a concept superior to most dinner theaters in that you dine out at participating restaurants and go to the theater for dessert at 8 p.m., followed by the curtain call. Dinner packages are $35 and $42. See the website for current and upcoming productions.

SeaStreak. 2 First Ave., Atlantic Highlands; (732) 872-2628; www.seastreak.com. This passenger ferry departs from the municipal marina on weekdays only. It goes to Wall Street and East 35th Street in New York.

Atlantic Highlands Farmers Market. 111 First Ave.; Atlantic Highlands, at Veterans Park across from Borough Hall. The market operates from noon to 6 p.m. Fri from May through Oct.

where to shop

Renaissance Emporium. 81 First Ave., Atlantic Highlands; (732) 291-9101. This is an emporium with 13 vendors to choose from, including Book Compound, which carries rare and out-of-print books, magazines, and sheet music. Other vendors carry toys, clothing, and specialty items. Open daily from 11 a.m. to 6 p.m., and until 9 p.m. on the weekends.

Zeek's Tees. 120 First Ave., Atlantic Highlands; (732) 291-2700; www.zeekstees.com. The store has been a mainstay here since 1984. Custom apparel is the specialty here, from screen-printing, digital photo printing, and embroidery to tackle twill. See the website for a catalog and services.

where to eat

Ama Ristorante Tuscana. 42 First Ave., Atlantic Highlands; (732) 872-4674; www.ama ristorante.com. Ama's co-owners are Chef Pat Trama and Laura Borawski. Pat admits to being a New Yorker, proud of it, but that doesn't stop Jersey boys and girls from following the buzz to the restaurant the pair opened in 2009. The petite dining room seats 38, with 18 seats outside. Cash is the password, and this is a BYOB operation—meaning bring your own vino. Make it a good bottle, to complement Pat's famous veal osso bucco, pasta classics, and seafood such as Raritan Bay scallops in brown butter sauce. Trama has a national reputation gained from mentors Charlie Palmer and Drew Nieporent, as well as a lifetime assimilating the rhythm and aromas in his family's restaurants. $$.

Copper Canyon Restaurant. 51 First Ave., Atlantic Highlands; (732) 291-8444; www.the coppercanyon.com. If you want to tip your sombrero to Southwestern cuisine, tequila shots, and just being glad to find the town, saunter on in. The dining room has about 90 seats, plus bar spots and some outdoor seats in the summer. The owner, Michael Krikorian, started the place in a nearby location in the 1990s and moved it here in 2003. To his credit, he is on the radar of the James Beard Foundation. Pepper steak and crab cakes are two of the locals' favorites, but the menu will tempt you to order one of each—or at least a few. Check the calendar for their version of a wine dinner. Copper Canyon calls it tequila night. $$.

The Flaky Tart. 145 First Ave., Atlantic Highlands; (732) 291-2555. The patisserie opened in 2007, and the hot items remain croissants, chocolate chip cookies, almond crème and other French tarts, and many Parisian favorites—ooh la la to the chocolate ganache and gooey coconut thingy. The early-a.m. crowd comes for a ham-gruyère croissant—a sort of Croque Monsieur on-the-hoof—and the lunch bunch likes the mac-and-cheese, topped with crunchy baguette crumbs. The chef/owner, Marie Jackson, has been a contender on more than one occasion in the pastry category of nominees for James Beard Foundation kudos. Open Tues through Fri, 6:30 a.m. to 4 p.m., Sat 8 a.m. to 4 p.m., and Sun 8 a.m. to 1 p.m. $.

The Harborside Grill. 40 First Ave., Atlantic Highlands; (732) 291-0066. This restaurant and lounge is a favorite with the locals. The menu is American food, from steaks to pasta and seafood. Prices are very competitive. $.

Memphis Pig Out. 67 First Ave., Atlantic Highlands; (732) 291-5533; www.memphispigout .com. This is an extremely popular barbecue spot that gets raves for its spare ribs, baby backs, chicken, pulled pork sandwich, filet mignon combo, and seafood selections. We have not tried the desserts, but the Tennessee Hot Fudge Cake may be worth cutting back on your entree. $$.

On the Deck Restaurant & Harborview Bar. 10 Simon Lake Dr., Atlantic Highlands; (732) 872-1424; www.onthedeckrestaurant.com. Conveniently located at the town marina, with indoor and outdoor seating, On the Deck is near the *Sea Streak* ferry terminal. This hangout has views of the Shrewsbury River, Sandy Hook peninsula, and, on a clear day, the skyline of Manhattan. Open for lunch, dinner, happy hour, or happy times. The owner has another spot in the nearby town of Highlands, Off the Hook. $.

Sissy's at the Harbor. 8 Simon Lake Dr., Atlantic Highlands; (732) 291-2218. If you are up and hungry, Sissy Smith has been yawning awhile, waiting for you to show up. She is open from 5 a.m. to 9 p.m. daily. The seating is outdoor, by the marina; not fancy but tasty fare. $.

where to stay

Blue Bay Inn. 51 First Ave., Atlantic Highlands; (732) 708-9600; www.bluebayinn.com. This 24-room establishment is a happy mix between bed-and-breakfast and charming boutique hotel. The deluxe guest rooms and elaborate suites are spacious, attractive, well-appointed, cozy, and comfortable. It has the same owner as its adjacent restaurant, The Copper Canyon, and the menu is as impressive as the service. The Blue Bay Inn is a gem and a sign of good fortune for the guest who happens upon it. It is a popular getaway for New Yorkers taking a 40-minute ride on the *SeaStreak* ferry, but why let them hog the place? For a special occasion, you can rent the whole inn. $$.

day trip 03

the shore

>>> **hook, (tan) lines & dinner:**
sandy hook, nj; highlands, nj;
sea bright, nj

The Jersey Shore begins at the Sandy Hook peninsula—not on reality TV. It takes a breather on various islands, bays, sounds, beaches, and riverbanks and packs it in after Holgate, where Beach Haven Inlet and Little Egg Inlet watch to see who blinks first. The region south to Cape May Point is known as the Southern Shore.

Water, water everywhere—the enviable lot in life for a barrier peninsula with riveting vistas that take in the Atlantic Ocean, the Intracoastal Waterway, Raritan Bay and Sandy Hook Bay. A pivotal unit of the Gateway National Recreation Area—covering parts of New Jersey and New York and overlapping portions of the Gateway region of New Jersey—Sandy Hook is, nonetheless, planted firmly in the Shore region.

Come to Sandy Hook for the natural assets—not the *Jersey Shore* variety—and stick around for maritime marvels. Take in views of Lower Manhattan as you soak up serenity and authenticity. Highlands is right next door, for dinner and a good night's sleep. At Sea Bright, grab a book, hit the beach, and work up an appetite, because the restaurant scene is broader than the town.

Rare indeed is virgin barrier ecology, and this one is a doozey. A well-protected anchor of a federal park system, Sandy Hook is dotted with coves, marshes, a bird sanctuary, parks, historic structures, a lighthouse, a fort, and some serious military provenance.

Beaches beckon on all sides. You may even bring your dog to the inlet side—not the ocean side—but always on a leash. A paved jogging path runs parallel to 7 miles of remote roadway with brush on both sides buffering the dunes. Parking areas are near designated beaches, and bayside walkways take you close to the water.

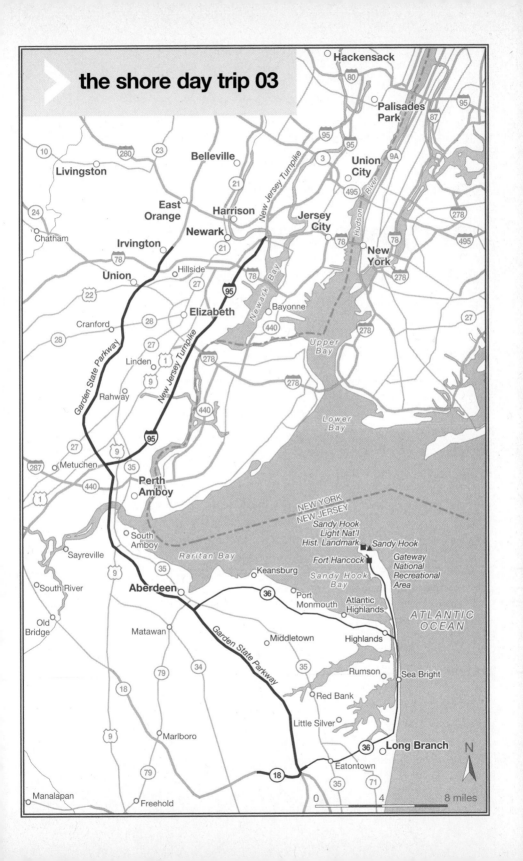

the shore day trip 03

The peninsula is a slender digit between two bodies of water, accessible by driving over the new $128 million Navesink River Bridge or riding a ferry for 40 minutes from Manhattan. All of New Jersey is hooked on Sandy—not to mention half of New York and Pennsylvania. If you are a newbie, there are almost 2,000 acres, including 264 acres of maritime forest, to explore and respect. And yes, it has a clothing-optional beach, the only legal one in New Jersey—thanks to its location on a federal preserve.

sandy hook, nj

getting there

Garden State Parkway to exit 117; head east on NJ 36 about 14 miles over the Navesink River Bridge. Turn left and follow the road north.

where to go

Gateway National Park. Hartshorne Drive, Sandy Hook; (732) 872-5970; www.sandy-hook .com. After you pass through the entrance, the Sandy Hook Visitor Center is about 2 miles north, by Beach Area D. It is housed in the historic Spermaceti Cove Life-Saving Station, along with exhibits and a bookstore. Park rangers provide maps showing dune trails, swimming areas and beach showers, restrooms, historic sites, observation decks, and wildlife habitats. If you ride a bike along any of the 12 miles available, note the abundant holly forest. There is seasonal food service—read hot dogs—at some of the beaches, but it's wise to bring your own provisions. The inlet side or western shore of the peninsula has plenty to see and do, but there are no lifeguards, no restrooms or refreshments. Park admission is free; parking fees are $10 per car and $50 for a seasonal beach pass. Sandy Hook is open every day from 5 a.m. to 10 p.m., Apr through Oct; until 8 p.m. Nov through Mar.

shifting priorities

Sandy Hook Lighthouse was financed by merchants in New York who hoped to stop losing so much cargo to the treacherous, wayward shoals of New York Harbor. The beacon was built at the northern tip of Sandy Hook peninsula, and it guided ships to ports in Jersey City and up and down the Hudson River. After 250 years of northward longshore currents and shifting sands, the lighthouse is about a mile and a half south of its original perch.

monmouth memories

Dr. Samuel Latham Mitchell, an explorer, botanist, and naturalist who served in both houses of Congress, is the namesake for the overlook in present-day Atlantic Highlands. A surveying expedition in 1813 put the cliff on the map, and from here, you can view Staten Island, Liberty Island, the Verrazano-Narrows Bridge, Romer Shoal Light, Sandy Hook Bay—even the JFK International Airport control tower and Rockaway Beach. And, of course, Lower Manhattan. What is chilling to realize, once you look into those magnifiers, is that visitors to the overlook on Sept. 11, 2001, may have been putting quarters into the machines at the precise time that terrorists attacked and destroyed the World Trade Center towers. Victims that day include 147 residents of Monmouth County; their names, ages, and hometowns are engraved here in the granite base of a monument. The site has a 9/11 timeline on a path leading to the centerpiece sculpture. An enormous stone eagle prepares to take flight, with a twisted piece of metal in its talons. There is a circular granite floor, a stone border, and benches with metalwork in the shape of leaves and acorns. The design summons dual reactions—a memorial to lost souls, and a monument to enduring creativity.

Sandy Hook Lighthouse. Erected in 1764, it is the dean of continuously operating American lighthouses. The Keepers Quarters has exhibits on other beacons in New Jersey. In the Keepers Barn, you can see a video on the littoral history of the lighthouse. The site is open daily in spring, summer, and fall, with lighthouse tours from 1 to 4:30 p.m. There is no charge to tour the lighthouse, but donations are customary.

Fort Hancock Historic District. (732) 872-5970; www.nyharborparks.org. The fort is on the bayside of Sandy Hook peninsula, toward the north end, and it was the outermost defense for New York harbor from 1895 to 1974. One point of interest is History House, a lieutenant's quarters built in 1898 in the Colonial Revival style. At the north end of "Officer's Row," and one of 17 similar bungalows ringing the bay, the 3-story 4,500-square-foot house has been restored to the 1940s. Battery Potter, the fort's oldest gun emplacement, is open for tours. Check with the visitor center on the status of the Fort Hancock Museum renovation.

Battery Gunnison. The big guns are on the dunes leading to clothing-optional Gunnison Beach, off Atlantic Drive on the northeast side of the peninsula. The battery was built in the 1800s as part of Fort Hancock, and is said to be named for John Williams Gunnison. Unlike most gun emplacements, Gunnison's guns and remnants of the battery are intact on the beach and involved in an Army Ground Forces Association restoration. Others on Sandy Hook include the Nine-Gun Battery, with "disappearing" artillery. The guns were loaded behind a concrete bulwark, lifted for firing, and stashed behind the walls. In such an environment, soldiers let off steam by skinny-dipping. Once the fort was decommissioned, Gunnison Beach stuck to its naked guns.

Sandy Hook Bird Observatory. 20 Hartshorne Dr., Sandy Hook; (732) 872-2500; www .njaudubon.org. The New Jersey Audubon Society leases one of the homes on "Officer's Row" at Fort Hancock. You can find literature and a sketch of the birding "hot spots" on Sandy Hook—from piping plover, osprey, heron, and raptor to orioles, warblers, and loons.

Charter Sails Inc. (732) 801-7472; www.charter-sails.com. Call to book a sailing charter for the waters around Sandy Hook and Lower New York Bay. Vessels range from sloops and catamarans to an 80-foot motor yacht for larger parties. The boats depart from Sandy Hook Marina and Monmouth Cove Marina.

where to eat

Sea Gulls' Nest. Sandy Hook Park Area D; (732) 872-0025; www.seagullsnest.info. This is the only restaurant and deck bar inside this unit of Gateway National Park, and it is located right before the Sandy Hook Visitor Center. Sit out in the open or under a canopy while soaking up the views. There is often live music at sunset. $.

highlands, nj

Quaint, charming, and nautical, sea-salty Highlands sits on a hill with the Eastern Seaboard at its feet. It always had appeal as a sleepy coastal stay-over, especially for bootleggers during Prohibition.

The town draws visitors to its ample seafood restaurants, lodgings, boating, water sports, and historic sites. On the Navesink River in summer, you'll spot a sea of wind-surfers, kayakers, and sailors. For no extra charge, admire the views of Sandy Hook, the ocean, the bays, and New York Harbor.

On a bluff in this picturesque borough west of Sandy Hook are twin lighthouses over-looking the peninsula, bays, and ocean. It is the home of filmmaker Kevin Smith, whose movie *Jersey Girl* was set there.

getting there

Garden State Parkway to exit 117; head east on NJ 36 for about 13 miles. Highlands is right before the new fixed-span bridge over the Navesink River.

where to go

Twin Lights of Navesink. Lighthouse Road, Highlands; (732) 872-1814; www.twin-lights .org. This is a New Jersey State Historic Site and stands 200 feet above sea level. The original beacons date to 1828. The southern light is on a square stone tower, the northern light on an octagon, and redbrick buildings connect them. After the lighthouse began to deteriorate, the current structure was built in 1862. The Navesink facility was the first twin lighthouse ever built, the first to use kerosene, and the first to use electricity. The road to the lighthouse curves and ascends through woodlands and residential neighborhoods. The cliffs provide bay and ocean views. To reach Lighthouse Road, turn right onto Portland Road, the last turn before the bridge. Tours are free but donations are customary.

Hartshorne Woods Park. Middletown, NJ; (732) 842-4000; www.monmouthcountyparks .com. Hilly and wooded, this 791-acre site south of Highlands overlooks the Navesink River. The county park is popular for hikers, bicyclists, and nature lovers who appreciate the trails, scenic views, and the chance to see deer, fox, and waterfowl. The park includes lands once important to coastal defense, and you can still see concrete and earthen bunkers in the forests. The namesake for the park is Richard Hartshorne, a Quaker from London who bought more than 2,000 acres in the area when he settled in 1669. Park hours are 8 a.m. to dusk daily, year-round. Admission is free.

SeaStreak. 325 Shore Dr., Highlands; (732) 872-2628; www.seastreak.com. This passenger ferry departs from Conner's Pier on weekdays. It goes to Pier 11/Wall Street and East 35th Street in New York.

where to shop

Aromatherapy Apothecary. 132 Bay Ave., Highlands; (732) 872-4629; www.christine michelle.com. The owners here are Kathryn and Albert Mongillo, and they cover a lot of ground. Their Christine Michelle Handmade line includes artisan batches of olive oil soaps, soy and beeswax candles, and herbal spa products. They sell an organic line of baby goo, too, laced with aloe, lavender, and chamomile, among other essences. You can consult with the staff to create your own shampoos, bath gels and salts, perfumes, scrubs, and lotions. Customize your lather from the shop's herbs and oils.

Endless Treasures Arts and Antiques. 126 Bay Ave., Highlands; (732) 872-2787; www .endlesstreasuresnj.com. This is a good browsing stop in the afternoons and evenings, Thurs through Sun. You will see fine art, furniture, glassware, and decorative accessories; vintage jewelry, handbags, and clothing; unusual greeting cards and handmade gifts. The owners spend the rest of their week running Endless Paintabilities. They specialize in faux finishes, murals, moldings, painted furniture, custom stencils, layouts, displays, and accessorizing homes and businesses.

collared & beached for good

*So what do you do after a robbery wipes out your necktie operation? You buy
a broke-down houseboat, of course, and some rowboats to rent, for a backup
plan. And after your "insurance" washes away in a storm the very next day? You
jack up the houseboat and jerry-rig a restaurant. You rent bunks on the houseboat to transient anglers, and serve your guests fried eels, buckwheat pancakes,
and eggs. Then you branch into stews, chowders, and catch of the day, making
it possible for four generations of the family to thrive in the same location since
1917. The founders of Bahrs Landing Famous Seafood Restaurant and Marina
cobbled together their unique compound in Highlands by adding on to that
barnacle-bottomed houseboat. John Bahrs, son of a tall-ship captain, owned a
necktie manufacturing business in Newark with his wife, Florence. The operation
folded after robbers made off with their silk goods. They headed to the Shore and
bought a boat-motel plus rental rowboats, losing the latter in a Nor'easter. As
the menu and reputation grew, the Bahrs' children—John Jr. (Bud), Al, Ken, and
Ruth—helped out.*

*The family put a bulkhead under the rust-bucket eatery and opened an office
upstairs. Since 1974, when Bud and Peg retired, Ray Cosgrove and his son Jay,
the great-grandson of Jack and Flo, run Bahrs Landing. A companion business
is Moby's Outside Deck & Lobster Pound. With 10 million customers, it is one of
the country's oldest family-run restaurants. On one side of the main dining room,
the floor is uneven—having survived some uncertain times. The old houseboat
rests somewhere in the mix.*

where to eat

Bahrs Landing. 2 Bay Ave., Highlands; (732) 872-1245; www.bahrslanding.com. Bahrs is
a local landmark, reeling in hungry diners since 1917. Getting here is even easier since the
new bridge opened in 2011 in the marina's lap. The main dining room has large windows
overlooking Sandy Hook Bay. Try the shrimp pesto pizza, which is excellent, with pesto
sauce on thin crust, luscious cheese, and shrimp cut into pieces so it absorbs the flavors.
This pie has a kick, plus slices of fresh Jersey tomatoes on top. Also good is the platter of
clam strips and grilled flounder with red potatoes and zucchini. Bahrs' bread is full of flavor
and has a cakey texture like biscuit dough. The wine list has whites, reds, blush, and bubbly
by the glass or bottle. $$.

Doris & Ed's Seafood. 348 Shore Dr., Highlands; (732) 872-1565; www.dorisandeds .com. New Jersey foodies and New Yorkers alike have been making their way to Doris & Ed's for decades. Owner Jim Filip took it over in 1978 and has been smeared with no small amount of gourmet ink ever since. His wine list is famous as well, having been featured in *Wine Spectator* for more than 26 consecutive years. The executive chef, Thomas Donohoe, is famous, too. The bargain here is the prix-fixe menu: three courses for $33; and wines at $25, $35, and $45 a bottle. There is a well-informed raw bar, appetizer menu, and soup/ salad selection. Main courses are heavy on the abundant local seafood, as well as steaks and roast duck. $$.

Havana Tropical Cafe. 409 Bay Ave., Highlands; (732) 708-0000. The menu is Cuban, which calls for Sangria, a Mojito, or something equally tropical. The restaurant is open from 4 p.m. to 10 p.m. during the week, and from noon to 11 p.m. on weekends. $$.

Windansea Restaurant & Bar. 56 Shrewesbury Ave., Highlands; (732) 872-2266; www .windanseanj.com. The big draw here is the food, but having a table on the outdoor deck, where you see Sandy Hook peninsula and the bay, and can watch people tying up their boats at the floating docks, is a big plus. The ceiling in the bar is barn height, with wooden plank floors and TVs on the walls. The indoor dining room has a fireplace. The contemporary American menu runs the gamut: raw bar, seafood, chicken, steaks, sandwiches, wraps, salads, and so on. The wine list is conversational, giving advice if you like, and there is plenty to order by the glass or bottle. $$.

"gloryview" too soon

The GrandLady by the Sea was built in 1910 on the first rise of Highlands by a local kid turned silent-screen matinee idol. William Wallace Reid—who called the place "Gloryview"—was best known to townsfolk as Wally, the tall, blue-eyed teenager who raced hot rods around the hills. Life on the way to art, some say. The son of Broadway producer Hal Reid, Wallace was married to actress Dorothy Davenport. Although he played the role of Jeff the blacksmith in Birth of a Nation, *he much preferred holding the camera to standing in front of one. In the 1920 song "At the Moving Picture Ball" is the lyric, "Handsome Wallace Reid/ Stepped out full of speed." He died impossibly young, at age 31, but not in a car crash—as the neighbors might have predicted. Reid was an alcoholic who became addicted to painkillers after being injured in a train wreck. His Hollywood studio sent him supplies to make certain he showed up on the set. His delight in "Gloryview" lasted a mere 13 years.*

where to stay

GrandLady by the Sea. 254 State Route 36, Highlands; (732) 708-1900; www.grandlady bythesea.com. This historic lodging with a handful of rooms and one 2-room suite is a short stroll from the ferry dock and well situated near town restaurants. The grand dame serves a full breakfast on weekends—omelets, cheese blintzes, French toast, oatmeal, yogurt, and such—and Continental on weekdays. $$.

Sandy Hook Cottage. 36 Navesink Ave., Highlands; (732) 708-1923; www.sandyhook cottage.com. This bed-and-breakfast was built in the 1930s and today is a 3-bedroom retreat. Each guest room is decorated with a beach or lighthouse theme. Breakfast is a Continental-style buffet Monday through Saturday, with a brunch affair on Sunday. The Cottage requires a 2-night minimum on peak weekends and a 3-night minimum on holidays. The rates may be combined with some fun packages. $$.

SeaScape Manor. 3 Grand Tour, Highlands; (732) 291-8467; www.seascapemanorbb .com. This bed-and-breakfast will have you eating out of their hands as you sip coffee or tea looking at the Sandy Hook peninsula and the bay. $$.

sea bright, nj

The once sleepy Shore community is a happy home for about 1,800 residents and an appealing stopping point for thousands of visitors each year.

A little larger than a sandbar, Sea Bright is about 0.25 mile wide and 4 miles long. A few miles south of the Sandy Hook peninsula, the borough has 6-foot stone buffers with walkways to the beach. You will notice plenty of private beach clubs, homes, and condominium developments as you make your way down the Shore.

Sea Bright gives a lot of novice anglers confidence in waters full of blues, albacore, and stripers. Surf casting is okay, as is fishing from the beach, but check the state license rules. Other pastimes are jetty surfing, rafting, and boogie boarding. Dining is a full-time job here, and the shops are unique.

getting there

Garden State Parkway to exit 117; head east on NJ 36 and go over the Navesink River Bridge. Sea Bright is south of Sandy Hook.

where to go

Sea Bright Municipal Beach. (732) 842-0215; www.seabrightnj.org. Beach badges are on sale at the Sea Bright Public Beach Office, which is open from 9 a.m. to 5 p.m. There are lifeguards, outdoor showers, and restrooms. If you have a beach badge, you also may use public-use areas in front of the borough's seven private beach clubs.

J.W. Ross Cultural Arts Center and Library. 1097 Ocean Ave., Sea Bright; (732) 758-9554; www.seabrightlibrary.org. Part of the Monmouth County public library system, Sea Bright's facility is near the beach and equipped with computers. The library displays the work of local artists on a monthly revolving schedule.

where to shop

Cocotay. 1080 Ocean Ave., Sea Bright; (732) 708-1010; www.cocotay.com. This women's apparel shop is in the same building as Northshore described below. In addition to stylish clothing and after-five designs, Cocotay sells accessories, jewelry, and handbags. Coco and Tay are identical twins whose jewelry designs combine gems and semiprecious stones with vintage settings. They aim to produce one-of-a-kind accessories that spell out a siren song of "chic . . . unexpected . . . smashing." Their aesthetic sense is the yin and yang of the natural world and the extravagant beauty therein. Cocotay's collections feature necklaces, earrings, pendants, rings, and cufflinks. Aside from Sea Bright and the online catalog, you can find their jewelry in Bergdorf Goodman in New York.

Look Back Antiques. 1050 Ocean Ave., Sea Bright; (732) 842-1005; www.lookback antiques.com. This trove of vintage treasures could occupy any serious browser or buyer. Looking for a left-handed Gibson Epiphone? Or a signed Steuben bowl? Look Back carries fine antique furniture, vintage jewelry, artwork, mirrors, posters, figurines, and all manner of decorative accessories. It's probably gone by now, but the 19th-century black walnut monastery chest was most handsome. The store is open from 10 a.m. to 6 p.m. daily; until 4 p.m. on Tues.

Northshore. 1080 Ocean Ave., Sea Bright; (732) 842-9909; www.northshoremenswear .com. It may have been awhile since you met a buttoned-down haberdasher who takes pride in classic tailored threads. That is the focus of Brian George's business, going strong since the 1980s. The one-off store also has lines of sportswear, shoes, and the Varsity Raggs collegiate line.

where to eat

Anjelica's Restaurant. 1070 Ocean Ave., Sea Bright; (732) 842-2800; www.anjelicas .com. With only 85 seats, you are lucky to get one at Anjelica's, a long-established and traditional Italian restaurant with wood floors and brick walls. Try the pappardelle with wild boar and mushroom ragú, the stuffed veal chop, or the "angry lobster" with a kick. The PEI mussels are delectable. There is some wine on the menu, but plan to bring your own. Open for lunch Tues through Fri; open at 5 p.m. for dinner Tues through Sat; Sun hours are 2:30 to 9 p.m. $$.

Donovan's Reef. 1171 Ocean Ave., Sea Bright; (732) 842-6789; www.donovansreef.com. This is a bar on the beach, with food in the background. Sunbathing, volleyball, beverages, and bands are the focus. $.

Harry's Lobster House. 1124 Ocean Ave., Sea Bright; (732) 842-0205. Harry's has been here since the 1980s, and people have come to depend on its signature dishes of stuffed lobster and lobster bisque. Open for dinner daily; closed Tues. Some say you pay through the claw for the privilege of dining here, but it's worth it. $$$.

McLoone's Riverside. 816 Ocean Ave., Sea Bright; (732) 842-2892; www.mcloones .com. Originally called McLoone's Rum Runner, it opened in 1987 on the banks of the Shrewsbury River. Shore diners are used to the name, as the owner has restaurants in Long Branch and Asbury Park, plus Woodbridge and West Orange. The menu is abundant, with plenty of sumptuous seafood, steaks, and a raw bar. $$.

Woody's Ocean Grille. 1 East Church St., Sea Bright; (732) 936-1300; www.woodys oceangrille.com. Located near Ocean Avenue, Woody's opened to a full house, and an hour's wait for a table, right after Hurricane Irene in 2011. The owners remodeled the former Ichabod's space, which is open for lunch and dinner. The menu is a mix of all-American, California coast, and Southwest: shrimp tempura tacos, pulled-pork sliders, braised short ribs, and fish dishes. $$.

Yumi. 1120 Ocean Ave., Sea Bright; (732) 212-0881; www.yumirestaurant.com. It's not pronounced "yummy," and that is too bad, because this neo-Asian spot gets raves for its fusion finesse and precise sushi. The chef's inspiration is Southeast Asian cuisine. Yumi means "most beautiful," which is an apt call for the so-attractive dishes. Open for lunch Mon through Sat; dinner Sun through Thurs. Bring your own wine. $.

day trip 04

the shore

counting on jazz, 'sink or swim:
red bank, nj

The elaborate piano riffs and bossy brass in *Red Bank Boogie* make you want to scoot on over to comingle with the melodic majesty of wherever Count Basie came into the world.

Situated on the south bank of the Navesink River in Monmouth County, Red Bank makes a big sound all its own. It celebrates its very personal musical heritage and regional roots, and cashes in on local biggies in countless ways. It also understands the sublime magic of quietude on the river at sunrise.

Easy to find and a hoot to explore, Red Bank is only 25 miles from Manhattan and only 1 mile off the Garden State Parkway. Every July 3 for more than half a century, the town has gone "Kaboom!" with a fireworks display by the river. At Christmastime, Broad Street paints the town red and turns up the lights. And year-round, Red Bank is down with high-end and novelty retail, dozens of world-class restaurants, parks, waterfront activities, art, literature, music, theater, and film.

A relatively young town, Red Bank's median age is under 40, and about 1,500 of them commute daily by train to New York City's Penn Station.

Noteworthy are all the rows of professional offices housed in restored vintage residences and a downtown decorated with Victorian-style street lamps and brick sidewalks. Red Bank knows where it came from, is quite pleased to look ahead, and invites you to boogie on down.

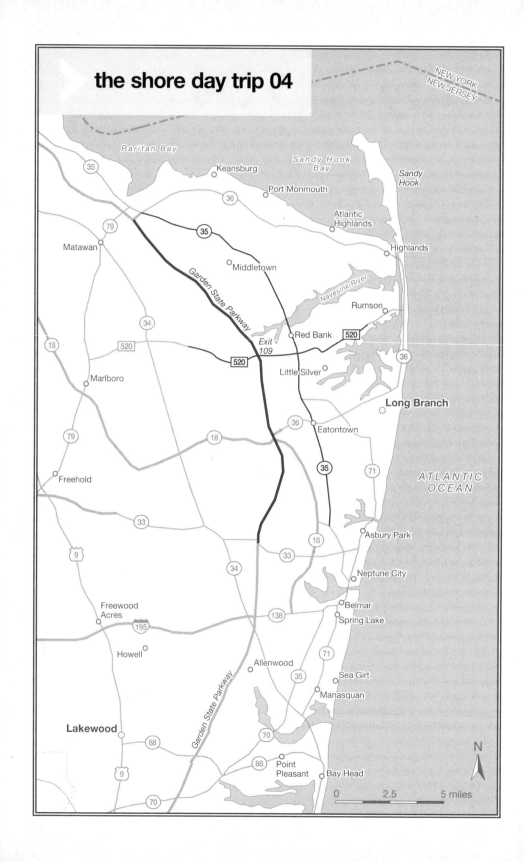

the shore day trip 04

red bank, nj

getting there

Take Garden State Parkway exit 109 onto Route 520; go east to NJ 35, head north, and you will arrive in downtown Red Bank. As is the case with many Jersey roadways, the borough has a doozey of a jug handle.

where to go

Red Bank Visitor Center. 46 English Plaza, Suite 6 upstairs, Red Bank; (732) 741-9211; www.visit.redbank.com. The center is open from 9 a.m. to 5 p.m. weekdays. You may also collect literature about downtown shops, galleries, and venues at the Daniel J. O'Hern Station, described below.

The Daniel J. O'Hern Station. 175 Monmouth St., Red Bank; (973) 275-5555; www.njtransit.com. This historic depot is owned and operated by New Jersey Transit. It was renamed in 2011 to honor O'Hern, a former mayor of Red Bank and a former judge of the New Jersey Supreme Court. Built in the 1870s in the Gothic style, it is a rare survivor of the Stick style, displaying decorative exterior "stickwork"—a Victorian-era half-timbering affectation—and jerkinhead roof lines. Today's passengers from Hoboken and Manhattan reach the same station as England's King George VI and his wife, Elizabeth, did in 1939. From here, the royals went by motorcade to Sandy Hook to board a warship bound for New York. The station is a vivid symbol of the end of Red Bank's dependence on steamboats.

Count Basie Theatre. 99 Monmouth St., Red Bank; (732) 842-9000; www.countbasie theatre.org. Some headliners in 2011 were Chris Botti, Lyle Lovett, Judy Collins, The Beach Boys, and Alice Cooper. The venue hosts nationally known performers, including David Sedaris, Tracy Morgan, Bill Cosby, Bob Newhart, Foreigner, Andy Williams, Brian Setzer, B.B. King, and others. Operated by a nonprofit organization, the theater also produces plays and full-scale musicals, and occasionally screens films. The venue is housed in the former Carlton Theatre, which opened in the 1920s as a vaudeville house and cinema. The Classical-Revival building was designed by architect William Lehman and still features a large lighted-sunburst dome in the ceiling.

Two River Theater Company. 21 Bridge Ave., Red Bank; (732) 203-2500; www.trtc.org. Now a top venue for off-Broadway productions, the company started in the mid-1990s by producing plays at Monmouth University in West Long Branch and the Algonquin Arts in Manasquan. The founders were able fund-raisers and built a visually inviting performance space, which opened in 2005. The firm of Hardy Holzman Pfeiffer Associates designed this architectural gem. Named for the Navesink and Shrewsbury Rivers, the company produces an eight-play season of classics, contemporary plays, new plays, and musicals. An episode

> ## hats off to "cap"
>
> *Being perched on a river crocheted in coves made Red Bank an important transportation hub early on. Schooners and sloops sailed to New York, carrying produce from Jersey farms, plus Navesink oysters and timber—and returning with manufactured goods. In time, steamships brought passengers who settled down, and by the mid-1800s, Red Bank was among the fastest growing boroughs in New Jersey. Prominent in the maritime expansion was Charles P. "Cap" Irwin, who took a dock and a lean-to in 1884 and grew his baby boatyard into Irwin Yacht Works. This local legend was the borough's constable for a time and was a well-known sportsman who built the ice yacht* Georgie. *Ice-boating on the river remains a favorite winter pastime here—as sails snap in the wind and sandbags cling to runner plates for dear life. Cap's marina-boatyard remains in family hands, with Channing Irwin, the third-generation owner, at the helm.*

of *VH-1 Storytellers* featuring Bruce Springsteen was filmed at Two River Theater Company. Two venues comprise the space—the 349-seat Joan and Robert M. Rechnitz Theater and the 99-seat, black-box Marion Huber Theater.

The Red Bank/Eisner Public Library. 84 W. Front St., Red Bank; (732) 842-0690; www .lmxac.org/redbank. The institution was founded in 1878, and the books were housed in various buildings until 1937. The heirs of Sigmund and Bertha Eisner donated the family home for use as a public library. Situated on the banks of the Navesink River, the house was built in 1856 and owned first by Stacey Pitcher. Two decades later, William H. Lowe bought and enlarged it considerably. The 16-room Victorian-style building had a tower and great river views. Lowe also installed a concrete-enclosed swimming pool on the river. A subsequent owner turned the house into an exclusive boarding school for boys before selling it to Sigmund Eisner in 1906. Eisner, the owner of a uniform-manufacturing company, removed the tower and Victorian millwork and covered the building with stucco in 1921. During two renovations, the Eisners also filled and terraced land behind the house. They built the main living room in 1920, finished it in mahogany, and installed a concealed heating system. The library was renovated in the 1960s and in 2007. The living room now houses the local history collection. The back porch is a gallery/cafe. Note the gleaming parquet floors, which were refinished after being masked by carpet for decades.

Marine Park. Wharf Avenue at the Navesink River, Red Bank. Public tennis courts make this an obvious choice, and it's a great picnic spot where you might piggyback onto a concert or festival. Children are fond of the waterfront adventures and the certainty of spotting something interesting from the pier.

Red Bank Armory Ice Rink. 76 Chestnut St., Red Bank; (732) 450-9001; www.redbank armory.com. After its beginnings in 1914 as a riding hall for the Red Bank Cavalry of the New Jersey National Guard, the armory was phased out and used to store tanks. In the late 1990s, the 14,400-square-foot main floor was converted to an ice rink. Check the website for the schedule on freestyle skating and pick-up hockey games. Admission is $9 for adults and $8 for children 12 and under. Skate rental is $4.

Riverside Gardens Park. 54 W. Front St., Red Bank; (732) 530-2782; www.redbanknj .org. This 2-acre award-winning municipal park opened in 2000. Its location on the Navesink River makes it ideal for families to picnic, attend outdoor jazz concerts, or see films—among the many summer activities scheduled by the borough. There is a sensory garden, boardwalk, snack concession, and entertainment stage. In the off-season, the arched entry displays a prominent Red Bank symbol, a lighted iceboat.

Maple Hill. 94 W. Bergen Place, Red Bank. This is a private residence built between 1860 and 1885, in the Second Empire architectural style, with a modest front porch, bay window, and dormers in the mansard-style upper level. From 1901 to 1915, it was home to Timothy Thomas Fortune, one of the leading black journalists of the late 19th century. Fortune, an editor, publisher, and poet born into slavery in northwest Florida, was an adviser to Booker T. Washington. Fortune is said to have coined the phrase "Afro-American," to reflect people of African heritage born in America. His home is listed on the National Register of Historic Places.

The "Lollipop Clock." 36 Broad St., Red Bank. Stalwart on the sidewalk, this treasured sentinel of time marching on stands at the curb outside Ballew's, a jewelry store that sells, among other things, fine watches. The clock was installed in 1902 by the previous owner, Alphonse Leon de la Reussille, a native of Switzerland, who had opened Reussille's jewelry store in 1886. He was an inspector of clocks and watches for the Central Railroad of New Jersey.

exactly like your father's buick

In addition to Tiffany & Co., Red Bank has the oldest family-owned Pontiac dealership in the country. Rassas Pontiac Buick on Broad Street was established in 1930. When General Motors sent out Pontiac's pink slip, the dealership persevered. In addition to its catalog of pre-owned Pontiacs, Rassas is one of the Top 50 Buick dealerships in the United States.

The Monmouth Chess School and Club. 51 Monmouth St., Red Bank; (732) 219-0916; www.monmouthchess.com. One possible conclusion is that the chess club has a checkered past. Another is that this site is much in demand—in that the chess-heads rent the space on Sunday afternoons; the nearby St. James Catholic School uses it for activities; and the landlord is the Community YMCA. The building and a monument in front of it are the star attraction. This 3-story brick Romanesque-Revival structure used to be the Shrewsbury Township Hall. Built in 1892, it was designed by local architect Robert D. Chandler. *Handing Down Old Glory* is the monument outside. Sculpted of Vermont granite by Frank J. Manson in 1926, it was a gift from borough firemen to honor fallen soldiers. It has the faces of Henry M. Nevins (center) in a Civil War uniform; an unidentified soldier who served in the Spanish-American War; and Major Peter P. Rafferty reaching toward the flag.

where to shop

Antique Center of Red Bank. 195 W. Front St., Building II, and 226 W. Front St., Building III, Red Bank; (732) 843-3393 and (732) 842-4336; www.redbankantiques.com. The town's celebration of its heritage is embedded all around you, and its reputation as a trove for antiques is well-earned. The center is housed in two locations, displaying wares from more than 150 dealers. Related services include jewelry repair and appraisals, vintage toy repair, metal polishing, clock and watch repair, and furniture restoration. With more than 46 years in business, the center is well on its way to being an antique.

Germany. 121 Broad St., Red Bank; (732) 576-8500; www.garmany.com. A linchpin for attracting some of the town's most high-profile tenants, this independent department store carries upscale, designer clothing for men and women, shoes, handbags, and accessories. Owner Larry Garmany moved his business here from Manhattan in the late 1980s.

Jay and Silent Bob's Secret Stash. 35 Broad St., Red Bank; (732) 758-0508; www .viewaskew.com. Filmmaker Kevin Smith and Jason "Jay" Mewes own this comics shop and novelty emporium. Say you need to find a signed hardcover copy of *The Green Hornet Vol. 1: Sins of the Father.* It is here, or can be ordered online, along with signed DVDs, Blu-ray discs, T-shirts, and all manner of memorabilia from Smith's various movies: *Jay and Silent Bob Strike Back, Chasing Amy, Jersey Girl, Mallrats, Clerks,* and more.

Red Bank Downtown. 20 Broad St., Red Bank; (732) 842-4244; www.onlyoneredbank .com. This restored Victorian enclave can keep you fascinated for hours, what with hundreds of shops, dozens of art galleries, and more than 50 restaurants within a few blocks.

The Red Bank Galleria. Bridge Avenue and Front Street, Red Bank; (732) 530-7300; www.thegalleriaredbank.com. Boutiques, restaurants, and offices took over the remnants of this historic building in the 1990s. The Galleria calls itself "the Soho of Red Bank." When it was built in 1903 as a factory for Sigmund Eisner's uniform manufacturing operation, the structure was much larger. During World War II, Eisner's military contracts created a boom

policing petals

When humorist James Thurber wrote "Memoirs of a Drudge," an essay published in 1942 in The New Yorker, *he recounted a city editor sending him to Red Bank to check out a tip: "Violets (are) growing in the snow over in Red Bank." Thurber placed a call to the Red Bank police department to check out the tip. A desk sergeant gave him the skinny: "Ain't no violence over here."*

for the company. Vizzini & Company has its furniture showroom here, should you need a Stephan secretary or Hanover console; its collections include Aidan Gray, Lillian August, and many more. A Step in Stone features tile and stone decor. At Moonstruck, you'll learn about proprietor Pamela Furlong's ideas on feng shui, chakras, meditation, numerology, and such. Other tenants here are a spa, a dance studio, a Pilates den, a gold vendor, a leather shop, art frames, and interior designer. Lots to linger over and plenty of refreshment stops. Hungry for Thai? The Galleria has Siam Garden. Longing for fondue? Stop by The Melting Pot. You also will find a pastry shop, espresso bar, pizza place, and Taste Cafe. Galleria hosts the local farmers' market.

where to eat

Basil T's Brewery and Italian Grill. 183 Riverside Ave., Red Bank; (732) 842-5990; www .basilt.com. This second-generation restaurant and bar serves lunch, dinner, and late-night menus and has nods from Zagat and *Wine Spectator* to show off. Regardless of the time of day, Basil T's stresses the importance of house-made pasta, sauces from scratch, and straightforward preparation—a tradition from the founder, Victor "Big Vic" Rallo Sr., and carried on by his son Victor Jr. One entree, Gnocchi Ragu di Maiale, is slow-cooked pork ragu with root vegetables, white wine, ricotta gnocchi, and fresh peas. Other promising choices are Sole Livornese and Chicken Scarpiello and the only-on-Sunday Sauce. Check the restaurant's calendar for live entertainment and seasonal wine tastings. The late-night menu includes plentiful pizza choices, calamari, and chicken wings. As for the microbrewery's offerings, you can order blond, auburn, or brunette ales—all described on the website. $$.

Blue Water Seafood. 9 Broad St., Red Bank; (732) 530-1906; www.bluewaterseafood redbank.com. The menu here is a well-informed selection of appetizers, raw bar, soups, salads, rolls, entrees, and desserts. The decor is crisp and comfortable, with brick walls, gleaming wood floors, and sparkling chandeliers. Open daily for lunch and dinner; bring-your-own wine or liquor. $$.

The Globe Hotel Company. 20 E. Front St., Red Bank; (732) 842-5572. Boffo burgers, tasty wings, pork-roll sandwiches, beer, and sports on TV—that is what you get, no apology expected, and no attitude to dodge. It is no longer a hotel, having lost much of its timber in a fire in 1936. It was built in 1840 as a home and converted to a hotel in 1844. If Red Bank had a pub of the *Cheers* variety, Ted Danson's Sam character would be pouring here. $.

red Restaurant & Lounge. 3 Broad St., Red Bank; (732) 741-3232; www.rednj.com. Do lowercase letters announcing a restaurant give you pause? Do libations taste better than cocktails? Is a kiwi mojito more wonderful than a dirty martini? All questions to be resolved at red, which draws crowds to its chic, minimalist spaces and inventive menu descriptions. "Lips on Fire," by the way, is made from hangar chipotle vodka, Thai chili pepper, and smoked paprika, and sushi is as it should be. red serves dinner from 5 to 10:30 p.m. Mon through Thurs; from 5 to 11 p.m. Fri and Sat; and from 3 to 9 p.m. Sun. $$.

Restaurant Nicholas. 160 Route 35 South, Red Bank; (732) 345-9977; www.restaurant nicholas.com. Chef Nicholas Harary, not yet 40, would seem too young to have amassed so much industry kudos and important food-critic ink. Yet here he is, just over a decade since opening this restaurant with his wife, Melissa—garnering fresh raves for his inventive New-American cuisine. In 2011 the Zagat Survey named this spot "New Jersey's Most Popular Restaurant," No. 1 for food and service. In addition to the main dining room, you may opt for the Chef's Table experience, seated at a four-person booth by the kitchen, to watch the

crème de clemons

For a while in the 1980s, Red Bank was home to a unique establishment, one that resonates even more with the passing of tenor saxophone giant Clarence Clemons in 2011. His nightclub on Monmouth Street was known as Big Man's West, a richly equipped venue to promote other artists but a doomed financial experiment for such a pudding-heart. When Clarence was not scorching some stage with Bruce Springsteen and the E Street Band, he offered this platform for the likes of Bon Jovi, Bonnie Raitt, and Joe Cocker, among many others. Members of Clemons's band, the Red Bank Rockers, were right at home here, and the customers never knew when they might be witnessing the kind of unscripted glory that goes down when jamming musicians collide. On such a night about three decades ago, Springsteen showed up to double-dog-dare the headliner, Dave Edmunds, into a rock 'n' roll guitare la guerre. Apparently no one with a sax was ready to duke it out with Clemons that night.

wizardry while sipping the house champagne. For more casual evenings, try the adjacent Bar N, for cocktails and a la carte tastings. $$$.

Soul Kitchen. 207 Monmouth St., Red Bank; (732) 842-0900; www.jbjsoulkitchen.org. Groundbreaking would be one way to describe the 2011 launch of this restaurant opened by pop star Jon Bon Jovi, his wife, Dorothea, and Chef Zeet Peabody. With a tagline of "Hope is Delicious," Soul Kitchen aims to feed you well and nourish your soul in the bargain. No prices on the menu—a priceless all-inclusive concept. You "donate" what you can, say $10 or so. Someone who has no money is welcome to eat and wash dishes or pitch in. The menu is nutritious comfort food, helped by an organic garden out front of the former mechanic bay. Reservations are advised, as people are lining up to break bread together as part of the owners' take on community spirit. Hours are Thurs through Sat, 5 to 7 p.m., and Sun from noon to 3 p.m. $.

where to stay

The Molly Pitcher Inn. 88 Riverside Ave., Red Bank; (732) 747-2500; www.molly pitcher-oysterpoint.com. Open since 1928, this splendid redbrick presence overlooking the Navesink River might have been a private mansion turned into a hotel. Not so. This Georgian-style building with green shutters and white wooden railings was built as a hotel in Colonial Revival style in 1928 and updated in the 1990s. Today, it is undergoing further expansion. "The Molly" is a favorite spot for dining, meetings, and events. There are 106 rooms and a handful of suites. The Dining Room at the Molly Pitcher serves contemporary American cuisine. For cocktails, guests go to the International Bar. The hotel's Sunday Brunch is a longtime award-winning favorite. The hotel's namesake is Mary Hays, a heroine of the Revolutionary War. In July 1778, in sweltering heat, Mrs. William Hays carried pitchers of water to soldiers fighting British troops in the Battle of Monmouth. Some say Molly "manned" a cannon after her husband fainted. $$.

The Oyster Point Hotel. 146 Bodman Place, Red Bank; (732) 530-8200; www.molly pitcher-oysterpoint.com. This 56-room establishment is a sister property of the Molly Pitcher Inn. In contrast to the historic treasures there, the Oyster Point is sleek, contemporary, and equally in demand. There is a fitness center, swimming pool, and other amenities, and the restaurant is called Pearl. Select among several 2-room suites and luxury guest room layouts. Also situated on the Navesink River, it has a marina and draws boaters for dockside dining. $$$.

day trip 05

the shore

born to run, a presidential preference:
long branch, nj

Fans associate superstar Bruce Springsteen with the town of Freehold, but Long Branch is where he was born and where he wrote the iconic "Born to Run," the title track to his breakthrough album.

History buffs recall Long Branch as a favored getaway for seven presidents of the United States—and one of the original seaside resorts. In its heyday, Long Branch was a virtual "who's who" of summering society, including such names as Astor, Fisk, and Drexel—as well as the colorfully notorious Diamond Jim Brady and Lily Langtree. Only 45 miles from Newark, it was a go-to glam spot, drawing famous writers, artists, and musicians. In 1870 a racetrack opened nearby, with casinos on its coattails.

First Lady Mary Lincoln visited in 1861, and in 1869 Long Branch had its first presidential visit. President Ulysses S. Grant returned to Long Branch every summer he was in office and for many years afterward.

Presidents Chester A. Arthur, Rutherford B. Hayes, Benjamin Harrison, William McKinley, Woodrow Wilson, and James Garfield were frequent visitors also. After an attempt on Garfield's life, he was brought to Long Branch in hopes the sea air would expedite his recovery. Indeed, a rail spur ran from the main line to his house to ease his travels. The president died here in 1881.

The 1920s saw a decline for the town's reputation as a fashionable summer spot. Gambling laws discouraged many of the rich and famous, and wicked storms eroded the town's famed beachfront. By the late 1960s, organized crime had tarnished the image further, and blight took its toll.

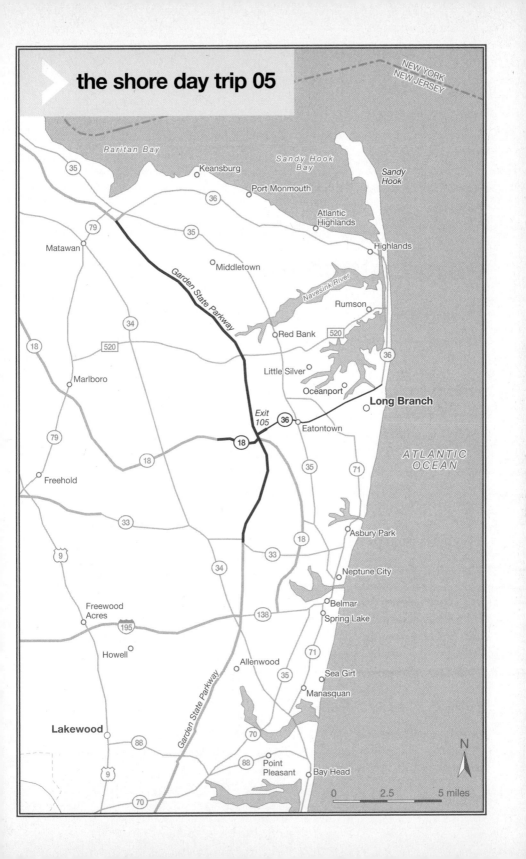

the shore day trip 05

Long Branch managed to pull up its bootstraps and rebuild an oceanfront destination. There are new resorts, spas, restaurants, nightclubs, shops, and high-rises. The new Seven Presidents Oceanfront Park, a 38-acre county park, draws crowds for swimming, boating, and picnicking.

Today, the young and hip—and the young at heart—are drawn to Long Branch, where you can enjoy the beach, the new boardwalk, some unique retail options, and scads of restaurants.

This branch of the Jersey Shore is most definitely in for the long haul.

long branch, nj

getting there

Take the Garden State Parkway to exit 105; go east on NJ 36 toward the ocean into Long Branch.

where to go

Seven Presidents Oceanfront Park. 221 Ocean Ave. North, Long Branch; (732) 229-0924; www.monmouthcountyparks.com. This is a relatively new public park with lifeguards. You can swim, surf, fish, play beach volleyball, launch a kayak or canoe, or watch children at a playground. There are restrooms, outdoor showers, and a snack bar. Lifeguards are on duty from 10 a.m. to 5 p.m. daily during the summer. You must buy a daily or seasonal beach badge, and there are parking fees—although the facility is free in the off-season. The park is open every day from 8 a.m. to dusk. At the north end of the park is a "Skateplex," with a paved trail, landscaped open areas, restrooms, drink vending machines, tables, and parking. One skate area is a 75-by-150-foot rink for inline skating and hockey. A skate park is for skateboarding and in-line skating, with a bowl, quarter pipes, wedges, and other features.

Long Branch Historical Museum. 1260 Ocean Ave., Long Branch; (732) 223-0874; www.churchofthepresidents.org. The former St. James Episcopal Church, where seven US presidents attended services, later was named Church of the Presidents. Built in 1879, it was deconsecrated in 1953 and is on the New Jersey and National Register of Historic Places. Its crenellated tower is distinctive. It is the one remaining structure that reflects the elegance of Long Branch's former glory.

Long Branch Boardwalk. The "new" Long Branch Boardwalk is centered on the updated Ocean Place Resort, new condo units, and Pier Village, a mixed-use shopping, dining, and entertainment area. The boardwalk is abuzz on summer evenings.

landmarks & boardwalks

The sight of Victorian-era women with parasols strolling along the boardwalk attracted Winslow Homer, who stayed in Long Branch in 1869 while painting the milieu. Writer Dorothy Parker of the Algonquin Round Table was born here in 1893—and the house at 792 Ocean Ave. is a national literary landmark. In modern times, "The Telltale Moozadell" episode of The Sopranos *featured actress Drea de Matteo in the role of Adriana La Cerva, whose fiancé, Christopher Moltisanti, bankrolled her nightclub. It was set at The Lollipop Club in Long Branch, which the character called "The Crazy Horse."*

Monmouth Park Raceway. 175 Oceanport Ave., Oceanport, about 3 miles northwest of Long Branch; (732) 222-5100; www.monmouthpark.com. Since 1870, this horse track has endured three incarnations driven by the politics of pari-mutuel wagering. In 1986 it came under the umbrella of the New Jersey Sports and Exposition Authority. Thoroughbred racing is only part of the attraction at "the Shore's greatest stretch." The track hosts the Jersey Home Expo; holiday arts and crafts shows; and family-fun days, with clowns, face-painting, a bounce house, pony rides, and live music. Dining options at the track range from casual to "proper attire," indoor and outdoor, and there is a picnic zone with 100 umbrella tables, should you choose to lug along a charcoal grill.

where to shop

Pier Village. 1 Chelsea Ave., Long Branch; (732) 923-0100; www.piervillage.com. This mixed-use destination has dozens of shops and plenty of food-court spots and restaurant variety. There also is a location for Gold's Gym.

where to eat

The Lighthouse/Strollo's Homemade Italian Ice. 65 New Ocean Ave., and 69 Brighton Ave., Long Branch; (732) 222-1990; www.lighthouseitalianice.com. One location is convenient for beachgoers. The other is in the west end of town. True to its history, the company features multiple flavors of soft-serve specialties. Born in Italy, Tony Strollo founded the business in his garage, where he made sandwiches and ices and peddled them from an old bus. His family expanded the operation in the 1970s and now has locations in both Red Bank and Point Pleasant Beach. $.

Max's Famous Hot Dogs. 25 Matilda Ter. (at Ocean Boulevard), Long Branch; (732) 571-0248; www.maxsfamoushotdogs.com. Talk about a stubborn streak . . . Max's has been a Jersey Shore constant since 1928, when Max Altman opened a 25-seat hot dog stand on the northern end of the pier. An associate, Milford "Mel" Maybaum, bought the place in 1950 and kept the name, earning himself the nickname "Mr. Max." After he married, his wife, Celia, was known as "Mrs. Max." Today, the third generation of Maybaums carries on the tradition, having expanded to a 200-seat restaurant farther south. The menu has hot dog classics, such as the chili cheese dog featured on a segment of Martha Stewart's TV show; plus steak sandwiches, burgers, clam strips and other seafood, corn on the cob, and fried zucchini. $.

mcloone's musings

In 2010 Harvard-educated entrepreneur-cum-musician Tim McLoone opened his first non-Jersey restaurant: McLoone's Pier House on the Potomac River, at the National Harbor hotel/restaurant/shopping site in Maryland. McLoone's roots in business, however, run to the Jersey Shore. A pianist who still performs, he opened his first restaurant in Sea Bright, the Rum Runner on the Shrewesbury River. The seller wanted a cool mil, and Tim got some investors to help him close the deal. McLoone's Woodbridge Grille in Fords operates like a mini-casino with food, drinks, and off-track wagering—a joint venture with the state. The gaming element is a natural fit, actually, as his dad once headed Freehold Raceway and Bowie Racecourse in Maryland. McLoone's Boathouse, inside the South Mountain Recreation Complex in West Orange, opened in 2011, was a homecoming of sorts, because Tim grew up in the area. As for Asbury Park, he reminisced about being old enough to see the original Planet of the Apes when it played first-run at the Paramount. On deck, what's cooking? Another gaming spot on Route 440 in Bayonne should open in time for the Kentucky Derby 2012. The solid success of McLoone's Pier House in Long Branch prompted Tim to take a chance on Asbury Park, where the Asbury Grille and Tim McLoone's Supper Club are vertically integrated, literally, on the Boardwalk. His $1 million gamble on the town's renaissance meant losing money in AP the first two years. But in 2010, sales were up 31 percent and up another 12 percent in 2011. Relief is the sensation of that bet paying off. And the Boardwalk is not the only homerun. In fact, downtown was ahead of that learning curve. Perhaps the popularity of the Asbury Grille is owed to its location in a former Howard Johnson's. The pointy-hat roofline is a vivid reminder of a time when forward-looking designs looked weird but now evoke a smile. Or, you could blame it on the clam strips still on the menu. How Ho-Jo poetic.

McLoone's Pier House. 1 Ocean Ave., Long Branch; (732) 923-1006; www.mcloones .com. The restaurant opened in Pier Village in 2005, part of the Jersey Shore restaurant group owned by musician/entrepreneur Tim McLoone. $$.

Sawa Hibachi Steakhouse & Sushi Bar. 68 Ocean Ave., Long Branch; (732) 229-0600; www.sawasteakhouse.com. Centrally located in Pier Village, Sawa is open for lunch and dinner. Choose among Japanese classics as well as the hibachi menu. $$$.

Sirena Ristorante. 27 Ocean Ave., Long Branch; (732) 222-1119; www.sirenaristorante .com. Upscale and casually elegant, the dining room with a choice of tables or banquettes features floor-to-ceiling windows overlooking the ocean. There are perky booths for dining in the bar, as well, and tables on the terrace. It is among our favorite Italian restaurants in these parts, and one yummy dish is Chitarra, or "guitar string" pasta with local tomatoes, olives, capers, anchovies, and basil. Sirena's interpretation of Snapper Acqua Pazzo, or snapper poached in "crazy water," has cockle clams and fennel. You can't go wrong with the Veal Chop Milanese accented with Grana Padano; or the Veal Valdostano rib chop stuffed with Fontina, prosciutto, spinach, and mushrooms. Sirena's is open daily for lunch and dinner and from 1 to 9 p.m. on Sun. Reservations are recommended. $$$.

The Sitting Duck. 104 Myrtle Ave., Long Branch; (732) 229-5566; www.sittingduckrestau rant.com. An all-around cozy, casual restaurant and sports bar a bit west of the beach area. The menu is new American, with raw-bar selections, plenty of seafood, steaks, sandwiches, wraps, salads, complete dinners, and a kids' menu. The bar boasts 20 beers on tap, some of them seasonal. Sit at the Duck for lunch or dinner seven days. $$.

where to stay

The Bungalow Hotel. 50 Laird St., Long Branch; (732) 229-3700; www.bungalowhotel .net. This is a boutique hotel located in Pier Village, and it is a feast for art lovers who may be intrigued with the design and hip decor. The Bungalow won't resemble the last place you stayed, for sure, and it also is pet-friendly. The beach is a short walk. You may want to splurge on a suite, with a separate living room, kitchenette, fireplace, powder room, and full bath with a whirlpool tub and walk-in shower. $$$.

Ocean Place Resort & Spa. 1 Ocean Blvd., Long Branch; (732) 571-4000; www.ocean placeresort.com. This relatively new resort, part of the revived Long Branch boardwalk, is a block from the beach. It has a swimming pool, fitness center, spa, and restaurants; pets are allowed. Guest rooms range from a limited view to coastal view and oceanfront, or you may want to splurge on a 1,300-square-foot oceanfront suite. Throughout the resort, you'll find a handful of indoor and outdoor dining and lounge locations. $$.

day trip 06

the shore

still staying attuned:
asbury park, nj; ocean grove, nj
(including sea girt)

As renaissances go, past ones in Asbury Park have been a bit dicey. Today, however, the joint is jumpin'—not jumpy. Downtown is hot, again, especially Cookman Avenue. And the boardwalk is abuzz with new and restored attractions, reflecting a decade of rebuilding. That trend to engage is holding, and local business owners cite this uptick with relief that their faith in a bounce-back was on the money.

Asbury Park was something of a ghost town after the urban angst of the 1960s. But abandoned towns most often suffer blight instead of being leveled. The shells not ruined by storms were a sturdy platform for new uses. Not all the neglect has been erased, but Ocean Avenue, the main drag by the water, is booming with oomph.

The famous boardwalk meanders parallel to buildings dating to the 1870s, when Asbury Park was the popular go-to among people from Philadelphia and New York who knew the best spots on the Shore. Once the swells built their seasonal digs, entrepreneurs ramped up to open hotels and restaurants. That reputation lasted for more than a century, and the surviving structures trigger nostalgia for that era. A coordinated redevelopment effort put a full-court press on the boardwalk in 2007, and many important sites show the results of ageless style and modern amenities.

Some noteworthy architecture is thriving in adaptive reuse. As for the tried-and-true measure of interest in the area, concerts draw droves and beach-pass purchases are up—confirming that sun and sand will win out over distractions from the national economy and partisan politics.

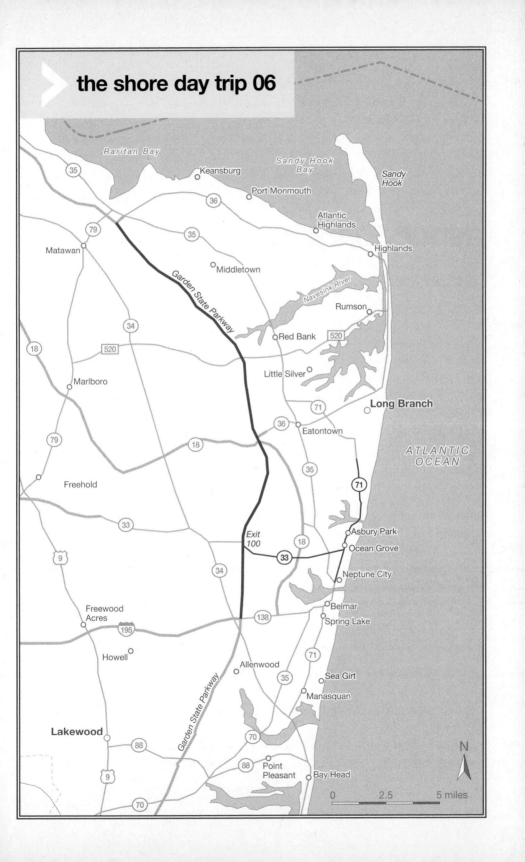

the shore day trip 06

The famous "Jersey Shore sound" of rock 'n' roll laced with R&B—and peppered with calliope tones—originated here, and the town is synonymous with music legends. Among those who played local clubs: Jon Bon Jovi, Count Basie, Southside Johnny and the Asbury Jukes, and Gary U.S. Bonds. The group most associated with the main stage was Bruce Springsteen and the E Street Band. To wit, The Stone Pony drew 5,000 soulful mourners when sax-to-the-max Clarence Clemons died in 2011.

asbury park, nj

getting there

Follow the Garden State Parkway to exit 100 (NJ 33 east); continue until you reach NJ 71. Head north for Asbury Park, which is about 1 hour from Newark.

"First Saturday" is a monthly promotion that is gaining traction as visitors catch up to the locals. Art galleries, restaurants, antiques dealers, and boutiques keep evening hours. Many serve hors d'oeuvres and present entertainment, another facet of a resurging resort town. In addition to a downtown art-house cinema, a new multiscreen complex is on deck.

where to go

Asbury Lanes. 209 Fourth Ave., Asbury Park; (732) 776-6160; www.asburylanes.com. This vintage bowling alley doubles as a performance space for musical acts, "neo-burlesque," art shows, and hot rods. Hours are Wed through Sat, 8 p.m. to 2 a.m.

Asbury Park Convention Hall. 1300 Ocean Ave., Asbury Park; (732) 775-3533; www.ap boardwalk.com. Built in the late 1920s, this 3,600-seat venue is on the eastern side of the complex closest to the ocean. It has many uses, including performance space by major musical acts and sporting events. It also is a derby venue for the Jersey Shore Roller Girls. The Grand Arcade, lined up with the boardwalk, is the entrance to both venues.

Chico's House of Jazz. 631 Lake Ave., Asbury Park; (732) 774-5299; www.chicoshouse ofjazz.com. The club located in The Shoppes at the Arcade was founded as a valentine to the late, great tenor sax stalwart Charles Rouse, a recording artist who performed with the

"greetings from asbury park"

In case you don't recall, it was 1973 when Shore Boy himself, Bruce Springsteen, released his debut album. There is a lighted sign atop Convention Hall that pays tribute to the man and his music.

likes of Thelonius Monk. His son, Charles "Chico" Rouse, is a veteran concert promoter. While you listen to the jazz du jour, the refreshment menu has appetizers, salads, sandwiches, desserts, and liqueurs—all named for a legend in this most American genre. The club's gift shop is the best place to buy a Charles Rouse Round Midnight T-shirt.

Hot Sand Glass Studio. 550 Cookman Ave., Asbury Park; (732) 927-5475; www.hot sandap.com. This unique studio and gallery is one of the only places in the country where you can walk in and cast your sandy feet or other shape in molten glass. Hot Sand was founded five years ago by Ocean Grove native Paul Elyseev and graphic designer-glass artist Thomas Stevens, a Fulbright scholar and former schoolteacher. Stevens studied in Amsterdam until a decade ago. Paul has a fine arts degree in glass and sculpture, and he studied in Germany. The buzzing environment on Cookman Avenue made them decide to relocate the studio from the Fifth Avenue Pavilion on the boardwalk. Check in spring 2012 for the date of their move.

The Paramount Theatre. 1300 Ocean Ave., Asbury Park; (732) 897-6500; www.apboard walk.com. This vivid, redbrick building dates to the late 1920s, accented with terra-cotta gargoyles and eagles, white stone arches, copper tall ships, sea creatures, and other nautical ornamentation. It poses the question of whether Italian-French lines work well with Art Deco. Inasmuch as it brings in the ticket-buying public in droves, the answer is yes. The 1,600-seat venue is connected to Convention Hall by The Grande Arcade, a soaring breezeway topped in skylights. All three were designed by Warren and Wetmore, a New York firm that designed Grand Central Station Terminal.

The ReVision Theatre. 700 Ocean Ave., Asbury Park; (732) 455-3059; www.revision theatre.org. This professional theater company beckons you to relive some of your favorite moments in the audience. As the name conveys, they "reenvision" the live stage experience. Summer 2011 brought in the New Jersey premiere of *Xanadu* and the regional debut of the Tony Award–winning musical, *Spring Awakening.* Right before Halloween, it opened the doors on *Little Shop of Horrors.* This company reinvents classics and produces new and obscure works and musicals. The format is cabaret, concert, and fully staged productions. Its primary venue is The Carousel House, a restored landmark on the southern end of the boardwalk. Look for the circular building with arched windows. The replicated Medusa-with-snakes motif appears in each window.

The Saint. 601 Main St., Asbury Park; (732) 775-9144; www.thesaintnj.com. The nightclub gives a stage to local acts, performers with a reputation, and emerging artists. The club's owner, Asbury Music Company, hosts the annual Asbury Music Awards.

The ShowRoom. 708 Cookman Ave.; (732) 502-0472; www.theshowroomap.com. Open since 2009 in a leased downtown storefront, this 50-seat art-house cinema presents indy films, live music, comedy, and other events. Late in 2011, the owners were preparing to buy a larger building across the street that would give them 125 seats. The ShowRoom also hosts monthly "Readings from Asbury Park," a program by The ReVision Theatre to put soft and encouraging lights on new plays and musicals being developed.

The Stephen Crane House Museum. 508 4th Ave, Asbury Park; (732) 775-5682. Most famous for his second novel, *The Red Badge of Courage,* the author, essayist, and war correspondent lived in Asbury Park from the age of 12 through the age of 20. He died in Germany eight years after his last summer on the Shore. His widowed mother bought the house in 1883 after moving from Crane's hometown of Newark. There are restored rooms and a lecture room for poetry readings and other occasions. The Asbury Park Historical Society meets here monthly.

The Stone Pony. 913 Ocean Ave., Asbury Park; (732) 502-0600; www.thestonepony.com. As live-music venues go, you can't go wrong at the Pony, where the logo is innocently profound. In a world where nothing is solely black or white, the silhouette of a white pony on a black background is both amateurish and enduring; just like music, a work in progress. Open since 1974—and forever branded as one of the greatest rock 'n' roll stages of all time—it gave many performers their start. The vibe behind these walls is serious, all business in the most-fun sense of the word: bare concrete floors and black walls that pop with the shimmering necks and bodies of guitars made famous here. The Stone Pony has about 6,000 square feet of indoor space, with beverage service and a small kitchen. Outside is the Summer Stage, which takes up the rest of the block. The performance schedule is Tues through Sun in summer and Thurs through Sun in the off-season. The stage is dark on Mon, except anytime house promoter Kyle Brendle books a concert tour. This iconic venue is a must-stop for anyone taking in the Shore. Come for the history—Bruce Springsteen, Clarence Clemons, et al—and an experience praised by concert fans the world over.

life imitating art, also

The Asbury Park Carousel House reflects its Victorian heritage. Its original architecture was vivid, and details included an ornate copper roof. The Philadelphia Toboggan Company created the carousel, and its elaborate, hand-carved wooden horses were beheld in high esteem. The amusement park was marred by storms and economic hardship. Even the horses were a casualty, sold off to circle in spirit in a warehouse. Artist Norma Tolliver created an enduring reminder, an acrylic painting on canvas, "Asbury Park Carousel House." She sold the original, but a limited number of giclée prints are available online at www.fineart america.com.

Watermark. 800 Ocean Ave., Asbury Park; (732) 455-3447; www.watermarkap.com. This sophisticated and upscale lounge has indoor and outdoor seating at the top of the First Avenue Pavilion. There are specialty cocktails with fresh juice ingredients, house-made ginger beer, brews on tap or in the bottle, a full wine list, espresso, coffees, and teas. Watermark opens at 4 p.m. weekdays and 2 p.m. on weekends. Happy hour is 4 to 6 p.m. weekdays and Sat, and from 2 to 5 p.m. Sun.

where to shop

Arcade at Convention Hall. 1300 Ocean Ave., Asbury Park. Galleries, shops, and restaurants are located in The Grand Arcade between Convention Hall and The Paramount. You'll find Robert Legere Beach for home accessories; photography, memorabilia, and African-American culture at Asbury Galleria; and the latest whimsy in accessories and furnishings at Shelter Home.

Carla Gizzi. 1300 Ocean Ave., Asbury Park; (732) 988-0000; www.carlagizzi.com. Also located in the arcade, this location sells gifts, jewelry, and custom pieces by artisan Carla Gizzi.

Flying Saucers. 658 Cookman Ave., Asbury Park; (732) 202-8848; www.flyingsaucerson line.com. This gift shop is located on the lower level of the Shoppes at the Arcade (not to be confused with the Arcade at Convention Hall). This complex is housed in a redeveloped downtown building. Owner James Kaufman and his dog Charlotte hang out there to explain his antiques and vintage, retro collectibles.

Lightly Salted Surf Mercado. 1000 Ocean Ave. (Third Avenue Pavilion), Asbury Park; (732) 455-3275; www.surfmercado.com. Some say surfboards are works of art. Some say art lets your soul catch air. You'll find both on the boardwalk, along with beachwear and accessories.

Posh Den. 1000 Ocean Ave. (Third Avenue Pavilion), Asbury Park; (732) 455-3284; www .poshden.com. Upscale merchandise here ranges from clothing for men and women to accessories, decor, and interesting imports.

Shoppes at the Arcade. Asbury Park. This retail, restaurant, and gallery complex has appealing locations on two levels. It is in a vintage Woolworth building in the 600 block of Cookman Avenue. There is a second entrance on Lake Avenue. The renovated complex also is the new home of the Asbury Park Historical Society, which hosted the first urban stop for "The Smithsonian Musical Heritage Exhibit: New Harmonies" in spring 2011. The museum hours are 11 a.m. to 5 p.m. Sat and 1 to 4 p.m. Sun. For details on other exhibits, see www.aphistoricalsociety.org.

The Sundry Times. 1100 Ocean Ave., Asbury Park; (732) 455-3490. This is a local newsstand and beach shop right on the boardwalk. Buy beach chairs, T-shirts, and headlines.

"batman" to the rescue

If anyone could give Asbury Park's newfound momentum an extra push, it is Michael Uslan, executive producer of the Batman *film franchise. Michael, son of a mason, grew up in nearby Deal Park. As a youngster, he was a dead-serious fan of the comic book superhero — riding his bike all over town to find the latest pulp edition. Somehow, his passion for the iconic crusader propelled him to Hollywood and a bonanza of blockbusters. Coming full circle in summer 2011 to Asbury Park, Michael brought the backstory home to promote the fall release of his memoir,* The Boy Who Loved Batman *(Chronicle Books). The AP Boardwalk brimmed over with bat-happy events — from book signings at The Sundry Times to oohing over Batmobiles in The Grand Arcade, courtesy of John Brown at Gotham City Supercars. The big moment came with a moonlight screening of the original 1989* Batman *movie directed by Tim Burton. Throughout the day, Michael soaked up the sentiment in salty AP, marveling at the glory in its grit.*

Words! Book Store. 612 Cookman Ave., Asbury Park; (732) 455-5549. This independent bookstore downtown has special events and discussions with authors. In 2011 the shop hosted a "Scrabble Scramble" to prepare contestants for Scrabble by the Sea. Store hours are noon to 5 weekdays, noon to 6 p.m. Sat, and 2 to 5 p.m. Sun.

where to eat

Dauphin Grille. 1401 Ocean Ave., Asbury Park; (732) 776-6700; www.berkeleynj.com. Located at The Berkeley Oceanfront Hotel, the grille has indoor and outdoor seating for its bistro menu. Drinks are available at The Berkeley Bar. $$.

Langosta Lounge. 1000 Ocean Ave., Asbury Park; (732) 455-3275. The cross-street here is Second Avenue. Langosta serves a tropical menu in casual surroundings, lunch and dinner daily. There is outdoor seating as well. $$.

McLoone's Asbury Grille. 1200 Ocean Ave., Asbury Park; (732) 774-1400; www.mcloones asburygrille.com. Keep your eyes peeled for a pointy roof on the boardwalk (site of the former Saltwater Beach Cafe). Tim McLoone's Supper Club occupies the space above the restaurant. The owner said he invested here " . . . because if we open and make one-tenth of 1 percent of Asbury Park's recovery, it would be worth it." The restaurant serves lunch and dinner seven days. $$.

Old Man Rafferty's Restaurant. 541 Cookman Ave., Asbury Park; (732) 774-1600; www .oldmanraffertys.com. Located on the first floor of the historic Steinbach Building; once a department store, now redeveloped as residential condominiums on the upper floors. This is a full-service restaurant and bar. The owner's flagship restaurant is in New Brunswick. The menu is American, and service is lunch and dinner daily. $$.

Stella Marina Bar & Restaurant. 800 Ocean Ave., Asbury Park; (732) 775-7776; www .stellamarinarestaurant.com. This highly rated restaurant has indoor and outdoor seating on two levels—giving diners views of the Atlantic Ocean and Wesley Lake. It is on the southern end of the Boardwalk, near The Carousel House. The menu is classic Italian. Open seven days for lunch and dinner; reservations are recommended. $$$.

Trinity and the Pope. 649 Mattison Ave., Asbury Park; (732) 807-3435; www.trinityand thepope.com.This Creole-Cajun house is among the Shore eateries operated by veteran restaurateur Marilyn Schlossbach. The specialty is creative dishes inspired by the cuisine of New Orleans. You may order many of the dishes in various plate sizes and price ranges during the week. Festive cocktails include a mission fig martini, a "big, pink and easy," and the Louisiana classic, a Sazerac. Happy hour is 5 to 7 p.m. weekdays. The restaurant serves dinner seven days. $$.

where to stay

The Berkeley Oceanfront Hotel. 1401 Ocean Ave., Asbury Park; (732) 776-6700; www .berkeleynj.com. This site near the Boardwalk was famously known for years as the Berkeley-Carteret Oceanfront Hotel. Choose among standard king and queen guest rooms and suites. $$$.

The Empress Hotel. 101 Asbury Ave., Asbury Park; (732) 774-0100; www.asburyempress .com. This long-established hotel has 101 guest rooms across the street from the ocean. It is owned by Shep Pettibone, who opened the Paradise Club in the building before remodeling the hotel. The in-house restaurant is Tabú. The Empress is recommended on www .gay-destinations.com. $$$.

Mikell's Big House Bed & Breakfast. 405 Fourth Ave., Asbury Park; (732) 869-0988; www.mikellsbighouse.com. This lodging offers historic caché with contemporary amenities. Choose from a big room, bigger, biggest, "huge," and "gigantic suite," which includes a private bath, wet bar, fridge, sitting area, and rooftop deck with ocean views. "Bigger" also has a private bath and a fireplace. Mikell's is located in a home that Albert Twining built in 1889. He was president of a local bank and apparently helped himself to its assets by investing in questionable gold mines. That was deemed embezzlement, which landed Albert a vacation at "the Big House"—hence the name Mikell chose for her bed-and-breakfast. Mikell, an interior decorator who lived in San Francisco, bought the Twining property, where she completed a historic restoration of the exterior. She updated the rooms with modern comforts and furnished them in a mix of antique, vintage, and modern. If you want something larger than a room or suite, ask Mikell about the adjacent Carriage House. It has three bedrooms, a pull-out sofa, two baths, kitchen, and living room. There is a porch, an upstairs balcony, and the property is pet friendly—with guidelines. $$.

ocean grove, nj (including sea girt)

This quaint seaside village just south of Asbury Park is a more sedate, "never on Sunday" town where vehicle traffic is restricted during church hours. "God's Square Mile on the Jersey Shore" dates to 1869, when the Ocean Grove Camp Meeting Association established a Methodist summer retreat—an open-air revival gathering that would last for several days. Today, it remains the longest-active camp meeting site in the United States.

The seasonal success of this society grew into a year-round resort community of well-tended homes on quiet streets—gaining the nickname "Queen of Religious Resorts." It hosted Christian preachers and secular orators ranging from Billy Graham to William Jennings Bryan and Booker T. Washington.

Most of the private homes have been maintained and restored to original styles. The Ocean Grove Historical Committee has stood firm on its reviews of architectural suitability. Cited as a unique 19th-century planned community, it became a national historic district in 1975.

A boardwalk now links Asbury Park to its southern neighbor, which hosts beach events, music events, and spiritual gatherings. And however buttoned-up Ocean Grove may remain, its well-kept Victorian bungalows and cottages provide plenty of eye candy.

A few miles south in Sea Girt are sandy lanes leading to substantial beach homes, giving this 1-square-mile patch the appearance of Malibu East.

where to go

Ocean Grove Beach Office. On the boardwalk at the end of Embury Avenue, across from the community fishing pier; (732) 988-5533; www.oceangrove.org. This is where you can purchase daily, weekly, or seasonal badges for one of the least commercial beaches on the Shore. Beaches are open from the end of May until mid-Sept.

The Great Auditorium. 54 Pitman Ave., Ocean Grove; (732) 775-0035; www.oceangrove .org. You cannot miss this vast church, with seating for 5,500 and a large illuminated cross on the central tower. The venue is part of a campus established by the Ocean Grove Camp Meeting Association. Every summer for more than 140 years, a "tent city" has appeared nearby, where camp participants live during a season of lectures, music, and discussions.

The Historical Society of Ocean Grove. 50 Pitman Ave., Ocean Grove; (732) 774-1869; www.oceangrovehistory.org. Call to schedule a 90-minute guided walking tour of the historic district and numerous landmarks: Centennial Cottage, The Great Auditorium, the tent colony, and Beersheba Well, where Carrie Nation delivered her Ocean Grove Temperance Lecture on Aug. 20, 1904. You may also schedule tours of historic homes.

Ocean Pathway. Ocean Grove. This street, once described as one of the top 10 most beautiful streets in America, is perpendicular to the boardwalk and leads toward The Great Auditorium.

where to shop

Ocean Grove Trading Company. 74 Main Ave., Ocean Grove; (732) 774-9200; www .oceangrovetrading.com. Brands include eyebobs, baggallini, Brighton, Watership Hats, and Not Your Daughter's Jeans.

Smuggler's Cove. 50 Main Ave., Ocean Grove; (732) 988-6938. The shop carries greeting cards, novelties, games, and toys.

where to eat

Barbaric Bean Coffee Roastery & Cafe. 48 Main Ave., Ocean Grove; (732) 775-8500. Open for breakfast and lunch weekdays and Sun; open Sat for breakfast, lunch, dinner, and live music. $.

Victorian Tea Room in the Lillagaard. 5 Abbott Ave., Ocean Grove; (732) 888-1216. Serving Fri, Sat, and Sun from 12:30 to 4 p.m. Reservations recommended. $.

where to stay

The Beacon House. 100/104 Beacon Blvd., Sea Girt; (866) 255-0005; www.beacon houseinn.com. Open year-round, this bed-and-breakfast has 21 guest rooms with private baths. Accommodations are in two houses with a pool in the middle and three cottages. Off-season rates are a bargain. $$–$$$.

The Henry Richard Inn. 16 Main Ave., Ocean Grove; (732) 776-7346; www.henryrichard inn.com. This comfortable and welcoming bed-and-breakfast is the site of the former Castle Arms. Henry Johnson and Richard Renzland and their wives took it over in 2000, hence the name. There are five single rooms, eight double rooms, and two apartments. All rooms have a sink and shared baths. The apartments have kitchens and private baths. $$.

The Inn at Ocean Grove. 27 Webb Ave., Ocean Grove; (732) 775-8847; www.theinnat oceangrove.com. This bed-and-breakfast has a dozen charming guest rooms plus some larger apartments. Many have private baths and some have refrigerators. There is a front porch and a rooftop deck. $$.

bed, breakfast, bands, clams

Who needs a free lunch when you can soak up Shore atmosphere in the back-yard of a vintage beach bungalow where sliders are $1.50, grilled lobster is $9.95, and half-shell treats are a quarter a pop? Need summer digs? The Parker House in Sea Girt (described below) rents guest rooms for the season. Break-fast goes on all morning, then lunch, happy hour, dinner, and live entertainment. There is a dining room inside, but most folks prefer a table on the wraparound porch. Even more so, they wander out back to the raw bar for some sweet deals. Weeknight dinner specials vary among broiled seafood, surf 'n' turf, lobster, and prime rib. Music is a daily pastime here, with live bands and DJs pushing your buttons. The tavern is downstairs, the nightclub upstairs. Happy hour at the bar is an all-day affair on weekends and holidays. It has been 134 years since The Parker House opened, and it still has a thing about tradition. Tony Sofia has been the manager since the 1970s.

The Majestic Hotel. 19 Main Ave., Ocean Grove; (732) 775-6100; www.majesticocean grove.com. Unlike many area bed-and-breakfast operations located in restored private homes, The Majestic was built as a hotel in 1870. It was most recently renovated in 2006. It has 15 king and queen guest rooms and a 3-room penthouse. In the ocean block, it is close to other attractions. The in-house restaurant is Bia, a European bistro that serves lunch and dinner. $$$.

The Parker House. First Avenue and Beacon Boulevard, Sea Girt; (732) 449-0442; www .parkerhousenj.com. This funky establishment is about 10 miles south of Asbury Park. Built as a hotel and restaurant in 1878, when congressmen and society swells sat on the veranda, it is open summers only. There are 32 guest rooms, half with private baths; twin beds or a double bed; available from Memorial Day through Labor Day; $3,200 to $3,800 per room for the season. $–$$.

day trip 07

the shore

>>> **taking in the view from "half moon":**
seaside heights, nj; seaside park, nj;
island beach state park, nj

Heading east across Barnegat Bay, you arrive onto another slender barrier island chocked full of paradox. Blue bay waters are busy with people catching air on Jet Skis and wave-runners. Piers jutting out into the Atlantic Ocean are jammed with a crazy-quilt of amusement rides. The Seaside Heights boardwalk is a neon jumble of honky-tonk hawkers with a relatively tame feature—cable car jitneys sliding on a wire.

Some "Jersey Shore" towns, Seaside Park for one, are laid-back odes to a sand castle mentality of beach indulgences. Others are stylish but unpretentious tributes to a coveted island lifestyle. And one or two are attractive nuisances—frenetic, noisy, kitschy—and absolutely spot-on for a reality TV show about tacky behavior.

Yet just a few miles away is an unspoiled treasure of nature that remains much the way it looked to Henry Hudson when he gazed upon the land from his ship, the *Half Moon*. Svelte and spectacular, the 10-mile bastion of nature known as Island Beach State Park has the Atlantic Ocean and Barnegat Bay locked in a dueling salute every day. For icing on top, the sun's job between dawn and dusk is a cakewalk.

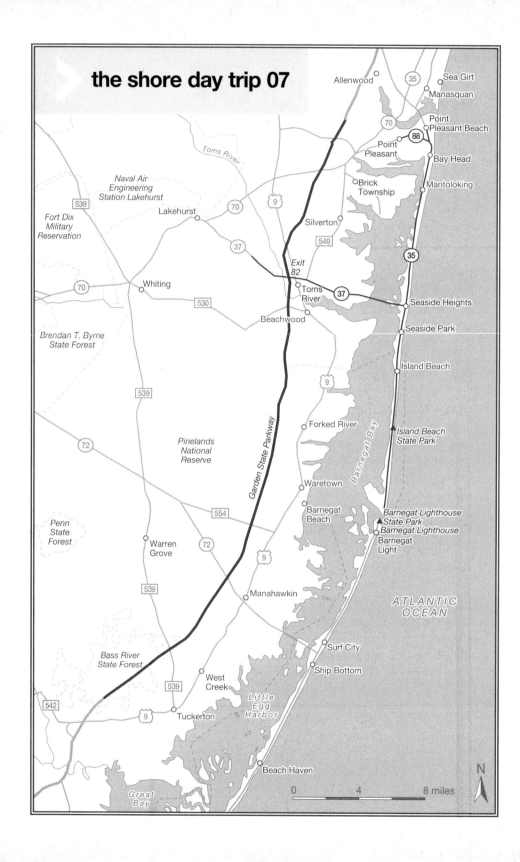

the shore day trip 07

seaside heights, nj

getting there

Take the Garden State Parkway to exit 82 at Toms River; take NJ 37 east and drive over the bridge across Barnegat Bay. After you clear Pelican Island, bear left on NJ 35 for Seaside Heights; bear right for Seaside Park, and Island Beach State Park. Take NJ 35 north for Point Pleasant Beach, Sea Girt, and Spring Lake.

To get a reading on Seaside Heights, consider that a circus comes to town now and then—and not to ride on the coattails of MTV's *Jersey Shore;* for one thing, a circus ringmaster seldom announces a daredevil headbanger—with or without attitude.

The town has hosted a clown festival and parade every year since the 1980s—and some say the amusement venues are a big-shoe scene every day. This berg is all about fun as you interpret it—whether hang-time at a body-piercing den, wolfing down fried Oreos, or losing your shirt at sundown. Cover-ups as a fashion statement? Who-ah-yu-tawkin-tu?

Special events range from the Seaside Heights half-marathon, to a vintage car show, Shamrock Festival, a bed race, Italian Street Festival, bike weekend, the New Jersey HOG Rally for Harley fanatics, and Q by the Sea—a barbecue contest.

where to go

Casino Pier. 800 Ocean Ter., Seaside Heights; (732) 793-6488; www.casinopiernj.com. This long-established amusement park includes 40 rides, a game arcade, and rooftop mini-golf. This is also where you will see the historic Floyd Moreland Dentzel/Looff Carousel, which dates to 1910; some animals making the circle were carved two decades earlier. This is one of two American-crafted, hand-carved antique carousels in New Jersey. It also has a 1923 Wurlitzer Military Band Organ, the only continuously operating carousel band organ in the state (www.magicalcarousel.com).

Breakwater Beach Waterpark. 800 Ocean Ter., Seaside Heights; (732) 793-6488. Breakwater Beach has waterslides of various challenge levels, splash pools, and cabanas for rent, including packages with towels, amusement ride vouchers, pizza, burgers, and ice cream.

***Jersey Shore* cast quarters.** 1209 Ocean Ter., Seaside Heights. This is the bungalow by the boardwalk where The Situation, Snooki, Pauly D, Vinny, Sammi, et al, did whatever it is that they did while filming the show in its early episodes. It occasionally is for rent, if you feel the need to see where their hormones in overdrive, or tanning oil overdoses, drove them to act on impulse without thinking.

Casino Fishing Pier. Sherman Avenue at the Boardwalk; Seaside Heights; (732) 830-2252; www.casinofishingpiernj.com. Fish the ocean for black sea bass, striped bass, fluke, bluefish, blue crabs, tuna, perch, and many more—all in their season. You also are likely to spot whales and dolphin. During the summer, the pier opens at 6 a.m. and at 3 p.m. in the fall and spring. It's near the amusement pier and water park. A daily pass lets you come and go all day, and you can find snacks, bait, and ice on-site.

Smuggler's Quay. 206 Grant Ave., Seaside Heights; (732) 830-4724; www.shore-guide .com/amusements/smuggler. "Adventure Golf" is the family sport here on this mini-golf spread covering almost 2 acres of hillside.

Seaside Heights Beach. Hiering Avenue at the Boardwalk, Seaside Heights; (732) 793-9100; www.seasideheights-nj.com. Look here for indoor hot showers and lockers. Beach badges are $5 a day, $45 for the summer season, and $10 forever for seniors over 65; children under age 12, free.

Wave Amusements. Funtown Pier at DuPont and the Boardwalk, Seaside Heights; (732) 830-7437; www.funtownpier.com. This is one of two amusement piers in the town, with rides galore for adults and children.

where to shop

Adrenaline. 1307 Boardwalk, Seaside Heights; (732) 854-1100; www.adrenalinetattoosnj .com. Let's say you don't have a tattoo but wish you did. Let's say you have a child/grand-child who has a tattoo and wish they didn't, but you need to buy a gift. You have come to the right place for a tattoo, a body piercing, clothing to mask your tattoo—or theirs—custom jewelry, novelties, and so much more than you might have wanted to know, ever. But hey, this is vacation, and you want to broaden your horizons, right? Stop in to look at custom air-brushed and printed T-shirts, and brands you won't find in your average department store: Wicked Quick, Black Market Art Co., Iron Fist, Tribal Gear, Tank Theory, and Miami Ink.

The Dock Outfitters. Route 35 South at Porter Avenue, Seaside Heights; (732) 830-8171; www.thedockoutfitters.com. All you might need in the way of beach supplies are stocked here, along with boat and Jet Ski rentals, tackle and live bait, and information about the waters.

Le Petit Garage. 1020 Ocean Ter., Seaside Heights; (732) 793-4004; www.lepetitgarage .com. Have fun poking around this seasonal trove for uncommonly interesting accessories, clothing, and jewelry. Owner Cara Hershey opened the place in 2005. The name of the shop says it all; it's in a made-over garage in an old brick house on the beach. Want a brilliantly executed Bogg Bag for the beach? How 'bout beaded bracelets handmade by villagers in Nepal? Le Petit Garage is open summers only.

Sand Tropez. 309 Boardwalk, Seaside Heights; (732) 830-8335; www.sandtropez.com. This company has other stores in town, such as One of a Kind and One of a Kind Lady, and locations in Seaside Park, Eatontown, and East Brunswick. They sell men's and women's shirts, pants, hoodies, and jewelry. None of the brands is shy: Bring It On Bro, Jersey Royalty, Jersey Girl, Jersey Shore, and NJ All Day.

where to eat

Gabriella's. Route 35 North and First Avenue, Seaside Heights; (732) 793-7400; www
.gabriellas.com. Long-established, this restaurant is well-known for its Italian specialties. $$.

Greek Peak. 716 Boulevard, Seaside Heights; (732) 854-1226. The Greek cuisine is part of the sea of ethnic choices in Seaside Heights. $$.

Hemingway's. 612 Boulevard, Seaside Heights; (732) 830-1255; www.hemingwaysnj
.com. This place aims to be one-stop-shopping for those bent on casual and comfortable. The menu reels you from seafood to steaks, pasta, sushi, and brick-oven pizza. There is a late-night menu, too, 20 TVs, a dance floor, dartboards, billiards, and live entertainment. Cold drafts and a full-service bar. $$.

Spicy Cantina. 500 Boardwalk, Seaside Heights; (732) 793-0612; www.spicycantina.com. The menu is Mexican, lunch and dinner, and the location on the top of the boardwalk guarantees a good ocean view. $.

Waterside Cafe. Top of Porter Avenue, Seaside Heights; (732) 830-7186; www.thedock
outfitters.com. This breakfast and lunch spot is part of The Dock Outfitters. You have your meal on a dock by the same place where you can rent boats and Jet Skis. Have an omelet or peppers-and-eggs on a hoagie roll; salads, soups, wraps, and more. The hours are 7 a.m. to 8 p.m. $.

where to stay

The White Pearl Hotel. 201 Sumner Ave., Seaside Heights; (732) 830-4242; www.the
whitepearl.com. This AAA-rated hotel was the lodging of choice for the cast and crew of *Jersey Shore*. There are 34 guest rooms on 4 floors—standard, king, small suite, or double-king suite. Some rooms have sleeper sofas and a hot tub. Some have mini-refrigerators. There are washer-dryer units next to ice machines. The Sixth Avenue Bistro inside the hotel serves pizza, burgers, and sandwiches. $$.

seaside park, nj

Seaside Park exists for beach devotees, period.

Okay. Zumba and yoga have a say and get play on the town calendar.

Otherwise, you will see row after row of cottages facing each other across narrow lanes with just enough leeway for two vehicles packed to the gunwales with beach chairs, coolers, water-sports gear, and Shore accoutrements. The lanes are perpendicular to the water. These one-story A-frames with siding are little more than lean-tos or pre-fabs, but home sweet home for the dune-happy throngs who want to live in bikinis, board shorts, and sandals all summer.

getting there

Take the Garden State Parkway exit 82 onto NJ 37 east; cross Barnegat Bay on the Thomas A. Mathis Bridge; bear right on NJ 35 south to Seaside Park.

where to go

Seaside Park Beach. Ocean Avenue, Seaside Park; (732) 793-3700; www.seasideparknj .org. There are almost 2 miles of scenic oceanfront beach in town, south of the boardwalk and amusement pier. Badges are available for daily use and seasonal with special rates for seniors. Parking Lot No. 1 on North Ocean Avenue between Farragut and Stockton Avenues has meters that allow you up to 7.5 hours. Parking Lot No. 2 and No. 3 will allow up to 4 hours. Other meters are available in the ocean blocks of Porter Avenue, Farragut Avenue, Stockton Avenue, Decatur Avenue, Lafayette Avenue, and O Street; another metered area is available on North West Central.

Seaside Park Farmers' Market. Marina Lawn at J Street and Central Avenue, Seaside Park; (732) 793-3700, ext. 105. The market operates from 11 a.m. to 5 p.m. every Mon from mid- to late June through the week of Labor Day; and every Sun, from September 11 to October 16.

Funtown Amusement Pier. 1930 Boardwalk, Seaside Park; (732) 830-7437; www.fun townpier.com. There are about 20 rides suitable for families and kids, almost that many rides suitable for adults and families; plus go-karts, a roller coaster, and the 225-foot "Tower of Fear."

Betty and Nick's Bait & Tackle Shop. 807 S.W. Central Ave., Seaside Park; (732) 793-9415; www.bettyandnicks.com. This establishment in place since the 1970s is a confluence of where to go, where to eat, and where to shop. You go there for information on fishing, plus supplies and bait, tide conditions, and timely tidbits from the locals. You can get breakfast there on the weekends—eggs, hotcakes, hash, you name it. Ask about the Friday evening fish fry, featuring shrimp, clam strips, flounder, grilled salmon, seared scallops, chicken, and flat-iron steak. There is a children's menu, and the side dishes include the usual, plus jambalaya, cheddar-mashed potato patty, asparagus, or green beans.

where to shop

B&B Department Store. 500 S.E. Central Ave., Seaside Park; (732) 793-1350; www .bandbdepartmentstore.com. The forerunner for this retail operation dates to 1900, when it was called The Bazaar. Owners in the 1930s renamed it B&B, a tradition that continued when the current owners took it over in the 1970s. B&B is open year-round and carries men's and women's clothing, swimwear, beach supplies, accessories, and gifts. The company also has stores in Lavallette, a Shore town to the north.

Sand Tropez South. 1815 Boardwalk, Seaside Park; (732) 830-3414; www.sandtropez .com. Look here for men's and women's shirts, pants, hoodies, and jewelry. For the brands they carry, see the description in the section on Seaside Heights.

where to eat

Atlantic Bar & Grill. 24th and Central Avenues, South Seaside Park; (732) 854-1588; www.atlanticbarandgrillnj.com. The oceanfront, dune-top location does not mean lunch or pub food. This is about fine dining in the evening, and it is serious business. Executive Chef Michael d'Ennery is from New Orleans, with some tours in Charleston, so he favors seasonal new-American fare with emphasis on fresh-caught seafood and whatever produce he can round up from farms within a few hundred miles. The raw bar includes East Coast oysters and clams on the half shell, and tuna tartare. The "small bites" menu gives a big shout out to N'Awlins with crab cake beignets in remoulade sauce. The onion-dusted sea bass is complemented with charred eggplant, artichoke hearts, roasted tomatoes, chive aioli, and fried leeks. A summer risotto is almost an all-Jersey marquee—sweet corn, tomatoes, and fresh herbs—plus black-truffle Parmigiano Reggiano and Vermont mascarpone. The wine list has a lovely Pio Cesare Cortese di Gavi, 2009, Piedmont, for $34, and plenty of tempting reds and by-the-glass selections. $$$.

Berkeley Seaside. 24 Central Ave., South Seaside Park; (732) 793-0400; www.berkeley restaurantandfishmarket.com. The Barulic family has owned and operated this restaurant and bar since the 1930s. They also own the fish market next door. Berkeley Seaside is prized by locals and visitors alike for its fresh Shore seafood, raw bar, and time-honored recipes. The upstairs dining room is open for lunch and dinner and has great views of the nearby state park. The first-floor Greenhouse Dining Room opens at 4 p.m. Lots of locals eat lunch in the downstairs bar, which is super casual and friendly. There, you can watch your on-the-half-shell orders being shucked atop the ice. Appetizers include coconut-fried shrimp and crab cake in remoulade sauce. The lunch menu has wraps, salads, and baskets. There is an early-bird menu, and the dinner menu offers an astounding choice of fish, seafood, chicken, and pasta entrees. $.

where to stay

Ocean Terrace Condominiums and Rentals. 1709 N. Ocean Ave., Seaside Park; (732) 793-7922. This popular property has efficiencies and 1-, 2-, and 3-bedroom units across the street from the beach and the boardwalk. There is an indoor pool and an outdoor pool. $$.

The Windjammer Motor Inn. 100 S.E. Central Ave., Seaside Park; (732) 830-2555; www .windjammermotorinn.com. This year-round lodging had been somewhat stuck in the past but drew a lot of repeat business even before the owners renovated the place. That's because the staff is friendly and the location is well south of the commotion and noise of the amusement rides on the boardwalk. Only a short walk from the beach, the Windjammer has a restaurant and bar, a heated swimming pool, and free on-site parking. You also get free beach badges while staying here. There are 39 guest rooms and 24 efficiencies. $.

island beach state park, nj

This remote paradise conjures up the voice of Donald Sutherland doing an orange juice commercial. Island Beach State Park is simply and unapologetically "un-fooled-around-with." Its snowy beaches, tidal marshes, and thickly thistled dunes are spectacular, *au naturel;* hence, the very best home for one of New Jersey's largest osprey colonies and many other species of waterfowl and wading birds.

The park's Northern Natural Area and Southern Natural Area cover 1,900 acres of coastal dunes, freshwater wetlands, saltwater marshes, designated trails, and hundreds of species of plants. On the north end, you may walk the shore on the ocean side or fish from it. On the south end, you may sunbathe, picnic, and fish. Leave the dunes and their thistles alone, however, as they are critical to the very existence of this fragile barrier island.

On the bayside, make time for a kayak trip through the tidal marshes, or slide into a canoe for some spectacular snapshots of falcons and other winged wonders at designated bird blinds.

getting there

Take the Garden State Parkway exit 82 onto NJ 37; across Barnegat Bay to NJ 35 south. The entrance is just past South Seaside Park.

a free lunch

If you have a New Jersey driver's license and are over age 62, admission to Island Beach State Park is free; no extra charge for the Brie and champagne in your picnic basket. Oops! Strike that last. Alcoholic beverages are prohibited in the park.

from earl to pearl of wisdom

The Earl of Stirling may or may not have enjoyed walking barefoot on the barrier island he acquired in 1635 as a land grant from King Charles I of England. However, he would have lost his socks over the outcome of that "unpleasantness" known as the Revolutionary War. In the 18th and 19th centuries, fishermen flocked here, building driftwood shacks on the dunes, and the US Lifesaving Service counted on the barrier beach for its rescue stations. Along came Andrew Carnegie's old partner, steel magnate Henry C. Phipps, who bought the island in 1926 with the idea of dolling up the dunes with resort structures. By the time Wall Street was brought to its knees in 1929, only three seaside manors had been built—putting a halt to Phipps's folly. Organizing itself as the borough of Island Beach, it became valuable during World War II, when the US Army and Johns Hopkins University experimented on anti-aircraft rockets here—code name "Bumblebee." In 1945 the world's first supersonic ramjet missile soared into the air going 1,300 miles per hour, heading southeast above these pristine dunes. New Jersey got so smart, it bought the Phipps estate and additional lands and turned the whole kit and caboodle into a wildlife preserve and natural recreation area. Island Beach State Park opened in 1959.

where to go

Island Beach State Park. (732) 793-0506; www.njparksandforests.org. A bicycle trail runs along both sides of the 2-lane road for 8.5 miles—and the state was nice enough to provide a tire-air station or two. Of the 10 miles of fiercely protected lands, a remarkable 4,300-foot stretch of beach 3 miles from the park entrance is nirvana for swimmers. Lifeguards are on duty from mid-June through Labor Day. There are restrooms, phones, showers, changing areas, and food and beach-supply concessions. You park in one of two lots with a total capacity for 1,850 cars, with boardwalk access to the beach and two beach-access ramps. Anglers are welcome, but not on the designated swimming beach between May 15 and Oct 15. These waters are popular for striped bass, bluefish, fluke (also called summer flounder), and kingfish. In three locations are access roads for mobile sport-fishing vehicles. You may surf or wind-surf, but only in the ocean at the south end of the designated swimming beach. Scuba diving is allowed near the inlet, but you have to register with the park office. The Recreation Zone in the middle of the park has an angler's walkway to the ocean and the bay. The southern third of the park at Barnegat Inlet is called the Sedge Island Marine Conservation Zone—with well-marked spots for launching a canoe or kayak. Find out about kayak tours, observation areas, and the self-guided trails with wildlife and ecosystem exhibits; and don't be surprised if your walk brings you toe to paw with a fox. The southern tip

the point is pleasant

Just 7 miles north of Seaside Heights is the more subdued, family-friendly Point Pleasant Beach. It is largely residential, with deeper streets and cottages closer to the ocean. Its boardwalk extends from the Manasquan Inlet south to Bay Head. In the middle of the boardwalk is Jenkinson's Amusements—lined with rides, games, mini-golf, fun houses, souvenir shops, and snack vendors. The bigger draw for kids is Jenkinson's Aquarium, at Boardwalk and Parkway, where you can see exotic fish, mammals, and birds. Farther north, in Ortley and Lavallette, the scenery appears more refined. Several streets have 2-story lofts and homes, with steps to the dunes at the end of each street. Churches and homes out-weigh the commercial scene. North of Normandy Beach, there are fewer rentals, and more upscale homes and condos. In many Shore towns, you see plenty of Victorian-style structures, plus Dutch Colonial–style homes with brown wooden shingles and white shutters and trim. By the time you reach Mantoloking, you'll see more luxury homes. Pinelands are the decor du jour for some landscaping, with more natural, less manicured drives.

also owns the best view of the Barnegat Lighthouse, a historic landmark across the inlet on Long Beach Island (explored in Day Trip 08). This vantage point makes Island Beach State Park a shutterbug's delight.

worth more time

The Robert J. Novins Planetarium. On the campus of Ocean County College, Route 549 South (Hooper Avenue), Toms River; (732) 255-0342; www.ocean.edu/campus/planetarium. The theater dates to 1970 and its digital video sky theater was renovated in 2010, with the latest projection technology. The dome is a virtual 3-D video space with a fiber-optic Zeiss Star projector, bringing you images of the brightest stars, constellations, and other celebrities of the universe you won't see anywhere else. Observing sessions and other events are held in conjunction with the local astronomy club, ASTRA. Visit the website for shows and times.

day trip 08

the shore

beam me up, barney:
barnegat light & long beach island, nj

A summer colony between ocean and bay, pristine beaches, and dunes knit with thistles—what else must you know to dive in?

One or two anomalies are easily navigated. For one thing, this is not a typical Jersey Shore situation—in that there is no boardwalk and only one amusement park.

Pronouncing the name Barnegat is easy enough, once you settle on whether you mean the borough on the northern tip of Long Beach Island, the humongous bay beside it, the ancient lighthouse nearby, the inlet past its pristine nose, or a few townships on the mainland—Barnegat, Barnegat Beach, and Barnegat Pines. Almost four centuries ago, a Dutch sea captain, Cornelius Jacobsen Mey, called this land of old salts Barendegat, or "inlet of the breakers," for the wildly unpredictable wave action on the shoals.

Long Beach Island is 18 miles long and less than 0.5 mile wide in a few places, hence its name. LBI has more towns than miles, and several of the smaller ones are part of Long Beach Township. Major boroughs from north to south are Barnegat Light, Harvey Cedars, Surf City, Ship Bottom, and Beach Haven—not to be confused with Beach Haven Heights, Beach Haven Gardens, Beach Haven Terrace, and Beach Haven Crest. When they ran out of BHs, they named one tiny stretch Haven Beach.

North end real estate is pricey, while the southern spots are more affordable, with considerably greater commercial development.

Barnegat Inlet was a pivotal point for course changes when cargo ships and whaling vessels plied the waters in the 17th century. The construction supervisor on "Old Barney,"

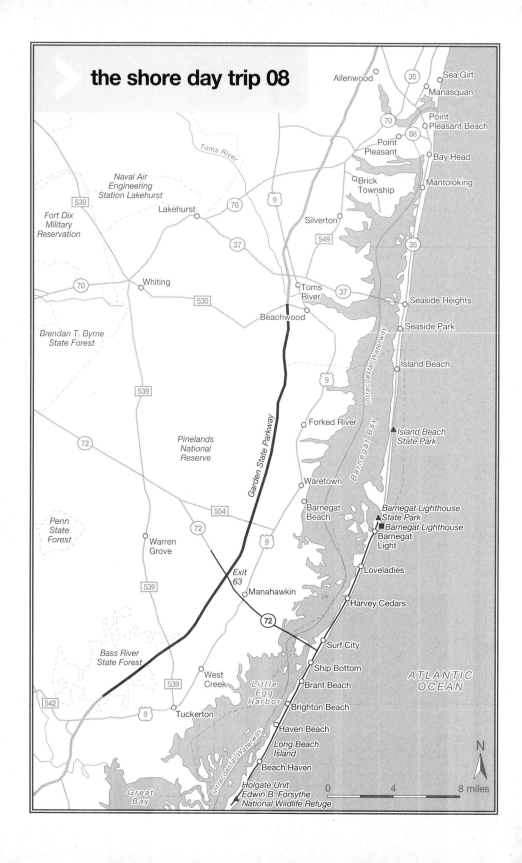

the shore day trip 08

the lighthouse, was George Gordon Meade, most famous for leading Union forces to victory at the Battle of Gettysburg.

Accessible only by a bridge from the mainland, LBI is a coveted destination for residents, celebrities looking for cover, and the savvy anonymous majority who know a good thing when their bare feet touch the sand.

barnegat light & long beach island, nj

getting there

Take the Garden State Parkway to exit 63; go east on NJ 72 to Manahawkin and cross over the Dorland J. Henderson Bridge ("the Causeway") to Ship Bottom on Long Beach Island. Head north for Barnegat Light; south for Beach Haven.

where to go

Barnegat Lighthouse State Park. On Broadway, Barnegat Light; (609) 494-2016; www .state.nj.us/dep/parksandforests.com. Fish, swim, and picnic, just as Captain Kidd did, at this 32-acre park, a maritime site on the New Jersey Coastal Heritage Trail. The star here is Barnegat Lighthouse, a conical tower of brick and iron on a granite base. It is 172 feet tall, the second tallest lighthouse in the United States, and was commissioned in 1859. The island's first light tower was built on the site in 1835, but erosion destroyed it a few decades later. "Old Barney" went dark in 1944 and was illuminated once again on its 150th anniversary. Adjacent to the lighthouse is the Barnegat Interpretative Center, which displays exhibits and encourages curiosity about the workings of beacons and some natural wonders of LBI. From Route 72 east, turn left onto Long Beach Boulevard; it becomes Central Avenue; turn left onto Broadway and the park entrance is on the right. Park hours are weekdays from 8 a.m. to 4 p.m.; lighthouse hours are 10 a.m. to 4:30 p.m. daily. Park entry is free; the lighthouse tour—including 217 steps—is $1.

Barnegat Light Museum. 501 Central Ave., Barnegat Light; (609) 494-8578; www.bl-hs .org. The museum is operated by the Barnegat Light Historical Society in a small house once used as a public school. The primary exhibit is "Old Barney's" 1857 first-order flashing lens built by French physicist Augustin Fresnel. The beacon could be seen 20 miles or more toward the horizon. The lens was removed in 1927, sent to a depot on Staten Island, and returned to Barnegat Light in 1954. A related exhibit is about Sinbad, a US Coast Guard dog who served in World War II; he "retired" to Barnegat Light and is buried at the base of the old Coast Guard station flagpole. The museum's exhibits reveal much about the whaling industry, fishing industry, old photographs of the borough, and details about the grand resort hotels that have long since vanished. The museum is open June through Sept. Donations are encouraged.

Surflight Theatre. 201 Engleside Ave., Beach Haven; (609) 492-9477; www.surflight.org. With more than 60 years of curtain calls, this equity theater is as much a part of LBI as its natural assets. It began as the dream of the late Joseph P. Hayes, who produced the first shows in a tent with a 12-piece orchestra. Fast-forward so many decades to Surflight's calendar, and it's easy to see that Hayes was on to something from the get-go.

Historic Viking Village. 19th Street and Bayview Avenue, Barnegat Light; (609) 361-7008; www.vikingvillage.net. Browse the shops and watch seafarers return to the docks with their fresh catch; shop for clothing, jewelry, and seafood. Check out The Seawife, an antique shop housed in a pioneer school. Every Fri at 10 a.m. is a 1-hour guided tour of the fishing dock. Each summer, Viking Village presents three art and craft shows and two antiques and collectible shows. This is a nod to the Norse heritage of the original fishing village developed in the 1920s. Sample seafood at Viking Fresh Off the Hook.

Edwin B. Forsythe National Wildlife Refuge. Holgate Unit; (609) 652-1665; www.fws .gov/northeast/forsythe. This pristine preserve has multiple units. This one is located at the southern tip of Long Beach Island. At 2.5 miles long, it has more than 400 acres of barrier beach, dunes, and tidal salt marsh. Visitors here have seasonal opportunities to observe its plants and animals on their own turf. Holgate has one of New Jersey's last undeveloped barrier beaches, and its path in the Atlantic Flyway makes it essential to beach-nesting birds—including the threatened piping plovers. More than 50 other bird species nest at Holgate during the spring and summer, including ospreys, black ducks, American oystercatchers, willets, and seaside sparrows. Visitors may walk Holgate's beachfront during non-nesting season, Sept 1 through Mar 31; during nesting season—Apr 1 through Aug 31—Holgate is closed to the public to ensure undisturbed nesting conditions. *Note:* no pets allowed in the preserve.

Alliance for a Living Ocean. 1101 Central Ave., Ship Bottom; (609) 494-7800; www.living ocean.org. This environmental group coordinates guided ecological tours of Long Beach

plenty to preserve

In addition to the unit at Holgate, the Edwin B. Forsythe National Wildlife Refuge has a unit on the west side of Barnegat Bay opposite Harvey Cedars (called the Barnegat Division). Another unit, the Brigantine, is on Homers Island south of Little Egg Inlet.

> ## loveladies lore
>
> *In the 1870s, the US Life Saving Stations established on Long Beach Island were often given names. After much debate about Station No. 114, it was decided that the namesake should be a 10-acre island in the bay whose owner, Thomas Love-lady, was a hunter and sportsman. For a time, the neighborhood was called Love-lady's. This affluent part of Long Beach Township changed its name to Loveladies.*

Island during the summer, for all ages. There are eco-kayak tours, "sea critter roundups," and a puppet theater.

Thundering Surf Waterpark/Adventure Golf. 8th Street and Bay Avenue, Beach Haven; (609) 492-0869; www.thunderingsurfwaterpark.com. Eight waterslides are here, plus a toddler zone called "Cowabunga Beach," snack shops, and cabanas. The adventure golf attraction, way beyond mini-golf, has two renovated 18-hole courses featuring water hazards and caves. Open daily. See the website for seasonal specials.

Fantasy Island Amusement Park. 320 W. Seventh St., Beach Haven; (609) 492-4000; www.fantasyislandpark.com. This is a family-friendly park with rides, games, entertainment, a food court, and ice cream parlor. There is the obligatory Ferris wheel, bumper cars, a carousel, and Rio Grande train rides. The casino arcade is designed for all ages, with hundreds of games.

Long Beach Township Beaches. 6805 Long Beach Blvd., Brant Beach (south of Ship Bottom); (609) 361-6675; www.longbeachtownship.com. This is the office where you pick up badges for many of the 20 beaches on LBI. The office is open from 9 a.m. to 4 p.m. weekdays, 9 a.m. to 3 p.m. on weekends and holidays.

Long Beach Township Beach Patrol. (609) 361-1200. LBI Township has a Beachwheels program. Call here to reserve a Surf Chair for up to 1 week, depending on availability.

The Long Beach Island Museum. Engleside and Beach Avenues, Beach Haven; (609) 492-0700; www.lbimuseum.org. The museum is housed in the former Holy Innocents' Episcopal Church, which was built in 1882. The Long Beach Island Historical Association owns and operates the museum. Museum hours from late June through Labor Day weekend are 10 a.m. to 4 p.m. daily, and from 7 to 9 p.m. Wed. From Memorial Day weekend through the end of June, hours are 2 to 4 p.m. on weekends; from mid-Sept to the first week of Oct, hours are 2 to 4 p.m. on weekends. Admission is a donation of $3.

The Long Beach Island Foundation of the Arts and Sciences. 120 Long Beach Blvd., Loveladies, just south of Barnegat Light; (609) 494-1241; www.lbifoundation.org. This nonprofit institution dates to 1948 and offers classes, workshops, performances, juried exhibitions, film and book discussions, concerts, lectures, and nature walks. Classes for grown-ups include painting, ceramics, sculpture, cooking, drawing, basketry, glass, jewelry, and fitness. Children age 3 and up can study art, marine science, and children's theater. You can even rent a studio for a day. The facility is closed Tues and Wed, and available to all. Order a catalog online for the upcoming season schedule.

Miss Barnegat Light. 18th Street Dock, Barnegat Light; (609) 494-2094; www.miss barnegatlight.com. This 90-foot, high-speed twin-engine catamaran reaches speeds of 25 knots, making it one of the swiftest East Coast party boats. This enables the vessel to reach open water faster, giving you more time to fish instead of "going" fishing. Equipped with advanced fish-finders, sonar, radar, and other electronics, *Miss Barnegat Light* can get you out and back safely. The boat makes daily 6-hour trips departing at 8 a.m. and returning at 2 p.m.; and on Fri and Sat evenings from 7:30 p.m. to 2 a.m.

LBI Parasail. Sixth Street and Bay Avenue at the Lighthouse Marina, Barnegat Light; (609) 361-6100; www.lbiparasail.com. Here is your chance to fly; to soar a few hundred feet above the Jersey Shore for unique views of the gin-clear water and confectionary sand; to hope the boat motor does not stall or otherwise cause you to spiral downward into the ocean, to wallow in the weight of the chute while the boat driver attempts to restart the engine before you run out of air. Just kidding; parasailing is a hoot, so try it. Once is good.

where to shop

The Boardwalk. 2306 S. Bay Ave., Beach Haven; (609) 492-3298; www.theboardwalklbi .com. This is a combination beach shop and ice cream parlor—featuring hand-dipped flavors, floats, frozen yogurts, Italian ices, and 28 varieties of gourmet milk shakes. "Chilled Monkey Brains," anyone? You can rent a bike here, or a surfboard, buy a wetsuit or swim-suit. The shop also repairs bikes and patches your flats. Open daily from 9 a.m. to 9:30 p.m. during the summer.

soothe the sunburn

Should you crave a little break from the sun's rays—or a rainy-day amusement— Long Beach Island has three cinema houses: Hoyts Beach 4, on Long Beach Boulevard in Beach Haven Park (609-492-6906); Hoyts Colonial Twin, at Bay Avenue and Centre Street in Beach Haven (609-492-4450); and Hoyts Colony 4, 35th Street and Long Beach Boulevard in Brant Beach (609-494-3330).

Morrison's Marina. Second Street and the bay, Beach Haven; (609) 492-2150; www.mor risonslbi.com. This multitasking operation is a ship store, gift shop, marina, and restaurant. Family-owned, it has operated on LBI since 1946.

Ric's Aloha Classics. 213 Bay Ave., Beach Haven; (609) 492-8896; www.lbi.net/aloha. If you know how to "hang 10" or ever wanted to, you will feel a kinship with owner Ric Anastasi. He has a thing for surf art, collectibles, apparel, decor, surf books, rare videos, posters, and surf music. Apparel includes Wave Wear surf trunks and women's wear by Toes on the Nose. Ric also carries Lee Sands of Hawaii jewelry and leather.

Under the Mistletoe. Long Beach Boulevard and 112th Street, Haven Beach; (609) 492-3333; www.underthemistletoe.org. For more than 25 years, shoppers on LBI have been able to find charming and unique holiday whimsy at Under the Mistletoe. Enjoy browsing among unusual ornaments in a dozen themes, handmade dolls, hand-blown glass, and a large array of Christmas decor items. Brands include Department 56, Snowbabies, Kringle, Byers Choice, Christopher Radko, Pipka, Cat's Meow, Possible Dreams, and Annalee. The store also carries Crabtree & Evelyn and Yankee Candle. The store is open from spring through New Year's.

where to eat

Blue Restaurant. 1016 Long Beach Blvd., Surf City; (609) 494-7556. The chef's *amuse bouche* is often an artisan bread and savory spread—perhaps pesto, olive or black bean. The menu is decidedly gourmet and international, yet the breezy, casual-chic atmosphere welcomes those possibilities. Appealing appetizers include a crab, avocado, and lobster mousse timbale and the vegetable empanada. The entrees invite you to be extra hungry: seared grouper, sea bass, scallops with pea risotto, and veal chop—each with a twist, each with a tempting surprise in the presentation and sides. Bring your own wine, and make it a respectable one, to complement the chef's creations and the display of modern art. $$$.

Kubel's. 28 Seventh St., Barnegat Light; (609) 494-8592; www.kubels2.com. This casual, popular hangout is full of locals who get their news, brews, and chews at the neighborhood tavern. It dates to the 1920s and has some colorful tales about that noble experiment known as Prohibition. Kubel's began as a food and lodging aside to Paul's rowboat business. The fact that alcohol was illegal until 1933 did not deter the locals, who sipped and supped there. The Kubelczikas family, experienced tavern owners from south Philly, bought the bar—then called Rudi's—deciding not to waste money on signage. They lopped off "czikas" and "Kubel's" appeared in neon. The bar changed hands a few more times, but the name stuck. Lunch and dinner daily year-round, from shrimp tempura and hot crab dip to seafood entrees and steaks. $$.

Pinziminio Trattoria. 8701 Long Beach Blvd., Brighton Beach; (609) 492-8700; www .pinziminio.com. Named for the simplest of Italian ingredients—seasoned olive oil—this restaurant is open for dinner daily, from Memorial Day through Labor Day, and Thurs through Sun in the off-season. Try the shrimp agliata appetizer or the Mediterranean salad. For chicken or veal entrees, or a pasta dish to remember, the Pinziminio sauce starts with pancetta and adds capers, olives, garlic, oil, and anchovies. The unusual ingredient in the sauce is currants. They add hot pepper flakes, too, so ask ahead of time if you want sauce without a kick. Orata is an entree showcasing Mediterranean black sea bass encrusted with feta cheese and a hot cherry pepper pesto, served over sweet-pea risotto. $$.

Rick's American Cafe. Fourth and Broadway, Barnegat Light; (609) 494-8482; www.ricks americancafelbi.com. This restaurant and nightclub with live entertainment is open summers and weekends during the off-season. The menu ranges from raw-bar classics to burgers, sandwiches, Rick's original Philly cheesesteak, soups, salads, and bar pizza. $.

Uncle Will's Pancake House. 3 S. Bay Ave., Beach Haven; (609) 492-2514; www.uncle wills.com. Breakfast is a colorful event every day, what with choosing among apple-pecan pancakes, blueberry waffles, dream-up-your-own omelets, and the whimsical menu descriptions. You can be served from 7 a.m. to "12:30-ish." Uncle Will's also serves a grilled dinner menu from 5 to 9 p.m. Thurs through Sun. $.

where to stay

daddy O hotel. 4401 Long Beach Blvd., Brant Beach; (609) 361-5100; www.daddyohotel .com. This boutique hotel half a block from the beach looks like a replica of a vintage Jersey Shore lodging from the outside but has a very contemporary interior. It has 22 rooms, a restaurant, rooftop bar, and outdoor lounge area; no swimming pool, however. The guest rooms are Euro-size, meaning smaller than many Americans are accustomed to, but the furnishings are sleek and the beds well turned out. If you don't love red leather, you might not spend a lot of time in the restaurant or bar. $.

The Engleside Inn. 30 Engleside Ave., Beach Haven; (609) 492-1251; www.engleside .com. The inn has several formats of guest rooms to choose from, including some with a hot tub in the suite. There are three in-house restaurants: The Leeward, with a full array of fine dining choices; Sushi Bar and Lounge, with a full menu and occasional entertainment; and The Sand Bar, for casual outdoor dining by the pool, patio, or bar. This is more popular than the other sites, with great clam strips, a good burger selection—say avocado, bacon, Asiago, and chipotle sauce; wraps, panini, a children's menu, and tons of tempting appetizers. Were we able to order another item, it would be the Big Bob salad: grilled marinated chicken, bacon, avocado, tomato, hard-boiled egg, crumbled Bleu cheese, mixed greens, and ranch dressing on the side. $$.

North Shore Inn. 806 Central Ave., Barnegat Light; (609) 494-5001; www.northshoreinn .com. This is a quiet, comfortable, family-owned establishment a block from the beach and the lighthouse. The inn requests guests to honor its "quiet" policy from 10 p.m. to 9 a.m. $.

The Sand Castle Bed and Breakfast. 710 Bayview Ave., Barnegat Light; (609) 494-6555; www.sandcastlelbi.com. Situated on the bay, just 2 blocks from the ocean, this mini-resort has 5 guest rooms and 2 luxury suites, a heated swimming pool, and spa. Each room is decorated individually, and each room has a private, exterior entrance, modern bath amenities, and a fireplace. The guest profile here is adults and couples, with no welcome mat for children under age 16. Parking is free and spaces are situated near room/suite entries. The Lighthouse Vista Suite is 2 stories, with a spiral staircase taking you to a loft and balcony with views of the pool and "Old Barney." There is an enclosed sunroom, library, and outdoor deck. Breakfast is no slouch, and the room rate includes complimentary beach badges, bicycles, towels, and chairs. This lodging operates from Apr 1 through mid-Nov. $$$.

worth more time

Tuckerton Seaport. 120 E. Main St., Tuckerton; (609) 296-8868; www.tuckertonseaport .org. This is a working maritime village along Tuckerton Creek on the west side of the Intracoastal Waterway, west of Long Beach Island. Take the bridge west from Ship Bottom and turn south onto Route 9. The Tuckerton Seaport is a unique attraction promoting the Jersey Shore's maritime traditions with exhibits and hands-on activities. You will see re-created buildings, historic structures, demonstrations, interpretive exhibits, events, festivals, and live aquatic displays. Artisans include decoy carvers, boat builders, basket makers, and baymen who entertain and educate. You may stroll along the boardwalk by Tuckerton "Crik" and see birds and plants on a nature trail. One of Tuckerton's most popular exhibits opened in 2010, featuring The New Jersey Surf Museum's celebration of surfing history. It opened with a 50-board collection that has already doubled. The exhibit displays mural-size canvases with pictures and text of surfers from the 1940s onward. The link between surfing and clamming is featured, giving good exposure to conservation efforts on New Jersey beaches. Memorabilia on display includes surfer duds, magazine articles, and photographs—with "hang 10" music playing in the background. The facility is open daily from 10 a.m. to 5 p.m.

greater
atlantic city

day trip 01

greater atlantic city

> > >

bling! ca-ching! a neon fling:
atlantic city, nj

All the usual suspects are here in plain sight: the "AC" Boardwalk, casinos, beaches, spas, restaurants, and bars; headline entertainers, family attractions, historic and cultural offerings, and enough shopping venues to shred your sandals.

That will prompt you to seek out the next favorite pair. Shopping in AC is as varied as the amusements and nightlife, with designer stores, brand-name outlets, unique boutiques, and the extra temptation of tax-free purchases on clothes and shoes.

Far from the neon marquees, the clatter of chips, and the clink of slots, Atlantic City has an overlay of islands—intriguing 24/7—so check out sightseeing by boat as another way to appreciate this unique playground.

The boardwalk dates to 1870, starts at Absecon Inlet, and runs parallel to the ocean for 4 miles. Once you reach the southern city limits, the boardwalk goes for another mile or so in Ventnor City.

Although most Shore towns sport a sizeable promenade, AC's boardwalk is the longest. It has casino resorts, restaurants, bars, and amusements. The turf gets a bit wider in spots, as piers extend the footprint over the ocean—walking on water, so to speak.

The boardwalk was already famous by the time the game Monopoly came out and positioned players in high-stakes Atlantic City real estate deals. In 2010 HBO launched a new drama series, *Boardwalk Empire,* inspired by the neighborhood.

Whether you want to put on a poker face or be in the audience when your favorite headliner performs, Atlantic City is a playful pastime. With good reason, gambling is part of the AC stereotype; however, there are some family-oriented resorts without casinos.

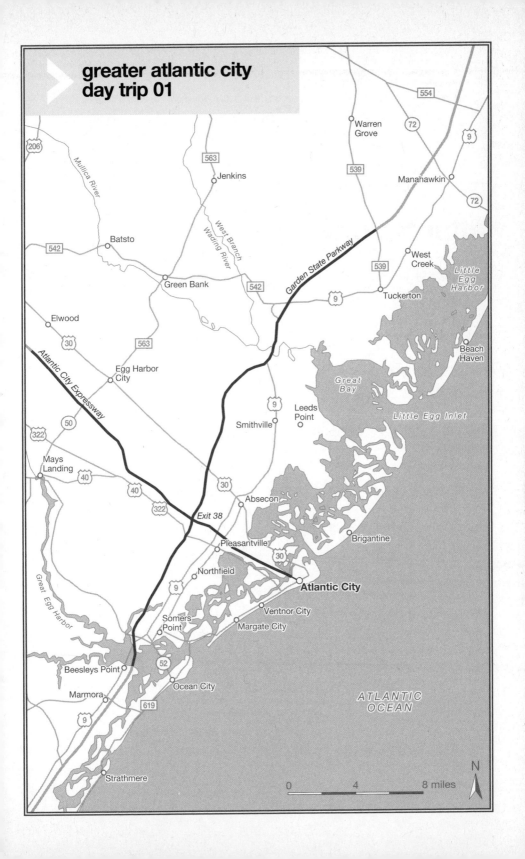

greater atlantic city
day trip 01

Newer casinos have drawn business from the oldies, tempting visitors with cosmopolitan amenities. So watch what happens with the newest one, Rebel, on the horizon at the north end of the boardwalk. Will it steal the fickle souls who scurried to the formerly new spots?

Why worry? The Marina District entices on many levels, and the boardwalk supersedes gaming here by more than a century. Who would come to AC without stopping by?

atlantic city, nj

getting there

Take the Garden State Parkway to exit 38; head east on the Atlantic City Expressway, and follow the signs. The city is laid out in districts, and the causeway has ample signage pointing the way to destinations in the Marina District and the boardwalk.

where to go

Atlantic City Aquarium. 800 N. New Hampshire Ave., Atlantic City; (609) 348-2880; www.oceanlifecenter.com. Located at Historic Gardner's Basin, and part of the Ocean Life Center, the aquarium has tanks with fish from the Amazon River, the Indo-Pacific, and the mid-Atlantic Oceans. You will see live coral and loggerhead sea turtles. Gardner's Basin also has artisan crafters on the premises.

Atlantic City Cruises. Located at Gardner's Basin, Atlantic City; (609) 347-7600; www .atlanticcitycruises.com. The company takes you out for 2-hour dolphin watching cruises, a 1-hour morning cruise, and other sightseeing voyages.

Capt. Mike's *Highroller*. Gardner's Basin, Atlantic City; (609) 348-3474; www.highroller fishing.com. This flat, houseboat-shaped vessel takes you for outings in the calm waters of the bay, to catch fluke, bluefish, stripers, and summer flounder.

Absecon Light. Vermont and Pacific Avenues, Atlantic City. With a height of 171 feet, it is the tallest lighthouse in New Jersey and first shone in 1857. It was decommissioned in 1933, but its fixed light still shines. You may climb the 228 steps to the top, and see the original first-order Fresnel lens in the Oil House. A museum in the replicated 1925 Keeper's House has references on shipwrecks and local lore.

Absecon Inlet. These waters in northern Atlantic City are an important eco-tourism look-see. Hundreds of acres of remnant beach and dune habitat are critical to breeding and migrating birds. Across the inlet are tidal salt marshes and creeks of the Absecon Wildlife Management Area and the Brigantine Division of the Edwin B. Forsythe National Wildlife Refuge.

lizzie's landlord license

Talk about being ahead of the game . . .

Elizabeth Magie Phillips created a game in 1904 that was published two decades later as The Landlord's Game—forerunner of the iconic board game Monopoly. Lizzie's purpose wasn't idle parlor entertainment for a rainy afternoon. She hoped the dice-roll-card-draw exercise would help laypeople understand the land-swap theories of economist Henry George. In a twist on that idea, Charles Darrow interpreted Lizzie's idea as Monopoly, and tried to get Parker Brothers and the Milton Bradley Company to bite. No dice. So Darrow got somebody to print thousands of copies of the game in time for the 1934 holiday shopping season at Wanamaker's in Philadelphia, and F.A.O. Schwarz in New York. After the department stores sold out their stock, Parker Brothers ate some crow. The rest, as they say, is all about the price of real estate on the Boardwalk.

The Steel Pier. Virginia Avenue and the boardwalk, Atlantic City; (866) 386-6659; www.steelpier.com. This icon of AC is a trip-capture for old times' sake, all by itself, as you explore the amusement park sprawling over the water—a super example of where the Boardwalk extends the imagination. From its inception in 1898, it was square-one for national headliners—from W. C. Fields performing in a minstrel group, to musicians and personalities such as Guy Lombardo, Benny Goodman, Mae West, The Three Stooges, Bob Hope, and Frank Sinatra. The pier was damaged by fire in the 1980s, and resurrected when The Trump Organization took the lead to put some oomph back into the pier's spine. Today, there are rides, rides, rides galore—from kid-friendly to extreme—plus helicopter spins, go-karts, and a game zone. Open daily in summer and weekends in the spring and fall.

Sammy's Beach Bar. Park Place and the boardwalk, across from Bally's, Atlantic City; (609) 236-6983. If you like to people-watch, sip a cold one, nibble from the Tex-Mex fusion menu, or take in the beach scene, Sammy has your number. It's named for rocker Sammy Hagar, formerly of Van Halen. Open for lunch and dinner, with live entertainment and DJs. If you object to your waitress wearing a red or white bikini, stay in your room. $.

The Atlantic City Historical Museum. Garden Pier along the "uptown" boardwalk, Atlantic City; (609) 347-5839; www.acmuseum.org. "Atlantic City, Playground of the Nation," a permanent exhibit, displays memorabilia, vintage postcards, artifacts, costumes, posters, photographs, and sheet music. You will be greeted by Mr. Peanut as you view a miniature boardwalk and "beach" collection of sand art. A documentary, *Boardwalk Ballyhoo: The Magic of Atlantic City,* runs throughout the day showing the Miss America Pageant, archival

Thomas Edison beach shots, and the famous high-diving horse. The video traces AC's history from an early seaside resort to the casino era. Inside the museum is the Al Gold Photography Gallery. The museum is open daily from 10 a.m. to 4 p.m., except for major holidays; admission is free. Signs in the lot across from the museum will post current parking restrictions.

Atlantic City Art Center. Garden Pier along the "uptown" boardwalk, Atlantic City; (609) 347-5837; www.acmuseum.org. The art center is inside the history museum. It has three galleries featuring paintings, sculpture, and photography. Free admission; open daily from 10 a.m. to 4 p.m.

Lucy the Elephant. 9200 Atlantic Ave., Margate City (2 miles south of Atlantic City); (609) 823-6473; www.lucytheelephant.org. An evergreen outing, for sure, and how could you drive by a 6-story "elephant" without stopping to ask her for directions? This structure is a National Historic Landmark, built of wood and tin in 1882. The idea was a promotion, credited to James V. Lafferty, who sought to boost tourism and sell property.

atlantic city casinos

ACH Casino Resort. Boston Avenue and the boardwalk, Atlantic City; (609) 347-7111; www.hiltonac.com. This resort is on the market, so call for special deals.

Bally's Hotel and Casino. Park Place and the boardwalk; Atlantic City; (609) 344-3483; www.ballysac.com.

The Borgata Hotel Casino and Spa. 1 Borgata Way (Renaissance Pointe), Atlantic City (Marina District); (609) 317-1000; www.theborgata.com. See the "where to stay" section for details on the companion property, The Water Club, a non-gaming hotel.

Caesars Hotel and Casino. Arkansas Avenue and the boardwalk; (609) 348-4411; www.caesarsac.com. See the "Where to Shop" section for details on The Pier Shops at Caesars.

The Golden Nugget. Huron Avenue and Brigantine Boulevard, Atlantic City (Marina District); (609) 441-2000; www.trumpmarina.com. This is the former Trump Marina (see the "where to stay" section for the new owner's renovation plans).

Harrah's Resort Casino and Hotel. 777 Harrah's Blvd. at Brigantine Bay, Atlantic City (Marina District); (609) 441-5000; www.harrahsresort.com. Staying here is one option; or just drop by the terrace, where people lounge by the swimming pool, have lunch, people-watch, and move along.

Resorts Casino Hotel. North Carolina Avenue and the boardwalk; Atlantic City; (609) 343-3119; www.resortsac.com. Based on what our cabbie said, Resorts leans toward some edgy promotions; that particular weekend, they hosted a naked circus. The resort touts an "all-gay bar."

playing the trump card

*Donald Trump has a different perspective on Atlantic City these days, compared to the years in which The Trump Organization ran things at three of the city's long-established casinos: Trump Taj Mahal, Trump Plaza, and Trump Marina (now the Golden Nugget). Donald's holding company got out of casino management after he turned some of his attention to his NBC reality shows—*The Apprentice *and* Celebrity Apprentice*—and his first love, developing real estate.*

Showboat Hotel and Casino. Delaware Avenue and the boardwalk, Atlantic City; (609) 343-4000; www.showboatac.com. This spot gets points for a rooftop swimming pool and the House of Blues. See www.houseofblues.com for the entertainment schedule.

Tropicana Casino and Resort. Iowa Avenue and the boardwalk, Atlantic City; (609) 340-4000; www.tropicana.net. The casino in this Old Havana–themed resort is one of AC's most appealing (see details about The Quarter in the "Where to Shop" section).

Trump Plaza Hotel and Casino. Mississippi Avenue at the boardwalk, Atlantic City; (609) 441-6000; www.trumpplaza.com. Bet on The Donald, any time.

Trump Taj Mahal. 1000 Boardwalk, Atlantic City; (609) 449-1000; www.trumptaj.com. See the "Where to Stay" and "Where to Shop" sections.

where to shop

The Pier Shops at Caesars. 1 Atlantic Ocean (Arkansas Avenue and the boardwalk), Atlantic City; (609) 345-3100; www.thepiershopsatcaesars.com. Located on a 900-foot pier over the water, this multilevel destination has about 75 upscale retail shops, some lower-end stores, and restaurants. Luxury brands include Hugo Boss, Burberry, and Gucci. At the end of the pier is The Water Show, a water, light, and sound scenario that runs every hour. On Level 3, you can watch the sunset while sitting in an Adirondack chair with your feet in the sand—all air-conditioned.

Princeton Antiques and Books. 2917 Atlantic Ave., Atlantic City; (609) 344-1943; www.princetonantiques.com. Robert Ruffolo bought this 3-story building in the 1960s and opened the bookstore in 1972. His son, Bob, runs the business today. There are more than 250,000 books in stock, many rare tomes, out-of-print volumes, and leather-bound books. Want to find Alexandre Dumas's *The Count of Monte Cristo,* or the complete works of Jane Austen? You can find them here, along with a wealth of literary expertise and research assistance. On the website, you'll see Princeton's collection of vintage Atlantic City photographs, memorabilia, antiques, paintings, Oriental rugs, clocks, watches, and pottery. About 3,000 books are displayed on a sidewalk "honor system." Hours are 8:30 a.m. to 5 p.m. weekdays and 8 a.m. to 1 p.m. Sat.

The Quarter at Tropicana. Brighton Avenue at the boardwalk, Atlantic City; (800) 843-8767; www.tropicana.net/thequarter. This mall inside the casino resort has about 20 shops, plus an IMAX theater, restaurants, lounges, and a spa.

Spice Road. 1000 Boardwalk and Virginia Ave., Atlantic City; (609) 449-1000; www.trump taj.com/shopping. This retail promenade is located inside the Trump Taj Mahal Casino Resort. Stores carry dreamy merchandise, from fashions at Marshall Rousse, to Swarovski crystal at Accents. Trump Exchange is a 4,000-square-foot store, with The Donald's line of dress shirts, ties, and accessories; apparel for men and women; jewelry, watches, and logo items. You also will spot fun memorabilia from *The Apprentice.* Decks of cards, dice, mugs, and T-shirts carry the pink-slip message—"You're fired!"

Talk of the Walk. Huron and Brigantine Boulevards, Atlantic City; (609) 345-9255; www .talkofthewalk.com. The women's apparel and accessories store is located at the Golden Nugget. It has other locations in Stone Harbor, and Haven Beach on Long Beach Island.

Tanger Outlets, The Walk. 1931 Atlantic Ave., Atlantic City; (609) 872-7002; www.tanger outlets.com. You will find a hundred or more ways to spend at well-known retailers, including outlets and factory stores. Brands include Tommy Hilfiger, Old Navy, and Brooks Brothers.

air to anybody down there

The airship America *departed from Atlantic City in October 1910, courtesy of explorer Walter Wellman. Jack Irwin, a Marconi wireless operator, made history by using a "spark gap" radio set installed in the airship's lifeboat to relay a crisis from call-sign "W." He used the frame as the antenna to call "CQD"—the original SOS distress signal—and his message is considered the first air-to-ground transmission. Irwin spotted a British steamship,* Trent, *when the* America *was west of Bermuda. He first used Morse code on a signaling lamp, followed by the CQD. He and the crew, plus a cat named Kiddo, got into the lifeboat and bid adieu to* America. *After the* Trent *picked them up, the captain gave them a ride to New York.*

where to eat

The Chart House. Brigantine Boulevard and Huron Avenue at the Farley Marina, Atlantic City; (609) 340-5030; www.chart-house.com. Located at the Golden Nugget Hotel & Casino (formerly Trump Marina), the restaurant is owned by Houston-based Landry's. Lunch on weekends; dinner daily except Mon. $$.

The Continental. Level 3 of The Pier Shops at Caesars, Atlantic City; (609) 674-8300; www.thecontinentalac.com. This casual, upscale eatery was launched by Philadelphia restaurateur Stephen Starr. It's open for brunch, lunch, and dinner, serving a tapas-style menu, which means you pick a continent and find a friend. We liked the French onion–soup dumplings, hot pepper calamari, and Pad Thai. The drinks menu is inventive and well-informed. $$.

Il Mulino New York. 1000 Boardwalk, Atlantic City; (609) 449-6006; www.ilmulino.com. Located inside the Trump Taj Mahal, this icon from Manhattan is a superb addition to AC fine dining. The chicken scarpariello is awesome. We enjoyed a marvelous grilled rib eye steak and Bucatini all' Amatriciana, a delectable pasta dish with pancetta and Romano. Open for dinner daily. Il Mulino's "Sunday Supper" is the epitome of Italian delicacies, with a four-course, $43 prix fixe menu. $$$.

Knife & Fork Inn. 3600 Atlantic Ave., Atlantic City; (609) 344-1133; www.knifeandforkinn.com. One of the most remarkable establishments in AC's long and colorful history, this 3-story building has been a restaurant since 1912, when it opened as a men's dining club. The steak and seafood operation got a makeover in 2005 when new owners renovated the building. $$.

Los Amigos. 1926 Atlantic Ave., Atlantic City; (609) 344-2293; www.losamigosrest.com. When you yearn for Southwest fare, c'mon down. The Tabasco Tequila Shrimp is marinated in cilantro and garlic, doused with tequila, and dimpled with hot sauce. There are traditional Mexican dishes, plus an interesting filet mignon Cuervo, and a choice of gluten-free items. $$.

Sack O' Subs. Park Place and the boardwalk, inside Bally's, Atlantic City; (609) 236-6474; and 777 Harrah's Blvd., inside Harrah's, Atlantic City; (609) 441-5034; www.sackosubs.com. The Sacco family's submarine sandwiches have been a Shore tradition since 1947. $.

where to stay

The Carisbrooke Inn. 105 S. Little Rock Ave., Ventnor; (609) 822-6392; www.carisbrookeinn.com. This luxury bed-and-breakfast is only a mile south of Atlantic City, and only 300 feet from the Ventnor boardwalk. The original hotel was built in 1891 and was the first luxury hotel in town, taking its name from Carisbrooke Castle in Ventnor, England, on the Isle of Wight. The current inn was built in 1909 in the American Foursquare style. Two buildings, across the street from each other, have a total of 14 rooms. Spa rooms are equipped with either a whirlpool tub or steam room. Some rooms are equipped as efficiencies—for the guest who wants a week at the beach versus a weekend in a B and B. Rates are highly flexible, based on the season and one's mood—$79 on a weeknight in winter, $400 on a Saturday in summer, and weekly specials. $$–$$$.

The Chelsea. 111 S. Chelsea Ave., Atlantic City; (609) 428-4380; www.thechelsea-ac .com. One of the newest luxury boutique hotels is a non-gaming resort with an emphasis on leisure and comfort. There are two restaurants, bars, a spa, and personalized, concierge-style beach service. There is a swimming pool on the ground floor and another on the roof. Choose from "luxe" rooms or suites in the 20-story tower and retro rooms in The Annex. $$–$$$.

Golden Nugget Atlantic City. Huron Avenue and Brigantine Boulevard, Atlantic City; (609) 441-2000; www.goldennugget.com. When it was Trump Marina, we really enjoyed staying here. The Deck Bayfront Bar and Restaurant is popular for its marina views. The hotel has a great swimming pool layout—an attractive and comfortable place to relax, read, sunbathe, and have lunch. As described elsewhere in this chapter, the resort was sold in 2011 and is under renovation. Visitors who took advantage of great deals were disappointed with the noise associated with construction. But the outlook sounds promising—as the new pool will be heated, with an H2O Lounge, hot tubs, and fire pits. Before booking a stay here, ask about the status of room renovations.

Trump Taj Mahal. 1000 Boardwalk, Atlantic City; (609) 449-1000; www.trumptaj.com. We've stayed here twice in recent years, and were impressed each time with the luxury of the room and extraordinary customer service. In 2011 we booked a king room in the newer Chairman Tower and loved it. These rooms are slightly larger, with high ceilings, marble baths, a granite-topped vanity with double sinks, and a large walk-in shower. The ladies'

good as gold

In 1980, just 2 years after gambling arrived in Atlantic City, casino mogul Steve Wynn built the Golden Nugget at Boston and the boardwalk. It was AC's first luxury resort and a worthy example of the developer's brand. Since Wynn sold it in 1987, it has changed hands a few times, and today is the ACH (for Hilton)— and on the market. Fast-forward to 2011, when Trump Entertainment Resorts sold Trump Marina Hotel & Casino to Landry's, a Texas company that owns res- taurants all over and the Las Vegas Golden Nugget. Landry's expects to spend a bundle to renovate Trump Marina, which was built in 1985. For starters, AC's newest name in the Marina District is a nostalgic one: the Golden Nugget.

vanity has a handy magnifying mirror on a retractable hinge. There is a spa, salon, fitness center, large indoor pool, and spacious sundeck. $$–$$$.

The Water Club at Borgata. 1 Renaissance Way, Atlantic City; (609) 317-8888; www.the waterclubhotel.com. With 43 stories of luxury, the Immersion Spa, five swimming pools, restaurants, lounges, and an outdoor SunBar, who has time to gamble? If you like to watch the pulse-racing gamers, however, The Water Club, a non-gaming hotel, is steps from Borgata's slots. $$$.

day trip 02

greater atlantic city

cap o' the cape:
ocean city & somers point, nj

Only 8 miles south of Atlantic City, this is the northernmost island in Cape May County. Originally called Peck's Beach—and often bragging about "America's Greatest Family Resort"—Ocean City is lovely, clean, safe, and popular.

Technically, Ocean City is part of The Southern Shore region, but because of its proximity to Atlantic City, we included it in the region next door.

It has attracted celebrities to spend vacations or a season. It was a summer home for Jimmy Stewart during his childhood. Jack Kelly, the Olympic oarsman from Philadelphia, built a summer home here and helped train its lifeguards. The locals knew his daughter, Grace Kelly, as a skinny adolescent long before she won an Academy Award, married a prince, and visited Ocean City as the glamorous Princess of Monaco.

Ocean City's boardwalk runs for 2.5 miles, with attractions to please nostalgia buffs as well as those seeking a new kick. A 140-foot Ferris wheel is visible for miles around—affording riders excellent views of the town and surrounding area. Rides include roller coasters, bumper cars, water rides, and 11 miniature golf courses.

The boardwalk is a draw to merely enjoy a sunrise, a stroll, a bike or surrey cart ride. And dining is pleasant at an oceanfront cafe.

Eight miles of beaches beckon—so maybe something in the salt air or sand inspires so many quirky special events. Regular features include the "Doo Dah Parade," "Weird Week," and "Miss Crustacean Hermit Crab Beauty Pageant."

Established as a religious retreat, Ocean City has been dry its whole history. The local mandate against selling alcohol or sipping suds in public stands firm. A vote on the matter,

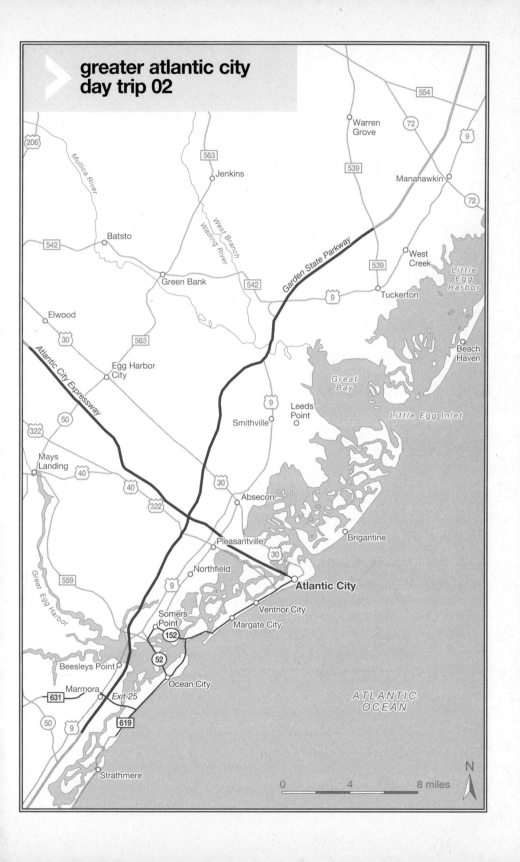

greater atlantic city
day trip 02

which had been scheduled for 2011, was removed from the ballot. For now, there are no restaurants in Ocean City where you can bring your own wine. The upside is no corkage fee.

In a different debate, Ocean City upheld a law for decades that required men on the beach to wear tops covering their torsos and abs. The city repealed the law in June 1949.

Over the causeway in Somers Point, take a look at some different points of historic significance.

ocean city & somers point, nj

getting there

Take the Garden State Parkway to exit 25 (Route 631/Roosevelt Boulevard-34th Street); cross a bridge over Great Egg Harbor Bay to the island and turn left. The road will take you into Ocean City. For a leisurely ride south from Atlantic City, drive along the coast through Ventnor City, onto NJ 152; at the Longport Boulevard fork, bear left and cross the JFK Memorial Bridge into Ocean City. To reach Somers Point from Ocean City, take NJ 52, the Stainton Memorial Causeway, over Great Egg Harbor Bay and head west to Shore Road.

where to go

Ocean City Arts Center. 1735 Simpson Ave., Ocean City; (609) 399-7628; www.ocean cityartscenter.org. Each month brings a new exhibit of a regional or national artist's work. The center has operated for more than 4 decades and hosts the nationally recognized Boardwalk Art Show, in addition to juried art and photography shows. The art center is located on the second floor of the Ocean City Cultural Community Center. Open Mon through Fri, 9 a.m. to 9 p.m., and Sat from 9 a.m. to 3 p.m.

Ocean City Historical Museum. (609) 399-1801; www.ocnjmuseum.org. Here, in the same building as the arts center, you can ponder authentic heirlooms and memorabilia from the city's Victorian days, along with lore about the wreck of the four-mast bark *Sindia*. Owned by John D. Rockefeller, it was bound from Japan to New York, laden with valuable cargo, before foundering off Ocean City in a storm in 1901. Open Tues through Fri, 10 a.m. to 4 p.m.; and Sat, 11 a.m. to 2 p.m. Admission is free, and donations are suggested.

Ocean City Fishing Center. 300 Bay Ave., Ocean City; (609) 391-8300; www.fishocnj .com. You don't have to know a tuna from a talywag to enjoy an outing on the 70-foot *North Star,* a fishing and party boat ideal for family outings. The captain and owner is Tim Barrus, a native of Ocean City who first held a fishing pole as a young boy. He started the company in 1950 and can customize a trip to catch whatever is in season: fluke, flounder, blackfish, sea bass, croaker, ling, porgy, dolphin, bonito, striped bass, and tilefish. Barrus runs half-day trips in the bay as well as deep-sea outings, private charters, and party cruises. You

a toll tale

Charging a fee to travel on roads and bridges is a time-honored concept in New Jersey. In 1693 John Somers established ferry service between Somers Point in what became Atlantic County and Beesleys Point in Cape May County. A marker at the site refers to Job's Point—named for Somers' 11th child. The vessel was a flat boat with tiller and oar to carry passengers and cargo across Great Egg Harbor Bay. The cost was 12 pence per person, one-way.

also can rent a pontoon, skiff, cuddy-cabin boat, and fishing rods at the center. Buy bait and tackle here, and have your catch filleted.

Pirate Cruises. 232 Bay Ave., Ocean City; (609) 398-7555; www.piratecruises.com. Indulge in a family-friendly fantasy aboard the *Sea Dragon,* where face-painting and tattoos are part of the package. The cruise lasts about 1 hour, and the vessel departs daily at 9:30 and 11 a.m., and 12:30, 2, 3:30, 5, and 6:30 p.m. The cost is $22 per person, and reservations are recommended.

Ocean City Parasail. Third Street at the Bay, Ocean City; (609) 399-3559; www.ocean cityparasail.com. This company has a long history of taking visitors for a bird's-eye view of the Shore. You can opt for a single hoist, a tandem ascent—even a triple-passenger adventure. The cost is $65 for a 500-foot "flight." Reservations are recommended.

Wet 'N Wild. 244 Bay Ave., Ocean City; (609) 399-6527; www.wetwildwaverunners.com. Located near the parasail outfit is a hub for renting Jet Skis and WaveRunners. See the website for online coupons and pricing specials.

Gillian's Island Water Park. Plymouth Place and Boardwalk, Ocean City; (609) 399-0483; www.gillianswaterpark.com. Getting soaked is the solution for children pretending to be bored and parents flailing against that uphill tide. At Gillian's, the kids can splash and slide to their hearts' content, while you relax in your cabana.

Congo Falls Adventure Golf. 1132 Boardwalk, Ocean City; (609) 398-1211; www.congo falls.com. For a fun family outing, this destination has three 18-hole courses—Congo Queen, Solomon's Mine, and the enclosed, air-conditioned Lost City, which is handy on a rainy day.

Atlantic Heritage Center. 907 Shore Rd., Somers Point; (609) 927-5218; www.atlantic heritagecenternj.com. This museum dedicated to the history of Atlantic County has displays of household items and decorative arts, fine arts, weaponry, maritime artifacts, and toys; even a Continental dollar. The library has more than 85,000 references to books, newspapers, family bibles, photos, maps, and historical and genealogical documents. Admission is free and the hours are Wed through Sat, 10 a.m. to 3:30 p.m.

Somers Mansion. 1000 Shore Rd., Somers Point; (609) 927-2212; www.somerspoint history.org. This 3-story brick home was built about 1725 by Richard Somers, a son of prominent settler John Somers. It is the oldest intact house in Atlantic County and was occupied by generations of the Somers family for more than 2 centuries. In 1937, descendants deeded it to the Atlantic County Historical Society. Four years later, the state of New Jersey took control and began to restore the house—removing some rooms added in the 19th century. The exterior brick was laid in the ornamental Flemish-bond pattern, and the walk-in fireplace holds a cooking crane. The interior woodwork features heart-shaped perforations. Furnishings and artifacts in the house belong to the Historical Society. It is listed on the state and national registers of historic places and the Historic American Buildings Survey. This structure is not to be confused with another home in town, also owned by the Somers family, that was lost in a fire. The Somers Mansion Historic Site is open Wed through Sun from 10 a.m. to noon and from 1 to 4 p.m.

The Shore Road Historic District. Somers Point. About a mile of this road was established as a district in 1989, and includes Somers Mansion. You will notice commercial, residential, religious, and institutional structures in various styles: Gothic Revival, Colonial, Queen Anne, Colonial Revival, Foursquare, and bungalow.

where to shop

Colette. 900 Asbury Ave., Ocean City; (609) 525-0911; www.colettewebsite.com. Girls who like a flirtatious outfit are sure to have fun at Colette's, which sells designer apparel, jewelry, handbags, and gifts. Lines range from Stop Staring to Betsey Johnson. The shop is open daily year-round.

Downtown Ocean City. Asbury Avenue between Sixth and 14th Streets, Ocean City; (800) 232-2465; www.downtownocnj.com. This 8-block area has specialty shops, boutiques, and restaurants.

The Gingham Whale. 636 Asbury Ave., Ocean City; (609) 391-0996; www.ginghamwhale .com. Browse here for antiques, collectibles, "Shore" stuff, woven and wire baskets, country cookware, ceramics, and furniture.

7th Street Surf Shop. 654 Boardwalk, Ocean City; (609) 391-1700; www.7thstreetsurfshop .com. This family-run business sells men's and women's apparel, Reef sandals, Rainbow soles, Uggs, wet suits, watches, sunglasses, short boards, and long boards. The boardwalk location is seasonal. The year-round store is at 720 Asbury Ave., and you can get deals on older merchandise at the 7th Street Surf Shop's outlet at 654 Asbury Ave.

Sun Rose Words and Music. 756 Asbury Ave., Ocean City; (609) 399-9190; www.sun rosebooks.com. This long-established retail shop is quite the multitasker. It began as a bookstore in 1973. The second owner added office supplies to the mix, and the next proprietor branched out into music—selling cassettes and then CDs. Nancy Miller and Rosalyn Lifshin bought Sun Rose in 1998 and expanded the business further. They carry all genres of new books—and offer 20 percent discounts daily on hardcover best sellers. There also is a section of books of regional interest. The store also carries greeting cards, games, puzzles, and toys.

where to eat

Cafe Beach Club. 1282 Boardwalk, Ocean City; (609) 398-7700; www.cafebeachclub .com. This seasonal restaurant is at the Beach Club Hotel described below. Come for breakfast (from 7 a.m. to 1 p.m.)—including coconut-custard French toast, eggs Benedict, omelettes, and such—lunch, and dinner; with ocean views and the option of patio dining. There also is a light-fare menu, a children's menu, and an early evening special. The proprietors are seasoned restaurateurs Stephen and Carolyn Nicoletti. $$.

Mallon's Homemade Sticky Buns. 1340 Bay Ave., Ocean City; (888) 880-2867; www .mallonsstickybuns.com. The secret is in the flour, apparently, and the right proportions of butter, sugar, and cinnamon. This family-run outfit dates to 1988 and has other Shore locations. The buns are the centerpiece here, but you can get hand-rolled bagels, crumbcake, homemade doughnuts, cinnamon swirls, and more. $.

Mike's Seafood. 208 55th St. at West Ave., Ocean City; (609) 263-3458; www.mikessea food.com. With a dozen tables on the deck, dive into "tonight's special," which might be a pound-plus steamed lobster split, cracked, and cleaned, with corn on the cob, slaw, and those cute little red bliss potatoes. Order ahead for take-out seafood platters, but be sure to try the "fresh-fried jalapeno shrimp jammers." The menu features some raw-bar items, plus steamed Alaskan king crab legs, snow crab legs, Maine mussels, wild Atlantic salmon, Nantucket scallops, Gulf shrimp, Jersey flounder—plus grilled Atlantic tuna, swordfish, pasta dishes, burgers, hot dogs, sandwiches, and homemade clam chowders. The owner, Mike Monichetti, is the third generation to run the place; his grandparents opened the doors in 1911. Open year-round for lunch and dinner. $$.

Sack O' Subs. 412 E. 55th St., Ocean City; (609) 525-0460; www.sackosubs.com. The Sacco brothers, Anthony and Ralph, banked on the family name for a clever moniker when they opened the first Sack O submarine sandwich shop in 1947 in Atlantic City. They later moved to Ventnor and now have a third location in Absecon. In addition, you can buy their inventive subs in two Atlantic City casinos. $.

where to stay

Beach Club Hotel. 1280 Boardwalk, Ocean City; (609) 399-8555; www.beachclubhotel
.com. This 3-story hotel has an oceanfront location and a three-Diamond AAA rating. The
in-house restaurant is the Cafe Beach Club. Choose from a guest room—pool view, ocean
view, or fronting the boardwalk—a studio apartment, or the penthouse. The latter, with
1,400 square feet, has a king-bed master bedroom, a guest bedroom with two queen beds,
kitchen, and dining room, and goes for $4,850 a week between mid-June and mid-Aug.
Room rates are the least expensive during May, June, and Sept. $$.

Watson's Regency Suites. 901 Ocean Ave., Ocean City; (888) 397-4673; www.watsons
regency.com. The accommodations give you 715 square feet of space with a bedroom,
bath, kitchen, living and dining area, and terrace. Amenities include an indoor swimming
pool and hot tub, which is open year-round. $$–$$$.

worth more time

Corson's Inlet State Park. Located south of Ocean City at the southern end of the island;
www.state.nj.us/dep/parksandforests. These lands were set aside as a park in 1969 to pro-
tect an undeveloped oceanfront tract. Natural habitats here include primary and secondary
sand dune systems, shoreline overwash, marine estuaries, and upland areas. Hundreds of
species of wildlife live and breed here. Corson's Inlet is popular for fishing and crabbing,
boating, sunning, and strolling. The boat ramp is open year-round.

WheatonArts. 1501 Glasstown Rd., Millville; (800) 998-4552; www.wheatonarts.org.
Located on the Maurice River about 30 miles inland from Ocean City, the Glasstown Arts
District is a national attraction. You will find specialty shops and museums, a major col-
lection of early-American glass, contemporary glass, and working glass artists—all in a
restored 19th-century glass factory. Downtown Millville has restaurants, bars, beer gardens,
and live entertainment. Shop here for antiques, unique gifts, hand-crafted clothing, art glass,
ceramics, and print galleries. Millville also is home to the New Jersey Motorsports Park;
www.njmp.com; on 700 acres with 2 road courses and a karting track. The website gives
the dates of major spectator races. Take the Garden State Parkway exit 20 west onto Route
50 and head north; at Tuckahoe, turn left onto Route 49 and proceed to Millville.

the southern shore

day trip 01

the southern shore

beach-to-bay bonanza, moonlight movies:
sea isle city, nj

Relax. You have come to the right spot to chill in the heat, be cozy in the cold, and revel in history dipped in drawn butter.

Sea Isle City is a year-round destination with a welcoming ambiance, a natural barrier island tucked away from crowds, traffic, and pretention. In recent years, this ocean-oriented berth has put its best foot forward, celebrating a "beach to bay" identity that embraces its heritage as the Port of Sea Isle. A Harbor Festival underscores the idea.

Thanks to a progressive mayor and council, the city owned up to its roots as a working seaport by promoting Historic Fish Alley. City leaders built a new bay-side boardwalk and put up a welcome sign defining the neighborhood. Wander over to Fish Alley for some serious seafood, and by the time you can say "catch of the day," it will arrive on a clean plate.

All over the city are lifestyle props encouraging you to enjoy a Sea Isle experience on a regular basis. A new band shell and beach pavilion are inviting new amenities. As one local put it, every Shore town is competing with the one next door for your business, so give people what they want. Maximize your assets, so to speak, and here, they are both natural and man-made.

Sea Isle City calls its oceanfront boardwalk The Promenade, a 1.5-mile stretch of pavement for pedestrians—no cars allowed. It is inviting for a stroll, jog, or bike ride, or just to sit and enjoy ocean breezes, spectacular sunups and -downs, outdoor concerts, and special events.

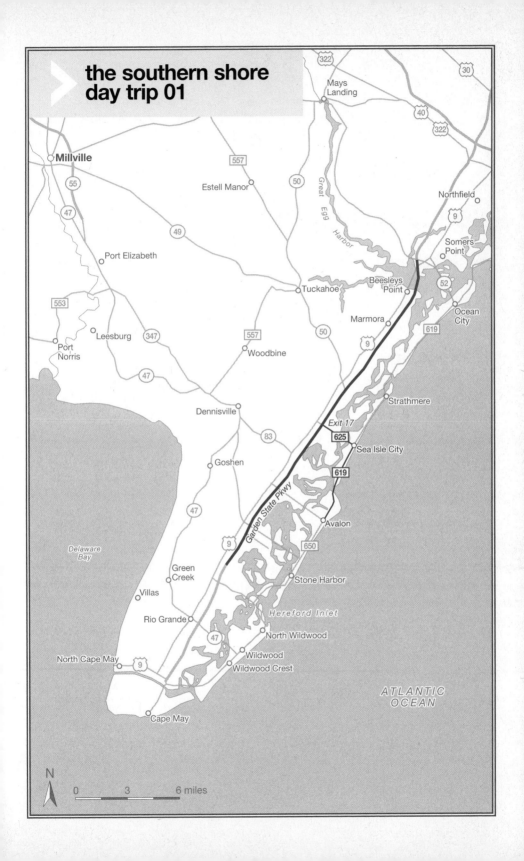

the southern shore
day trip 01

Five miles of wide, clean beaches have designated areas for swimming, rafting, surf fishing, and sailing. There are outdoor movies, concerts—even a Friday night version of the TV phenom, "Sea Isle City's Got Talent," with cash prizes.

In addition, there are party boats, a trolley route, and a new amusement park to keep the whole family entertained.

sea isle city, nj

getting there

From the Garden State Parkway, take exit 17 onto Route 625 (Sea Isle Boulevard). The road will split so bear left at the fork and go over the bridge, where Sea Isle Boulevard becomes JFK Boulevard.

where to go

Dealy Field. 59th Street and Central Avenue, Sea Isle City. There are soccer and softball fields, tennis courts, basketball courts, a skateboard park, playground, walking path, and restrooms.

Gillian's Funland. 42nd Place and Ludlam Bay (JFK Boulevard), Sea Isle City; (609) 399-7082; www.gillians.com. This amusement park in the Marina District was built in 2009. It is very kid-friendly, with about 17 rides, with more being added each year. The same owner has Gillian's Wonderland Pier in Ocean City.

Marina Waterfront Park. 42nd Place and Ludlam Bay, Sea Isle City. This is a boat launch and picnic site, with restrooms.

Sea Isle City Historical Museum. 4208 Landis Ave., Sea Isle City; (609) 263-2992; www.jerseyseashore.com. Back in the day, indeed. The museum displays vintage furniture,

a sound policy

New Jersey topography involves a lot of "sounds" and other bodies of water that flow into eco-sensitive lands. From the Intracoastal Waterway, you will see references to Great Sound, Jenkins Sound, Grassy Sound, Richardson Sound, Jarvis Sound, Cape May Inlet, Cape May Canal, and many more names associated with marshes, wetlands, basins, and estuaries. Around Sea Isle City, south of Ludlam Bay, you'll see Stites Sound and Townsend Sound.

antique toys, an exhibit of postcards, archives with articles and photos of major storms, and old photos from the locals' childhood.

Star Fish Party Boat. 42nd Place and Ludlam Bay, Sea Isle City; (609) 263-3800; www .starfishboats.com. You'll learn the turf once you see it from the water. This company hosts nature and sunset cruises and private charters.

Townsends Inlet Waterfront Park. 94th Street and Landis Avenue, Sea Isle City. This site at the southern end of the barrier island is handy for fishing and picnics. There is parking, a shaded pavilion, a nature trail, and restrooms.

where to shop

The Book Nook. 3800 Boardwalk, Sea Isle City; (609) 263-1311. The shop carries best sellers, a variety of book genres, plus children's items, newspapers, and magazines. It is located at Spinnaker Stores, inside a residential condominium. Open in the summer.

Dalrymple's Gifts. 20 JFK Blvd. #20, Sea Isle City; (609) 263-3337. This downtown shop is just a short walk from the Promenade, and you will find collectibles, souvenirs, candles, greeting cards, stationery, books, newspapers, and magazines. The store is open year-round.

Sands Department Store. 6208 Landis Ave., Sea Isle City; (609) 263-3351. If you haven't found what you are looking for, Sands very likely has it: clothing, footwear, house wares, beach essentials, gifts, toys, games, sporting goods, gear for anglers, and hardware items. The store is open year-round.

where to eat

Mike's Seafood and Dock Restaurant. 4222 Park Rd., Sea Isle City; (609) 263-3458; www.mikesseafood.com. As described in the trip to Ocean City, Mike's Seafood is a must. The Sea Isle City restaurant and market is the flagship operation, with 50 tables at the Ludlam Bay Harbor. The owner, Mike Monichetti, runs the business begun in 1911 by his grandparents. Conscious of families working to afford a vacation at the Shore, Mike's Seafood frequently offers specials such as buy 1 pound of crab legs, get 1 free; "kids eat cheap"; or the lobster special, one and a quarter-pound steamed, split, cracked, and cleaned, with Jersey corn, coleslaw, and red bliss potatoes. Order ahead for take-out seafood platters, or take home seafood from the market. There are raw-bar items, steamed Alaskan king crab legs, snow crab legs, mussels, wild salmon, scallops, shrimp, and numerous varieties of fish caught "today." In addition, choose among pasta dishes, sandwiches, and chowders. You are welcome to bring your own spirits. Open year-round; lunch and dinner daily from May through mid-Oct, weekends only in the fall, winter, and early spring. $–$$.

O'Donnell's Pour House. 39th and 40th Streets at Landis Avenue, Sea Isle City; (609) 263-5600; www.odonnellspourhouse.com. Yes, this takes up more than one address,

the net effect

Many immigrants who settled in Sea Isle City were directed to the back-bay area, where they built shacks and lean-tos and carved out a livelihood. One such couple was Lodovico and Rosina Monichetti, who arrived in 1911 and opened a "market" in a building they bought for $500. They sold the day's catch downstairs and lived on the second floor. After Lodovico died, his son ran the business. By then, the family was successful enough to own a 54-foot trawler, the Dewey, which fished local waters through the 1980s. Today, Rosina's grandson runs Mike's Seafood and Dock, shaping the current chapter of Fish Alley. And at still-viable Port of Sea Isle—one of only a handful of working seaports on the East Coast—you will see nets hanging, lobster boats, swordfish boats, and other long-liners pulling in and leaving the dock. As he points to a century in Sea Isle City, Mike Monichetti recalls that his grandfather passed away on the corner and his father died upstairs: "This is home . . . I'll die here happy."

because it is two establishments. The Irish pub-style restaurant opened next to the legendary Ocean Drive Bar in 1999. Hang out here for live music and upscale bar cuisine. The menu hops around a bit, with plenty to choose from. If you have already eaten your weight in seafood today, try a New York strip in peppercorn sauce or onion butter. Open for dinner weekdays and lunch and dinner on the weekends. $$.

where to stay

The Colonnade Inn. 4600 Landis Ave., Sea Isle City; (609) 263-8868; www.thecolonnade inn.com. This is a daily reminder of a bygone era, as it was built in 1882 as a Victorian-style summer hotel popular with tourists from Philadelphia and New York. After periodic changes in ownership and a historic restoration in 2004, the Colonnade is a bed-and-breakfast 1 block from the beach and the Promenade. There is a large wraparound porch to take in the breeze or read. In the lobby is a large-screen TV, where guests gather for football games on fall weekends. Units have private baths and range from 1 room to 3-bedroom suites. Each unit has wireless Internet, cable TV, air-conditioning, and heating. $$–$$$.

Concord Suites. 7800 Dune Dr., Avalon (7 miles south of Sea Isle City); (609) 443-8202; www.concordsuites.com. A short drive from Sea Isle City, you will find an ideal lodging for families. The suites have a private bedroom, a sleeper sofa, a kitchen, and eating area. There are two swimming pools, and the hotel is only a block from the beach. To reach Avalon, drive south on County Route 619 and over the toll bridge at Townsends Inlet. $$.

day trip 02

the southern shore

>>> **winging it, too:**
stone harbor & avalon, nj

The resort town of Stone Harbor is on Seven Mile Beach, a 2,700-acre nook of the cape wedged between the Atlantic Ocean and the Intracoastal Waterway. In 1722 the whole kit and caboodle sold for $380—which today might get you a weekend stay in the off-season.

Families and couples love it here, so chances are, you will too. Stone Harbor's beautiful beaches are pristine, which does not go unnoticed by the many tourists from out of state.

The quaint downtown is an appealing mix of shops, art galleries, and restaurants—many owned by chefs. The setting is street-savvy, with nostalgia lamps and decorative pavers. Recreation is well organized here; including rooftop mini-golf. Some of the yacht clubs and golf clubs welcome reciprocal members.

The island is especially well-known as a National Natural Landmark, with a bird sanctuary that is the only municipal-sponsored heronry in the country.

A stroll to the north is Avalon, which calls itself "cooler by a mile."

stone harbor & avalon, nj

getting there

Take the Garden State Parkway to exit 10 and go east on Route 657. The road becomes Stone Harbor Boulevard.

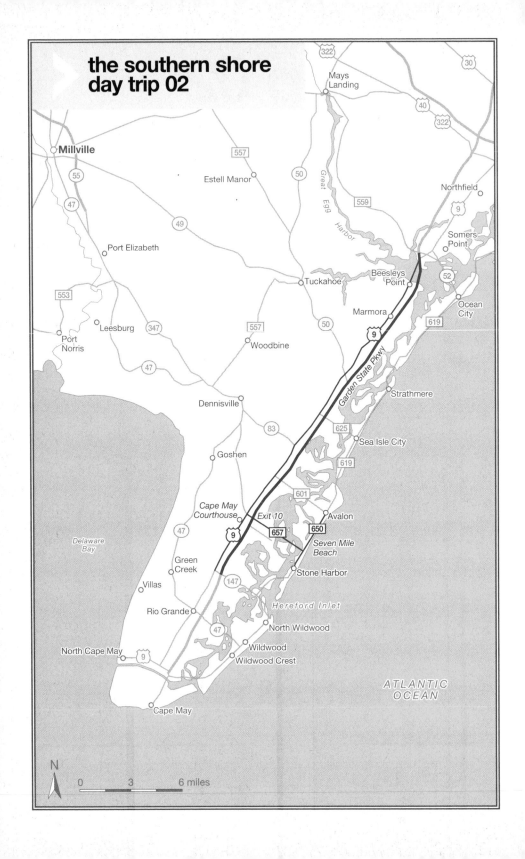

the southern shore
day trip 02

where to go

Stone Harbor Point. 122nd Street, Stone Harbor. Remote is one way to describe this "secret" beach at the southern end of Seven Mile Beach by Hereford Inlet. At this tidal estuary, you will see birds drifting above their best-kept hideaway, an unspoiled strand with the ocean and the Intracoastal Waterway lapping at its heels. Sand bars and salt marshes loiter, too. Parking is free and there are restrooms.

Stone Harbor Public Marina. 81st Street and the bay, Stone Harbor; (609) 368-5102. There is a concrete ramp, restrooms, daily rates, and seasonal fees.

Stone Harbor Museum. 235 93rd St., Stone Harbor; (609) 368-7500; www.stone-harbor .nj.us. The exhibit, "On the Street Where You Live," is a collection of old and new photos— arranged by street—to show the past and present of landmark homes and businesses which have been preserved. You will see how exteriors have been retained while structures were modernized for contemporary lifestyles. Admission is free and the museum keeps regular summer hours. You also may make an appointment to visit in the off-season.

Stone Harbor Bird Sanctuary. Third Avenue at 114th Street, Stone Harbor; www.stone harborbirdsanctuary.com. With a barrier island below their wings, migratory birds using the Atlantic Flyway know a good thing when they spot it, and so will you. White egrets, night egrets, blue heron, and ibis are among the hundreds of species which visit, roost, and linger on this unique 21-acre preserve. Follow the 410-foot path through a maritime holly forest whose centerpiece is a 300-year-old specimen perched on a 15-foot dune. At Heron Overlook, pause to listen for the songbirds. Meadow Walk, a 210-foot path, lets you observe a fresh-water meadow, salt marsh, and spring-fed pond—the ibis playground. Egret Espy is a 280-foot path to the birds' feeding grounds, with a footbridge at the beginning and gardens galore. After your stroll along the paths, park yourself on a teak bench with a book and relax in a setting that takes you away from it all.

The Wetlands Institute. 1075 Stone Harbor Blvd., Stone Harbor; (609) 368-1211; www .wetlandsinstitute.org. Located east of Jenkins Sound, this unique facility is an ideal outing for children to get acquainted with the aquatic world. There is a touch tank, aquarium, exhibits, kayak tours, boat cruises, and nature classes. Open in the summer from 9:30 a.m. to 4:30 p.m. Mon through Sat and from 10 a.m. to 4 p.m. Sun.

Cape May County Historic Museum. 504 Route 9 North, Stone Harbor; (609) 465-3535; www.cmcmuseum.org. The museum's collection includes furniture, decorative objects, maps, and charts that elaborate on the cape's history. Visit the museum store and browse among the books, gifts, souvenirs, and memorabilia. From June through Sept, the museum is open Tues through Sat from 10 a.m. to 3 p.m. From Oct through May, it's open Wed through Fri from 10 a.m. to 2 p.m. and on Sat from 10 a.m. to 3 p.m.

Cape May County Zoo. 707 Route 9 North, Cape May Court House; (609) 465-5271; www.capemaycountyzoo.org. Say hello to Rocky, a Siberian tiger who was born in New Jersey, and Kaba and Sabu, twin boy snow leopard cubs born in 2010. Himani, a mother snow leopard, welcomed a new cub, Nubo, in 2011. They are just a few of the wildlife royalty living here.

where to shop

Coastal FX. 270 96th St., Stone Harbor; (609) 368-3800; www.coastalfx.com. This is a fun destination for an experience you won't run across in most department stores.

Paisley Christmas Shoppe. 9512 Third Ave., Stone Harbor; (609) 368-7873. Forgot to pack your sock monkey or need some souvenirs? Paisley has three decades of tradition here, carrying Christmas decorations and kooky novelties.

Skirt. 272 96th St., Stone Harbor; (609) 948-4912; www.shop-skirt.com. This is the home of beach-chic, where you can find lightweight sweaters, just the right sundress, jewelry, and anything else you forgot to pack. Brands here include Theory, Calypso, and Milly, plus Pink Pineapple and Joie. *Philadelphia Magazine* said Skirt was "Best of the Shore" in 2010.

Talk of the Walk. 248 96th St., Stone Harbor; (609) 368-0008; www.talkofthewalk.com. Ladies will appreciate this Shore landmark with fashionable apparel, sportswear, evening wear, shoes, handbags, and jewelry. Talk also has locations in Haven Beach and Atlantic City.

Trendz. 209 96th St., Stone Harbor; (609) 368-3313; www.trendzstoneharbor.com. This is the home of guilty pleasure, aka fashion jewelry, in business here since about 1990. Lines include David Yurman, Paul Morelli, Temple St. Clair, and many more. In the vicinity, you will find Trendz Home, which carries fine linens—Frette and the like.

where to eat

Captain Marriner's Seafood. 365 96th St., Stone Harbor; (609) 368-0075; www.club soup.com. This is the spot for dining on the bay, savoring a lobster roll and a pinot grigio brought from home. The captain specializes in chowders, soups, bisques, crab cakes, clam strips, and a new item, lobster ravioli. It's open daily for dinner in the summer. $$.

Concord Cafe. 7800 Dune Dr., Avalon (1 mile north of Stone Harbor Boulevard); (609) 368-5505; www.concordcafe.net. This friendly tavern has upscale food and a comfortable atmosphere. The menu is a dizzying array of appetizers, pasta entrees, Strombolis, calzones, pizza, cheesesteaks, salads, soups, burgers, and sandwiches. Try one Concord-style: sliced London broil, Italian roast pork, or chicken cutlet with broccoli rabe, roasted red peppers, and provolone, and baked on a long roll in the brick oven. There is a full bar service, draft beer, domestic and imported bottles, and a few "house" wines by the glass. Open for lunch and dinner. $–$$.

Jack's Shack. 261 96th St., Stone Harbor; (609) 368-4565; www.jacksshackstoneharbor .com. If you want an omelette before leaving the dock, Jack has it covered. The burgers, hoagies, panini, and grouper sandwiches are family favorites. Open for breakfast, lunch, and dinner in the Harbor Square Food Court. $.

Stone Harbor Golf Club. 905 Route 9 North, Cape May Court House; (609) 465-9270; www.stoneharborgolf.com. The club is just west of the Garden State Parkway. And don't worry if you are a duffer, never swing a club, or are not a member. You are welcome to visit for lunch, dinner, or challenging golf. $$.

where to stay

Golden Inn Hotel and Resort. 7849 Dune Dr. at the ocean, Avalon; (609) 368-5155; www .goldeninn.com. Accommodations range from standard guest rooms to efficiencies, deluxe oceanfront rooms and suites. See the website for rates by the season and room size. The hotel's fine-dining Seaglass Restaurant faces the dunes. You can opt for casual fare indoors or at the Beach Bar. Call for details on entertainment and dancing. $$–$$$.

The Windrift Hotel and Restaurant. 80th Street and the beach, Avalon; (609) 368-5175; www.windrifthotel.com. This luxury hotel on the beach is where you can park it and relax for the duration of your visit. In 2011 the hotel opened a few new suites and renovated the swimming pool, adding zero-entry, underwater music, a waterfall, and hot tub. Accommodations include deluxe rooms, efficiencies, suites, and units with more than one bedroom. Signature Lounge is for sushi and cocktails; the adjacent dining room serves breakfast and dinner; Blue Wave Lounge overlooks the pool and serves lunch and casual dinners; the Beach Bar is open for lunch and dinner; the oceanview Deck is open for lunch and happy hour; and the Tiki Bar is open for lunch, drinks, and happy hour. See the website for a live entertainment schedule. $$–$$$.

day trip 03

the southern shore

>>> **honky-tonk heaven:**
wildwood, nj

Just a few miles south of stylish Stone Harbor, and a world apart, welcome to "the Wildwoods," the cape's outermost barrier island stretching for about five miles from Hereford Inlet to Cape May Inlet.

Five municipalities claim the area, but Wildwood is their mascot, if you go by the centerpiece on the boardwalk. Playful-looking concrete beach balls stand their ground here, as if to say that beach-going is the American way—carved in stone, if not the Constitution.

Should you find yourself whistling a long-forgotten tune, it's probably because the recording artist performed it live here, long before finding fame. Half a century ago, this berg was "Little Las Vegas."

So retro it almost stings, Wildwood has an exaggerated honky-tonk tone set by a neon-blazing boardwalk that runs for a couple of miles. The atmosphere is at once nostalgic and a bit down on its luck—which is as much a part of its perennial charm as the aroma of pizza and cotton candy. Nonetheless, the stunning beaches enjoy a constant uptick, because they are wider than anywhere else on the cape—and free, unlike most Shore beaches.

Built at the turn of the last century, the boardwalk is packed with a convention center, three amusement piers chocked with rides, water parks, game arcades, two cinemas, restaurants, ethnic food vendors, souvenir and novelty shops, and of course, saltwater taffy every few blocks.

If you eschew neon after a while, head for a Wildwood marina, where you will find party boats and fishing vessels for daily outings in the bay and ocean, plus sightseeing excursions, whale-watching cruises, sailing, and Jet Ski rentals.

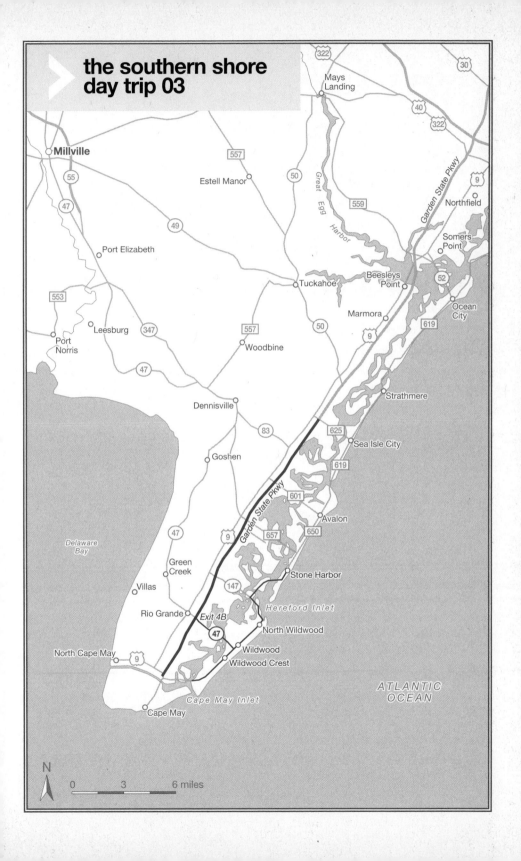

the southern shore
day trip 03

If Wildwood seems a little schizophrenic, consider some of what it has on the calendar: Fabulous 50s Weekend, Sensational 60s Weekend, War at the Jersey Shore Wrestling, Boardwalk Nationals Car Show, Knights of Columbus, Wildwood International Kite Festival, Beach Jam, Elks Conventions, American Legion Convention, VFW Convention, Cape Express Beach Blast Soccer, Radio Disney Music Fest, Thunder in the Sand Motocross Races, Youth for Christ, WWE Raw, Sunset Hydrofest Boat Races, a HOG Rally, Firemen's Convention, and Roar to the Shore.

There also is miniature golf, grown-up golf, nightclubs, and special events from May through October.

wildwood, nj

getting there

From the Garden State Parkway, take exit 4B onto NJ 47 east to the barrier island; from Stone Harbor or Avalon, drive south along the ocean and over the toll bridge across Hereford Inlet into Wildwood.

where to go

Hereford Inlet Lighthouse. Central Avenue, Wildwood; (609) 522-4520; www.hereford lighthouse.org. This is a working lighthouse and museum open for tours. The site calls itself Anglesea, which was the original name for Wildwood. A park surrounds the lighthouse with gardens in the Victorian cottage style near the ocean. A gift shop has books and gift items in nautical themes. The museum is open daily from mid-May through mid-Oct. Admission is $4. Tours of the park and gardens and gift shop are free.

Morey's Piers & Beachfront Waterparks. 3501 Boardwalk, Wildwood; (609) 522-3900; www.moreyspiers.com. The family's second generation heads the operation begun in the 1960s. New rides and attractions have been added almost every year since the first pier opened. There is Adventure Pier, Mariner's Landing Pier (and Ocean Oasis), and Surfside Pier (with Raging Waters). Two eateries serve beer and wine, and there are heated outdoor decks. Call ahead if you want to rent a cabana.

Adventure Maze. 2701 Boardwalk, Wildwood; (609) 770-7259. This maze of mirrors may confound your sense of direction, but the operators say that after 20 minutes, someone will come to look for you.

Doo Wop Experience Museum. 4500 Ocean Ave., Wildwood; (609) 523-1958; www .doowopusa.org. "Dwop by" if you'd like to step back into the 1950s. There are rooms decorated in period furnishings, artifacts, and photographs about post-World War II pop culture. In the summer, you can take a guided bus tour of the astonishing array of seaside motels preserved from that era. Many have outrageous signage and architectural gimmickry designed to grab the motoring tourist. No surprise that some of the wacky rooflines and detailing resemble the tailfins on those beloved ragtops.

Seaport Aquarium. 3400 Boardwalk at Oak Ave., Wildwood; (609) 522-2700. An ideal outing for families awaits you, with marine life from Australia's Great Barrier Reef and the Pacific Ocean, the Amazon River, and the Florida Everglades. You can pet a shark and ray in the touch pool, hand-feed fish and turtles at the indoor waterfall, and hold a really big snake. Play games with marmoset monkeys and lizards, and watch while a Moray eel ignores you. The aquarium's gift shop carries toys, books, clothing, jewelry, and souvenirs.

Avenue of the Stars. Pacific Avenue, Wildwood. Stroll here to see the names of entertainers that might just as well have jumped off the marquees of venues. Starting decades ago, these inductees shaped the Wildwoods as a headliner hub on the East Coast. You will recognize the names of national acts, Jersey bands, comedians, DJs, composers, and music arrangers who had a role in Wildwood's music history.

George F. Boyer Historical Museum. 3907 Pacific Ave., Wildwood; (609) 523-0277. The Wildwood Historical Society operates the museum, which has collections about the settlement of the original Anglesea. At one time, the area was grazing land for farmers and summer camp for Lenni-Lenape Indians. In the 1870s, fishermen of Scandinavian heritage settled here. And in 1884, the West Jersey Railroad put in tracks to Cape May Court House. There are "then and now" photographs, memorabilia, and artifacts representing highlights about the boardwalk, the beach, and those who made history. The museum, also home to the Marbles Hall of Fame, is open Mon through Sat from 9 a.m. to 2 p.m. from mid-June through Sept, and Thurs through Sat the rest of the year. Admission is free but donations are requested.

where to shop

Beach Whiskers. 4909 Pacific Ave., Wildwood; (609) 846-7339; www.beachwhiskers .com. You don't have to sport a five o'clock shadow to appreciate this whimsical shop. Fun is the concept, while you browse for clothing, accessories, shoes, gifts, jewelry, kooky novelties, toys, sundries, and candy. The store is open year-round, and in the off-season from Thurs through Sun.

5 Mile Marketplace. 2502 Boardwalk, Wildwood; (609) 522-7140. Browse here for men's and women's clothing, children's duds, home decor, and souvenirs.

Gemini. 3704 Boardwalk, Wildwood; (609) 729-5411. The store carries clothing for men and women. But if you want a tattoo or something pierced—or your hair braided—the proprietor can oblige.

"let's twist again, like we did last summer"

The first time anyone heard Chubby Checker sing "Twist," it was 1960 and he was performing at the Rainbow Club in Wildwood. Three years earlier, American Bandstand had its national debut, featuring Dick Clark at the Starlight Ballroom on the Wildwood boardwalk.

Hooked on Books. 3405 Pacific Ave. at Oak Ave., Wildwood; (609) 729-1132; www .hookedonbooks.com. The primary focus is all genres of used books at discount prices, although the shop also carries new releases. Located 2 blocks from the boardwalk, Hooked has been attached to this location for 22 summers. Open May through Sept.

where to eat

Dogtooth Bar and Grill. 100 E. Taylor Ave., Wildwood; (609) 522-8383; www.dogtoothbar .com. This is a nice, cozy sports bar with a full menu of high-quality cuisine. The signature starter is Dogtooth Bites—seared and blackened Ahi-grade tuna bites served with sweet chili, wasabi, and soy sauce for dipping. Lunch items cover all the bases, and dinner entrees are much more inventive than you see on most sports-bar menus. Steaks are shipped from farms in Pennsylvania, and the dinner menu offers filet mignon, rib eye, and New York strip. Seafood entrees are delectable: salmon from the Bay of Fundy, mahimahi from the Carolinas, yellowfin tuna from the Pacific, and whatever Jersey anglers caught today. You can eat inside or have some solitude on the patio. Dogtooth has live entertainment on the weekends. Open year-round. $$.

Doo Wop Diner. 4108 Boardwalk, Wildwood; (609) 522-7880. If you love being lost in the 1950s, hurry on over to this seasonal diner for a burger and milk shake, sandwich, or dessert. Open from Apr through Oct, for breakfast, lunch, and dinner. Bring your own spirits. $.

Marie Nicole's. 9510 Pacific Ave., Wildwood Crest; (609) 522-5425; www.marienicoles .com. *Wine Spectator* likes this classic restaurant, as does *South Jersey Magazine*. Try the eggplant Napoleon or lobster quesadilla for a starter, and the salad with Granny Smith apples, spinach, candied walnuts, and Gorgonzola. Among the noble entrees are seared salmon, ahi tuna with wasabi and a sesame crust, and seafood risotto. The well-informed wine list has some pricey bottles, but a few are under $40. The restaurant is open for dinner. Sit indoors or on the patio. Reservations are recommended. $$–$$$.

Pacific Grill. 4801 Pacific Ave., Wildwood; (609) 523-2333; www.pacificgrillwildwood.com. If you are looking for an upscale, sophisticated haven for an exotic dinner, Pacific Grill will be a delightful find. The casually elegant dining room has a choice of cozy banquettes and well-spaced tables with proper linens. Much of the menu is inspired by cuisine from the Pacific Rim and Bourbon Islands. For an appetizer, try the edamame and Thai-style boneless pork ribs with papaya pico de gallo. The Pescado Del Dia, whole grilled fish with risotto, is divine, and others in our party liked the blackened scallops and marinated hanger steak. The Kobe burger comes with caramelized onions and Boursin cheese. Bring your own wine to complement the chef's inspired dishes. And leave room for dessert, even if you usually skip the sweets. There are fruit sorbets, a yummy apple tart, crème brulee, and chocolat pots du crème. The restaurant is open from May through New Year's Eve, and has another location in Cape May. $$–$$$.

where to stay

Bolero Resort & Conference Center. 3320 Atlantic Ave., Wildwood; (609) 522-6929; www.boleroresort.com. This lodging doubles as a hotel and a motel, with a wide range of accommodations to suit most budgets. In the hotel tower, rooms range from deluxe to luxury to 2-room suites, while the motel section has efficiencies and "breezeway" rooms. There is a large, well-equipped fitness center, indoor and outdoor swimming pools, and a new tiki bar. The in-house restaurant and lounge is the Blue Water Grille, a 2-story space with live entertainment. $–$$$.

Esplanade Suites. 230 E. Taylor Ave., Wildwood; (609) 522-7890; www.esplanadesuites .com. Located near the beach, boardwalk, and convention center, this year-round lodging has studio and 1-bedroom suites with ocean views. Modeled like condo units, they have kitchenettes, table and chairs, flat-screen TVs, and DVD players. Rooms have one or two double beds and a queen-size sleeper sofa. There is an outdoor heated swimming pool and attached kiddie-splash, plus picnic tables, barbecue grills, and a video game room. The manager, Beachtree Properties, runs other boutique hotels in Atlantic City, Cape Cod, Hawaii, and Palm Beach, FL. $$.

worth more time

Starlight Fleet. 6200 Park Blvd., Wildwood Crest; (609) 729-3400; www.jjcboats.com. The whole family will enjoy whale-watching and dolphin-watching cruises, with a marine biologist onboard to explain what's going on. There are touch tanks, so that an intelligent mammal can experience a human. In addition to three cruises daily, the fleet has sunset dinner cruises.

day trip 04

the southern shore

victoria would be proud:
cape may, nj

Imagine you are Jane Seymour on the arm of Christopher Reeve, enchanted by an era *Somewhere in Time.* That is the way Cape May rushes you beyond the moment, to a place in memory or literary travels.

As you ride along the boulevard by the ocean, grand homes in pristine condition remind you of the way aesthetics and craftsmanship once ruled everyday lifestyles. Pastels and vivid floral hues dot the streets, where rooflines tinker with gravity and tickle your imagination.

When you leave the expressway, it is time to back-pedal slowly as you enter a time-warp of tone toward generations of gentility. On street after street—Pittsburgh and New Jersey are two of them—you cannot resist a grin over the elaborate millwork. Many homes have been converted to inns, some with restaurants; one or two have a putting green in the side yard.

The Inn of Cape May must be seen to be believed: a large white beauty on a corner near Ocean Avenue, its purple awnings daring you to ride on without stopping on the veranda. This is where Victoria's secret stash of really good bones lolls in the breeze, her awnings fluttering like lace on a parasol.

The city is highly organized and abundantly well-prepared to show you around—from historic walking tours, to themed trolley routes, sightseeing cruises, shopping, and whale- and dolphin-watching excursions.

And even though it was drizzling on a recent visit, nothing could dampen the spirits of throngs of spectators camped under beach umbrellas to watch the National Lifeguard

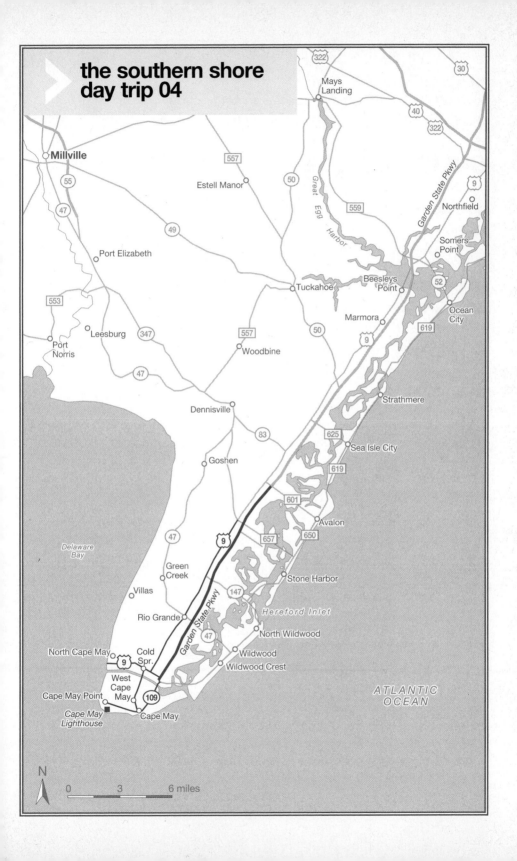

the southern shore
day trip 04

Mays
Landing

322

30

40

322

Garden State Pkwy

Millville

55

557

50

9

47

Estell Manor

559

Northfield

49

Great Egg Harbor

Somers
Point

Port Elizabeth

Beesleys
Point

52

Tuckahoe

Ocean
City

553

Marmora

9

619

Leesburg

347

557

50

Port
Norris

Woodbine

Strathmere

47

Dennisville

83

625

Sea Isle City

Goshen

619

Delaware
Bay

47

601

9

Avalon

657

650

Green
Creek

Stone Harbor

Villas

147

Hereford Inlet

Rio Grande

9

47

North Wildwood

North Cape May

9

Cold
Spr.

Wildwood

Garden State Pkwy

Wildwood Crest

ATLANTIC
OCEAN

West
Cape
May

109

Cape May Point

Cape May
Lighthouse

Cape May

N

0   3   6 miles

Championships. The sight of très fit physiques going through their paces had a lot in common with Cape May—very good eye candy, indeed.

cape may, nj

getting there

Take the Garden State Parkway as far south as it goes; it turns into NJ 109. From there, you simply can't miss Cape May.

where to go

Cape May Stage/The Robert Shackleton Theatre. Bank and Lafayette Streets, Cape May; (609) 884-1341; www.capemaystage.com. This professional Equity theater company presents traditional plays, contemporary and new works. In addition, its Second Stage presents post-show forums on relevant themes. One such event was a discussion on "the role of an artist," following the Cape May Stage production of John Logan's Tony Award–winning play, *Red.* The venue is conveniently located near the Washington Street pedestrian mall.

Cape May Lighthouse. Cape May Point, Cape May; (609) 884-5404. Located at the state park described below, the 157-foot lighthouse is open to the public for spectacular views of the cape, peninsula, and Delaware Bay. The lighthouse was built in 1859, using bricks from an earlier structure. Arrange a tour through the Mid-Atlantic Center for the Arts and Humanities, (609) 884-5404.

Cape May Point State Park. Cape May Point, Cape May; (609) 884-2159; www.state.nj .us/dep/parksandforests.com. The park's blazed trails lead you to wildlife habitats at the most southern point in New Jersey. There are ponds, coastal dunes, marshes, and forests with observation platforms to view park "residents," including many species of birds on a year-round basis. The area also is a significant stopover for migratory birds, especially hawks. It is the nesting ground for horseshoe crabs and home away from home for Monarch butterflies. The park is popular for surf-fishing and picnics. And if you happen to visit at low tide, you will see remnants of a World War II bunker which used to be 900 feet inland. The park is open from dawn to dusk. Admission is free.

Historic Cold Spring Village. 720 Route 9, Cape May; (609) 898-2300; www.hcsv.org. This open-air living history museum is a great learning experience in Early Americana, with more than 2 dozen restored buildings on 30 acres. There are wagon rides, animals, and farms for flowers, vegetables, and herbs. Observe the intricacies of weaving, book-binding, blacksmithing, woodworking, and other crafts and trades essential to life in the 1800s. The village puts on themed events every weekend, from antiques shows to military maneuvers and concerts. There is a village bakery, ice cream parlor, and the Old Grange Restaurant.

Naval Air Station Wildwood Aviation Museum. 500 Forrestal Rd., Cape May; (609) 886-8787; www.usnasw.org. Hangar #1, the centerpiece here, is listed on the National Register. The 92,000-square-foot wooden structure was built during World War II and was a training facility for dive-bomber squadrons. There are more than 2 dozen aircraft displays and exhibits of military memorabilia, engines, photographs, and artifacts. On display are a Boeing-Stearman, a T-33 Thunderbird, and a MiG-15, plus a Bird Dog, Avenger, Trojan, and Skyhawk—for those of you who have winged it. If you relate to the Vietnam era, you'll see Cobra, Loach, and Huey choppers. Courtesy of the Franklin Institute of Philadelphia, NAS Wildwood has some interactive exhibits on the science of flight. There is a library, gift shop, and food vending area. Located at the Cape May Airport, just west of Route 9 and Route 47, the museum is open daily, 9 a.m. to 5 p.m., from Apr 1 through mid-Oct. See the website for other hours. Admission is $8 for adults and $5 for children.

Cape May Whale Watcher Fleet. 1218 Wilson Dr., Cape May; (609) 884-5445; www .capemaywhalewatcher.com. The company operates two 110-foot ships that are docked at the Miss Chris Marina. Tours run from Mar through Dec, with cruises at 10 a.m., 1, and 6:30 p.m. The website lets you know about dining onboard and a dockside gift shop.

The Historic Emlen Physick Estate. 1048 Washington St., Cape May; (609) 884-5404; www.capemaymac.org. This authentic Stick-Style Victorian residence is operated as a museum by the Mid-Atlantic Center for the Arts and Humanities. It was built in 1879 in a variation of Gothic Revival. Architect Frank Furness designed the home for Dr. Emlen Phys- ick Jr. of Philadelphia. Exterior features are pure Furness: brackets, jerkin-head dormers, and corbelled chimneys. Some furnishings on display are originals. This is Cape May's only Victorian house museum. It is open daily in season, and part of the experience includes luncheon or tea in the restored carriage house or garden patio.

where to shop

All Irish Imports. 401 Lafayette St., Cape May; (609) 884-4484. The shop carries Water- ford crystal, Beleek china, mohair throws and scarves, and Connemara jewelry.

t-shirt testimonial

Without the authentic period architecture in such abundance and good condition; without all the intricate gingerbread designs and the mountains of ornate custom millwork, this could have become a ho-hum yawn of a sleepy town with a lighthouse on the tail of the Jersey Shore. But Cape May is awash in quantifiable evidence that historic preservation feeds a very fat cash cow. On the flip side of that coin, as spelled out on a T-shirt, it is "A Drinking Town with a Victorian Problem."

Cape May Linen Outlet. 110 Park Blvd., West Cape May; (609) 884-3630; www.cape maylinen.com. If you love grand linens at less-grand prices, stop by this outlet for bath and bedding basics, decorative items, and baby gifts.

Caroline Boutique. Carpenter's Lane between Decatur and Jackson Streets, Cape May; (609) 884-5055. Browse here for casual, contemporary, and stylish apparel for the ladies. Brands include Eileen Fisher, Three Dot, and Diane Von Furstenberg, among others.

Henry's Jewelers. 407 Washington St., Cape May; (609) 884-0334. Henry's is a local gem of long-standing. Even before the store was renovated, it was tough to get in and out without buying something sparkly and special.

Rea's Farm Market. 400 Stevens St., West Cape May; (609) 884-4522. If you love the aroma of fresh fruit and vegetables, homemade pies and flowers, the market is a short ride from the beach. You also may pick your own pumpkins and strawberries. Open from 9 a.m. to 5 p.m., May to Oct.

Splash. 513 Carpenter's Lane, Cape May; (609) 846-7100. This little gallery carries hand-crafts and jewelry.

Washington Street Mall. This 3-block pedestrian promenade from Ocean to Perry Streets is lined with antiques shops, estate jewelers, gift shops, and stores selling art, apparel, and whimsy. People-watching is fun, too, from vintage iron benches surrounded by flower boxes, nostalgia lamps, and brick pavers. Plenty of restaurants have sidewalk tables on the mall, as well, and there are stands where you can catch a ride in a horse-drawn carriage.

Whale's Tale. 312 Washington Mall, Cape May; (609) 884-4808. This store opened more than 35 years ago and carries beach-theme jewelry, gifts, seashore books, and toys.

where to eat

The Ebbitt Room. 25 Jackson St., Cape May; (609) 884-5700; www.virginiahotel.com. A fine dining room located in the prestigious and pricey Virginia House—Zagat has said to expect service that is "Swiss-level." This legendary establishment is a favorite among people who can afford to eat out every night of the week. When you own your own farm, you can brag about farm-to-table and farm-to-glass, because the menu here includes arti-sanal beverages. All because the hotel owns the 62-acre Beach Plum Farm west of Cape May—leaving nothing to chance with the ingredients. The style is casually elegant, whether eating in the newly renovated dining room or at a table outside. Cocktails on the Virginia's front porch are a cape tradition, with some pale-ale calamari or a farm-cheese board to start the evening. The dinner menu is classic American, accented with tinkling ivories in the background. $$$.

410 Bank Street. Cape May; (609) 884-2127; www.410bankstreet.com. This restaurant and Frescos next door are sister properties, jointly co-owned for almost three decades. 410 Bank Street is a straightforward invitation to sprint over and savor anything put out by Chef Henry Sing Cheng. The classic appetizer of escargot Bourguignonne is a divine interpretation served over toasted peasant bread. Sing's take on shrimp is New Orleans–style, sautéed in "voodoo beer sauce." He prepares a roast of the night, and the baby rack of lamb is delectable when served with a pinot noir demi-glace and truffle butter. We also loved the pan-blackened prime rib, Sing-spiced and applewood-roasted. $$–$$$.

Frescos Restaurant. 412 Bank St., Cape May; (609) 884-0366; www.frescoscapemay .com. We chose this seafood trattoria on our most recent visit and were delighted with the quality of the food, the service, and the ambiance. We had a table on the enclosed front porch, with pleasant candlelight, blown-glass light fixtures, and vines pressing against the glass. The Caesar salad was extremely fresh, delicious, and not over-dressed, so we could actually taste the ingredients. We sampled Rigatoni Arrabiata, which was excellent, and Spaghetti Omuntiacata—absolutely superb. The pasta was tossed with generous strips of prosciutto, green peas, garlic, and red pepper flakes. The bread was served with rosemary sprigs in the olive oil. The menu is predominantly Northern Italian, with a focus on seafood, but you can get a rave-factor veal osso bucco if you get there before it runs out. $$–$$$.

Lucky Bones Backwater Grille. 1200 Route 109; Cape May; (609) 884-2663; www.lucky bonesgrille.com. From the very busy parking lot, you know something tasty is going down, and it's not just baby back ribs; although they are a menu staple. Seared filet mignon is yummy, and the grilled pork chop was prepared with a Cuban spice rub. There are seafood and chicken dishes, a menu for lighter fare, plus pizza, burgers, and sandwiches. On tap are domestic and imported beers, some you won't find just anywhere. The wine list is a no-brainer—plenty of reds and whites to choose from, all the same price. $$.

The Mad Batter. 19 Jackson St., Cape May; (609) 884-5970; www.madbatter.com. This address is square one for a fabulous breakfast, especially the eggs Benedict. All manner of sinful temptations keep us coming back every time we visit Cape May. $$–$$$.

The Merion Inn. 106 Decatur St. at Columbia Ave., Cape May; (609) 884-8363; www .merioninn.com. Named for a golf club in Pennsylvania, this is one of our favorite restaurants anywhere. The decor, service, and food are consistently splendid. For starters, try the seared crab cake and clams casino, with diced top necks, a tasty mirapoix, and bacon. The filet mignon is magnificent, and the Merion's stuffed lobster tail with lump crab is a serious contender for best of the best. No matter what entree you order, make sure to choose the Merion potato cup for a side. It comes in a little crock with creamy potatoes, sour cream, cheddar, and chives. The grilled asparagus with noisette butter is a good second call. If you don't love lobster, try the Atlantic salmon with a horseradish crust and smoked salmon-chive cream sauce. This is not an inexpensive place, but they do offer an "express" menu. $$–$$$.

Panico's Bistro. 422 Broadway, Cape May; (609) 884-7170. Located in an old church, it draws in the crowds, so it's noisy. There are only a few tables for two—most are set up for large families—and the high ceilings magnify the noise factor. The menu is heavily Greek and Italian fare. Pizza is a big attraction, and many menu items may be ordered in family-style portions. $–$$.

Peter Shields Inn & Restaurant. 1301 Beach Dr., Cape May; (609) 884-9090; www.peter shieldsinn.com. This gourmet Zagat-rated site is a 1907 Georgian-Revival–style mansion. Eat in one of the interior dining rooms by the fireplace or on a wide veranda while taking in the ocean breeze. The chef prepares classic seafood dishes and many farm-to-table touches. On a recent visit, we tried the roasted beet and Maine lobster salad with wild arugula, fennel, and carrots, all super-fresh, then pan-seared crab cakes and garden risotto. Superb is the word, if you like a special experience. Open for dinner daily in season. See the website for information about the inn's 9 guest rooms. $$–$$$.

Washington Inn. 801 Washington St., Cape May; (609) 884-5697; www.washingtoninn .com. Dinner here is always a special occasion, as is dessert, especially the chocolate mousse tower with a goblet of Remy Martin. $$–$$$.

where to stay

Angel of the Sea. 5 Trenton Ave., Cape May; (609) 884-3369; www.angelofthesea.com. This is a Victorian-style bed-and-breakfast, no extra charge for browsing the vintage jewelry in its lobby gift shop. The 27 guest rooms have private baths. Many have ocean views, and all guests enjoy the ambiance of wraparound porches. It has no elevator, but some guest rooms are on the first floor. There is a 2-night minimum stay on weekdays and a 3-night minimum on weekends. $$–$$$.

Congress Hall. 251 Beach Ave., Cape May; (609) 884-8421; www.congresshall.com. Established on a much smaller scale in 1816—and rebuilt after a fire in 1878—this renovated landmark is a self-contained destination with a very high profile. It was a favorite summer getaway for President Grant, President Pierce, and President Buchanan, and President Harrison turned it into a "summer White House." The original owner, Thomas Hughes, was elected to Congress in 1828, which allowed the locals to drop its former nickname, "Tommy's Folly." Families with children are welcome, and the resort offers beach service for its guests. There is a spa, fitness center, swimming pool, shops in the lobby, a restaurant, lounge, and nightclub. Live entertainment draws people from all over the cape. Congress Hall has 108 guest rooms and a handful of luxury suites. $$–$$$.

Sea Crest Inn. 101 Beach Ave., Cape May; (609) 884-4561; www.seacrestinn.com. All of the oceanview suites were remodeled in 2011 at this inn, which faces the beach and is only a short walk to the tip of the cape. We have stayed here a few times, so booking it is almost automatic. On the most recent visit, we stayed in a king-bedroom suite, which has hardwood floors and a sleeper sofa in the living room for company. The kitchen has a ceramic cooktop, fridge, microwave oven, and a table and chairs by the balcony. There is a whirlpool spa by the large heated swimming pool. You see local owners Bob and Cyndi Progner on the grounds and in the reception area every day, always on the outlook for a detail to be improved upon. Albert and Irma Progner, immigrants from Russia by way of Germany, built the current inn in 1978, after "retiring" from Philadelphia. $–$$.

The Virginia House. 25 Jackson St., Cape May; (609) 884-5700; www.virginiahotel.com. This genteel vintage hotel is a local legend that caters to grown-ups, so couples looking for a respite from parenting will enjoy the lull. Regulars flock here year after year, and re-book a year in advance, as the staff is first-rate and the setting addictive. The veranda is a pleasant spot to loll for breakfast or evening cocktails (see the "Where to Eat" description of The Ebbitt Room at the Virginia House). The hotel provides its guests with beach service for refreshments. $$–$$$.

worth more time

Willow Creek Winery. 168 Stevens St., West Cape May; www.willowcreekwinerycapemay .com. This 50-acre winery is a relatively new operation, with gardens under development. Check the website for tours and wine tastings.

day trip 05

the southern shore

dutch treat:
lewes, de; rehoboth beach, de

Only 17 miles from Cape May and a 90-minute ferry ride across Delaware Bay, Lewes (pronounced "Loo-iss") is a delightful diversion. It is scenic, quaint, fond of galleries, kind to foodies, and down with interesting shops (ah, tax-free temptation).

Downtown Lewes has a dandy called Second Street, and it is way ahead of whatever took first place. This hub of a well-restored central business district is a lively nod to the town's heritage as a Dutch whaling colony founded in 1631.

The vicinity is loaded with kudos to its maritime and military history, as well as major natural attractions. And Lewes's main drag has a Kilwin's Ice Cream shop, a sure indicator it knows where its bread is buttered. Inquiring minds must ask: scoop or cone?

lewes, de

getting there

Take the Garden State Parkway south to the end; turn right onto NJ 109 north, then left onto US 9 south (Lincoln Boulevard). Go to the Cape May-Lewes Ferry Terminal at 1200 Sandman Blvd., North Cape May; (800) 643-3779; www.cmlf.com. Reserve in advance to take your car on the ferry; foot passengers may be walk-ons. For the return, the Lewes-Cape May Ferry Terminal is about a mile east of downtown, and buses are ready for you.

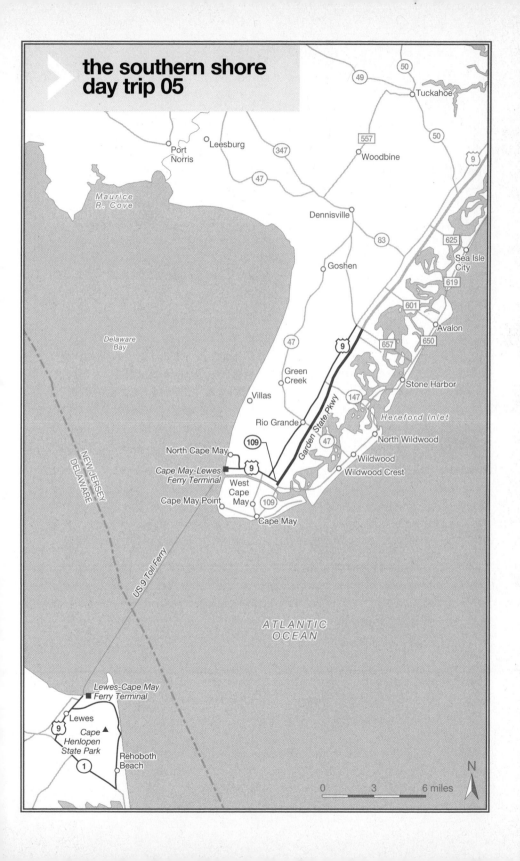

the southern shore
day trip 05

where to go

Lewes Historical Society. 110 Shipcarpenter St., Lewes; (302) 645-7670; www.historic lewes.org. You can get literature here on points of interest and sign up for a tour.

Ryves Holt House. Second and Mulberry Streets, Lewes; www.historiclewes.org. The Lewes Historical Society's Visitors Center has its reception area here, along with a marvelous gift shop chock-full of quaint maritime items. This shingled house was built in 1665 and is believed to be the oldest house in Delaware standing on its original foundation. Its credentials were established by an analysis of wood borings in the structure. Once a colonial inn, the house is named for Ryves Holt, a naval officer of Port Lewes who took his post in 1721. Holt also was a high sheriff and chief justice of the Delaware Supreme Court.

Zwaanendael Museum. 102 Kings Highway at Savannah Rd., Lewes; (302) 645-1148; www.history.gov/delaware/museums. The state built this museum in 1931 to mark the 300th anniversary of its first European settlement. The Dutch called the colony Swanendael (valley of the swans). Inspiration for the building's design came from the city hall in Hoorn, Holland. Exhibits include artifacts from the H.M.B. *DeBraak,* a recovered British warship that sank off the coast of Cape Henlopen in 1798; artifacts from the bombardment of Lewes during the War of 1812; and provenance from the Cape Henlopen Lighthouse. Other exhibits pay tribute to bay and river pilots and coastal ecology. Open Tues through Sat, 10 a.m. to 4:30 p.m., and Sun, 1:30 to 4:30 p.m. Admission is free, but donations are welcome.

Saint Peter's Episcopal Church. Second and Market Streets, Lewes; (302) 645-8479; www.stpeters.episcopaldelaware.org. This parish was identified in 1681, but it was not Lewes's first congregation of the Church of England. The original building was begun in 1707 and the current one dates to 1858. An interesting stone in the churchyard indicates that Margaret Huling was born in 1631. This is also the resting place of four governors.

Cannonball House-Marine Museum. 118 Front St., Lewes. Built about 1760 and enlarged in the 1790s, this house with cypress shingles was the home of David Rowland, a pilot on Delaware Bay. The nickname came about because it was struck by a cannonball when the British bombarded Lewes during the War of 1812. It was restored by the historical society. Themed rooms have exhibits on local maritime culture and history. Area gardeners designed the landscaping.

Cape Henlopen State Park. 15099 Cape Henlopen Dr., Lewes; (302) 645-8983; www.destateparks.com. From sandy beaches and nature trails, there is enormous variety for visitors to enjoy thousands of acres of the peninsula just a mile east of the historic downtown. The park is good for swimming, surf fishing, and birding. There are basketball courts, hockey and softball fields, and an 18-hole disc golf course. The area was part of a land grant to William Penn, who said its natural resources should be preserved "public lands." Here also is the Fort Miles Historic Area, an important aspect of World War II heritage. Several wartime bunkers are now scenic overlooks; one has been renovated to enable a panoramic view of the peninsula.

The Lightship *Overfalls*. 219 Pilottown Rd., Lewes; (302) 644-8050; www.overfalls.org. Overfalls Shoal at the mouth of Delaware Bay is the namesake for four lightships or "floating lighthouses" that illuminated the East Coast from 1898 to 1960. Visitors will see LV118 *Overfalls,* which served from 1938 to 1971. The vessel is 114 feet long and 26 feet wide. Its 15,000-candlepower light flashed every three seconds and was visible for 12 miles in clear skies. Its foghorn sounded every 30 seconds and was audible for 5 miles. The lightship museum on the canal at the foot of Shipcarpenter Street is open for tours from late May through mid-Oct.

Kalmar Nyckel. Lewes Ferry Terminal, Lewes; (302) 429-7447; www.kalmarnyckel.org. This wooden tall ship drops anchor at this port in August and September, when you can take 90-minute sails. There are pirate cruises, and you are able to haul the lines as the crew spins sea yarns about the original vessel. The cost is $60 for adults and $40 for children 17 and under.

where to shop

Biblion. 205 Second St., Lewes; (302) 644-2210; www.biblionbooks.com. You will be able to browse among a curated collection of contemporary books, antiquarians, rare finds, used books, unique greeting cards, stationery, art, and literary gifts.

Sand N Stones Delaware and Nature Shoppe. 112 Front St., Lewes; (302) 645-0576; www.sandandstones.com. Lapidary artisan Michele Buckler creates unique jewelry using gemstones, beach glass, and other natural specimens. She hand-crafts each piece by wrapping the stone in either 14-karat gold-plate, rose gold, anti-tarnish sterling silver, or a combination. You may choose a loose stone or ask her to frame something of yours—a coin, an orphan earring, even a shard of your grandmother's fine china.

where to eat

The Buttery Restaurant and Bar. 102 Second St., Lewes; (302) 645-7755; www.buttery restaurant.com. You can't take a wrong turn here, whether you want a bite or the entire menu, course by course. The motto here is "feed the senses, treat the soul, cure the common happy hour." The Buttery opens for brunch and serves lunch and light fare through to 5 p.m. From then on, it's either the dinner menu or the pub menu, meaning you won't go hungry while coordinating your return ferry ride to Cape May. On the pub menu, The Buttery on a Bun is a Kobe burger—superb any day and half-price on Tuesday. The tenderloin salad is a marvelous array of filet mignon on romaine, with roasted red peppers, artichoke hearts, crumbled bleu cheese, olives, tomato, and red onion. We also enjoyed the crab cake sandwich and Vietnamese-style imperial eggrolls. We were not here for dinner, but the gourmet menu indicates a sophisticated take on satisfying everybody; beef tenderloin, duck leg confit and rabbit sausage, PEI mussels, vegetarian ragu, Scottish salmon, crab cakes, and pork osso bucco. Three-course prix fixe dinners are $30, and the desserts are award-winners. $$–$$$.

Kindle. 111 Bank St., Lewes; (302) 645-7887; www.kindlerestaurant.com. This quaint perch in downtown Lewes sports brown shingle siding on the upper level, a Dutch-style calling card, and perky white siding on the first level—both with bright blue trim and a sign spelling out its motto: "eat, drink, glow." Drop in for lunch or dinner, inside or on the patio. The menu is American with some French persuasion. There is a cocktail menu and wine list—and this is one of the few places you will see wine offered "by the half-glass." $–$$.

where to stay

Hotel Rodney. 142 Second St., Lewes; (302) 645-6466; www.hotelrodneydelaware.com. Hotel Rodney is a classic, boutique-style hotel that dates to 1926. A lovely New York–inspired lobby is stylish and welcoming, with sofas and tables, computers and TVs. There are 24 renovated guest rooms, tastefully furnished with restored antiques, and the bathrooms updated with chic, designer styling and luxury. You can book king or queen beds, adjoining rooms with twin beds, or a suite. There is a workout facility and conference center and the hotel is now pet-friendly. $$.

The Inn at Canal Square. 122 Market St., Lewes; (302) 644-3377; www.innatcanalsquare .com. This charming, Nantucket-style lodging is on the waterfront at Lewes Harbor and next door to the Canal Front Park. The year-round inn has 22 lovely guest rooms with private baths, a pair of two-bedroom luxury suites, and two conference rooms. There is a fitness center and room rates include a complimentary European-style breakfast. Many of the accommodations feature a balcony overlooking the harbor, and it's a short walk to shops and restaurants. $$–$$$.

rehoboth beach, de

One of Delaware's best-known resort towns is a nationally recognized East Coast vacation destination. Rehoboth Beach is also convenient to Cape May, NJ, via the Lewes Ferry Terminal.

There is a 1-mile boardwalk, a lively retail district, first-rate restaurants, art galleries and museums, and a 130-store outlet shopping center.

getting there

The town is about 7 miles southeast of downtown Lewes; take US 9 west/Road 268, then bear right on US 9 west; turn left onto DE 1 south/Coastal Highway East; turn left onto DE 1A/Rehoboth Avenue until you reach the boardwalk.

where to go

Rehoboth Beach Film Society. 107 Truitt Ave., Rehoboth Beach; (302) 645-9095; www .rehobothfilm.com. This organization screens films year-round in diverse genres. In 2011 the group gained an additional perk, hosting the "On Screen/In Person" touring program. It brings the work of leading American indie filmmakers, including animation, documentary, experimental, and narrative works, accompanied by the filmmaker. One program featured *In Good Time, the Piano Jazz of Marian McPartland*.

Rehoboth Beach Museum. 511 Rehoboth Ave., Rehoboth Beach; (302) 227-7310; www .rehobothbeachmuseum.org. Check out the website for the 2012 schedule of exhibits.

where to shop

AerieArt Gallery. First Street Station, Rehoboth Beach; (302) 227-4776. The gallery carries fine art from the 19th century and more contemporary works, plus photography and furniture. The work of local artists is exhibited on a regular basis.

First Street Station. 70 Rehoboth Ave., Rehoboth Beach; (302) 224-7700. There are apparel shops, shoe and accessory stores, plus gifts, novelties, toys, and souvenirs.

Tanger Outlet Center. 36470 Seaside Outlet Dr., Rehoboth Beach; (302) 226-9223; www .tangeroutlet.com. Tanger Bayside and Tanger Seaside are on opposite sides of Route 1; Tanger Midway is a little north, creating a combined "mile of style" on the way to the beach and boardwalk. There are more than 130 stores such as Nike, Abercrombie & Fitch, Lenox, and the L.L. Bean Factory Store. You can save money while spending tax-free.

where to eat

The Back Porch Cafe. 59 Rehoboth Ave., Rehoboth Beach; (302) 227-3674; www.back porchcafe.com. Off the sidewalk, down a wooden walkway, is an entrance to the little porch that could. Its three owners have cobbled together a hideout that begs to be discovered for its positive energy and unassuming gourmet presentation. The bar and main dining room appear to have been joined as an afterthought, by adding a roof over separate cottages— as if they were undersea somewhere for a long time, dredged from the deep, dusted off, and opened for business. There are wooden beams, ceiling fans, and a skylight. A "Jack Sparrow" wooden ladder leads from behind the bar up to a secret loft where provisions are stashed away from prying eyes. The Porch speaks pirate, and the food is good enough to bootleg. A simple chicken salad turned into colossal contraband when paired with roasted beets and corn and served with crunchy pita. Eat alfresco in a courtyard outside the Porch's perky blue siding and white shutters. Quirky and whimsical, the place is decorated with people and places spelled out in charms, beads, and pearls. Fresh linens lend a civilized spin to varnished wooden tables. Credit cards are accepted, but not American Express. *Delaware Magazine* awarded The Back Porch kudos awhile back for "The Best Flaming Coffee Drink." $$–$$$.

Dos Locos Stonegrill. 208 Rehoboth Ave., Rehoboth Beach; (302) 227-3353; www.dos locos.com. Eat it raw? Nah, just grill it yourself at this restaurant, which delivers your selection on a 700-degree stone. You decide whether you want the fajitas rare or well-done. The restaurant has a good spirits selection, and each entree comes with a salad. The menu is Mexican, with some Tex-Mex lobster items, and several American dishes. Not recommended for children, as the stone grill is way too hot to touch. $–$$.

worth more time

Delaware Seashore State Park. Rehoboth Beach; (302) 227-2800; www.destateparks .org. With 6 miles of ocean and bay shoreline, it's a perfect spot for a family day at the beach. Enjoy surfing, fishing, swimming, sunbathing, a campground, a boat ramp, and a 295-slip marina with charter boats. You also can find furnished cottages, open year-round.

delaware river region

day trip 01

delaware river region

>>> **martyrs, drama & drums:**
princeton, nj

If you haven't checked out Princeton's assets lately, a sound "drumthwacking" might be in order. Well before this berg was synonymous with "Ivy League"—and before any Gothic edifice on campus would have been perfectly cast in a Harry Potter adventure— Princeton University was busy educating Presbyterian scholars.

Founded in 1746 in Elizabeth, NJ, and after spending a year in Newark, the institution moved to Princeton a decade later. Home base was Nassau Hall, named to honor King William III of the House of Orange-Nassau. In summer 1783, the hall doubled as the capital of the United States when the Continental Congress convened, and it is on the National Register of Historic Places.

Princeton also is historically significant for the battle in which Gen. George Washington's forces defeated British troops. It occurred at the end of the "Ten Crucial Days" campaign, after the dual battles at Trenton.

Princeton also is home to Drumthwacket, the official residence of the governor of New Jersey. To balance the atmosphere of high-minded pursuits and military history, downtown has plenty of upscale shopping, rare finds, and cutting-edge restaurants.

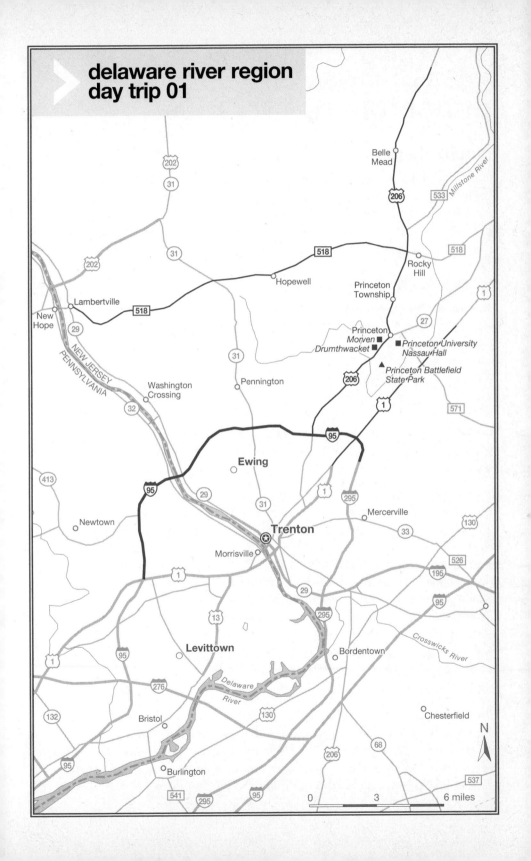

delaware river region
day trip 01

princeton, nj

getting there

From northern New Jersey, take I-287 south to exit 17; take US 206. Once inside Princeton Township, the ride is lovely; but watch for a road quirk. A traffic circle gives multiple exits. Princeton is about 43 miles southwest of Newark Liberty Airport; take the New Jersey Turnpike (I-95) to exit 9; and follow US 1. From Philadelphia, about 40 miles, take I-95 to exit 7 and head northwest on US 206.

where to go

The Morven Museum and Garden. 55 Stockton St., Princeton; (609) 924-8144; www .morven.org. In 1701 Richard Stockton bought a 5,500-acre tract from William Penn, and in 1754 his grandson, also named Richard Stockton, acquired 150 acres here for his house. Stockton was a prominent attorney and a signer of the Declaration of Independence. His wife, poet Annis Boudinot Stockton, named the house "Morven" after a mythical Gaelic kingdom described in the works of 3rd-century bard Ossian. In the 20th century, Morven was used as the governor's mansion. It was converted to a museum in 1982 and renovated in 2004. From Jan through Nov, there are docent-guided tours of the mansion and exhibited collections. The site is open Wed through Sun, excluding major holidays. A popular annual event here is the Festival of Trees, from the end of November through early January, when local businesses and garden clubs decorate holiday trees in the galleries.

Princeton Battlefield State Park. 500 Mercer Rd., Princeton; (609) 921-0074; www .njparksandforests.org. Away from modern doings in town, a rolling green field rises quietly, and its emptiness resounds. It conjures images of Mel Gibson as the reluctant patriarch who defends his family in *The Patriot*. A monument memorializing a martyr sits on a rise in the field. Above it, Old Glory flutters, then whips in the breeze. Shade trees line the drive, and it's not unusual to see one person or a group of students sitting on the grass studying or reading charts describing the site's historic significance. On Jan. 3, 1777, on this unlikely patch, Gen. George Washington's forces defeated British troops. The fighting occurred late in the "Ten Crucial Days" campaign, after the iconic crossing of the Delaware River. High on a hill is the Thomas Clarke House. Gen. Hugh Mercer, born in 1720 in Scotland and fighting beside Washington, lay wounded here after the battle. He later died in the Clarke home.

Drumthwacket. 354 Stockton St., Princeton; (609) 683-0057; www.drumthwacket.org. The property is a three-way: listed on the National Register, a historic house museum, and the official residence of the governor of New Jersey. Most governors since the 1980s have lived in the manor only part-time. The last governor to reside here was James McGreevy. Chris Christie holds occasional dinners and ceremonies at Drumthwacket. The first governor to live here was Charles Smith Olden, whose father, William, bought the land in 1696 from William Penn. Olden, born at the site in 1799, began building the current Greek Revival–style estate in 1835. Olden named the place Drumthwacket, a version of Scottish Gaelic words for "wooded hill." The original structure had a two-and-a-half-story center hall with two rooms on each side. It has a large portico with six Ionic columns. Moses Taylor Pyne bought it in 1893 and enlarged the estate and acreage, adding a formal Italian garden. In 1941 Russian immigrant industrialist Abram Nathaniel Spanel bought the house and 12 acres from Pyne's granddaughter. The state bought the estate in 1966.

Nassau Hall. Princeton University, downtown Princeton; (609) 258-3603; www.princeton .edu. This Renaissance-style edifice built in 1754 is the oldest building on campus. It houses administrative offices now, but in 1783 it was the seat of our national government. The Continental Congress met in the library on the second floor. See the website for campus tour information.

where to shop

Nassau Place. 20 Nassau St., Princeton; (609) 924-9201; www.nassauplace.com. This address is home to 15 specialty shops, art galleries, and antiques stores in the heart of historic Princeton.

Palmer Square Shops. 40 Nassau St., Princeton; (609) 921-2333; www.palmersquare .com. Located across from the university, this is a collection of fashion boutiques and shops carrying apparel, shoes, jewelry, accessories, and gifts. There are restaurants here, as well, and specialty food shops.

Terhune Orchards. 330 Cold Soil Rd., Princeton; (609) 924-2310; www.terhuneorchards .com. This is a family-run farm market open year-round. They grow dozens of fruits and vegetables and also sell cider and baked goods. You can pick your own produce, stroll the gardens, and follow the farm trail.

where to eat

Elements. 163 Bayard Lane, Princeton; (609) 924-0078; www.elementsprinceton.com. Executive chef Scott Anderson's menu is American with a lot of international influence. The decor is crisp, inventive, and an artful setting for his famous dishes. The restaurant serves brunch and lunch daily except Saturday and dinner seven days. For lunch, the smoked pork croquet madame is intriguing, on an English muffin with organic egg, Mornay sauce, and avocado. The house tagliatelle is a delectable toss of pasta, onion, and Parmesan. Pheasant and Colorado lamb are dinner entrees, but the chef also looks closer to home for his provisions. In 2011 Anderson was named among the best new chefs in *Esquire Magazine*. The write-up said he is "in the vanguard of modern global-American cuisine." Also in '11,

Anderson took home top honors in the Jersey Seafood Challenge, which Mary Pat Christie hosted at Drumthwacket. $$–$$$.

Mediterra. 29 Hulfish St., Princeton; (609) 252-9680; www.terramomo.com. Inspired by the cuisines of 20 or so countries hugging the Mediterranean Sea, what's not to like about this menu? In a rush, you may sample some spirits and tapas in Mediterra's taverna—maybe baby octopus or bacon-wrapped dates. For dinner, we opted for the paella, made with calasparra rice, mussels, chicken, shrimp, clams, calamari, chorizo—and of course, saffron. $$–$$$.

where to stay

Nassau Inn. 10 Palmer Square, Princeton; (609) 751-0903; www.nassauinn.com. Both traditional and historic, with updated amenities, this downtown lodging has more than 200 guest rooms and suites, a fitness center, business center, and the Yankee Doodle Tap Room—a restaurant, bar, and patio where you can enjoy breakfast, lunch, and dinner from the American menu. There is a stone fireplace and a 13-foot-wide Norman Rockwell mural hanging behind the bar. This full-service hotel also has some pet-friendly rooms. The location is near shops, galleries, salons, and Princeton University. $$–$$$.

worth more time

Lambertville. Hunterdon County, NJ; www.lambertville.org. On the east bank of the Delaware River—which New Jersey refers to as its "west coast"—this historic outpost is a country slice of laid-back, river-run charm with quaint hangouts, art galleries, gift shops, vineyards, and a great mix of locals. A town time loved and left alone, Lambertville is known as the "Antique Capital of New Jersey." If you happen to drive here from Princeton, it's a short ride west on US Route 206 north to Route 518. Stop by The Lambertville Station for lunch, dinner, or Sunday brunch—inside or out—and admire the restored 19th-century train station. The Inn at Lambertville Station can put you up for a sojourn while you get your bearings. The Delaware and Raritan Canal State Park winds through town, with four-season recreation activities for the whole family. Victorian bungalows inspire respect, especially from *This Old House.*

day trip 02

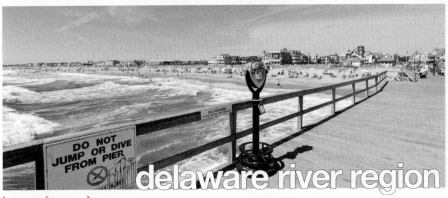

delaware river region

digging in, dodging bayonets:
trenton, nj; titusville & hamilton, nj

Yes, almost all are weary of political gridlock, so why are we suggesting you visit the state capital?

Because Trenton has some treasures that merit a fresh look. There are museums, fields of major battles, and restored examples of an important residence in pre-Revolutionary times.

And if you can't leave town without a dose of legislative atmosphere, make time for the 145-foot ceiling in the rotunda of the New Jersey State House—in continuous use since 1792.

History buffs will appreciate that the state capital began as the country home of Philadelphia merchant William Trent during the mid-1600s. In addition to its current status, Trenton was a significant Revolutionary War battlefield.

trenton, nj

getting there

From I-95 (the New Jersey Turnpike), take exit 7A onto I-195 west.

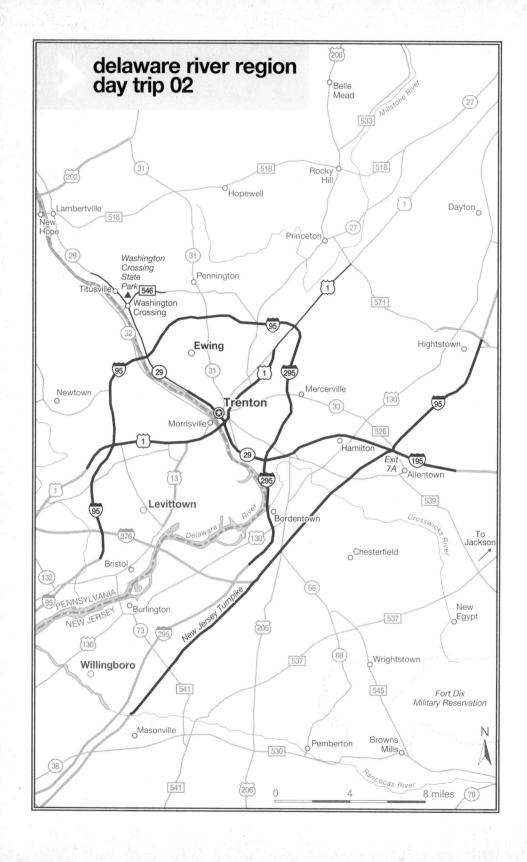

delaware river region
day trip 02

where to go

The New Jersey State Museum. 205 W. State St., Trenton; (609) 292-6464; www.state .nj.us/state/museums.com. This is four museums in one. Archaeology/Ethnology showcases artifacts of the state's Native Americans, especially the history of the Lenni-Lenape Indians, arriving here 11,000 years ago. Collections illustrate everyday life among them, and include a dugout canoe, tools, weapons, clothing, ornaments, and jewelry. This museum also takes a look at the heritage of those from Africa and South America. The Cultural History museum shows decorative arts from Colonial times to the present, with folk art, furniture, fire-backs, and silver objects. The Fine Art collections have 20th-century American art, with important works by Georgia O'Keeffe, Alexander Calder, John Marin, and Louise Nevelson; plus a focus on New Jersey artists. You also will see a collection of American and European prints, drawings, and photographs. The Natural History galleries show New Jersey's dinosaurs, Ice Age mastodons, and today's wildlife. Exhibits relate the mix of the Garden State's highlands, piedmont cities, farms, coastal plains, and seashore. The state museum also has a hi-def Planetarium, a state-of-the-art projection facility showing 6,000 stars in full-dome video, with 140 seats designed to recline. Open Tues through Sat, 9 a.m. to 4:45 p.m. and noon to 5 p.m. on Sun. Admission is free.

New Jersey State House. 125 W. State St., Trenton; (609) 292-4840; www.njleg.state.nj .us/legislativepub/visiting. This is the nation's second oldest state capitol in continuous use, after Maryland. It originated in 1792; after additions, modifications, and periodic restoration, it is said to reflect America's finest craftsmanship. Some of the re-created period rooms reflect styles of the 1892 General Assembly and the 1903 Senate. A third-floor exhibit has artifacts, engravings, and memorabilia related to the building and the Legislature. Artwork on display includes Hiroshi Murata's elaborate inlaid-wood designs in the walls of a conference room. Paintings and sculpture adorn the halls, many on loan from major museums. The rotunda has a 145-foot domed ceiling. The chandelier in the Assembly Chamber, lit since 1892, was made by Thomas Edison's General Edison Electric Company. In a senate conference room are original stained-glass skylights. You may tour the State House with a self-guiding map.

William Trent House. 15 Market St., Trenton; (609) 989-3027; www.williamtrenthouse .org. Scotsman William Trent came to Philadelphia in 1682 and became a wealthy merchant and ship owner, exporting tobacco, flour, skins, and furs; and importing wine, rum, molasses, and dry goods. Slaves from Africa arrived on Trent's vessels. In 1716 he began building a summer estate on the banks of the Delaware River, and laid out the "Trent's Town" settlement. In a 1-hour guided tour, you will see a beautifully restored Georgian manor, furnished in 1728 style. Three pieces in the Drawing Room are "japanned," or coated with black lacquer or enamel. A tea set imported from China has cups with no handles—as the custom was to pour chá into a cup and then a saucer. The Library, which was Trent's office, has an Elizabethan Game Box—for chess, checkers, backgammon, and tric-trac. In the dining room, a hand-crafted chandelier has lift-off arms, so that guests could light their way to another room. The house is open daily from 12:30 to 4 p.m.

Old Barracks Museum. Barrack Street, Trenton; (609) 396-1776; www.barracks.org. This Historic Landmark was built in 1758 to house British troops during the French and Indian War. "Of War, Law, and the Third Amendment" is an exhibit about forced quartering in America (at a time when soldiers commandeered private homes). "The Battle of Trenton" exhibit features period weapons and equipment surrounding the standoff against Hessian troops during the Revolution. "Hail the Conquering Hero" is about Washington's arrival at Trenton. There are restored and refurnished Officers' Quarters, as well as exhibits recalling military life before and during these battles. The museum presents reenactments, family workshops, concerts, lectures, and a summer history day camp. Open Mon through Sat from 10 a.m. to 6 p.m., closed on major holidays.

where to shop

Boehm Porcelain. 25 Princess Diana Lane, Trenton; (800) 257-9410; www.boehmporcelain.com. The current gallery is the legacy of an enterprise begun in an atelier in 1949. Sculptor Edward Marshall Boehm and his wife, Helen, built an unrivaled reputation for the finest sculptures of animals, birds, and flowers. Praised by the Metropolitan Museum of Art for their superior quality, these works were presented as gifts to national and world leaders, from the White House to the Vatican.

Classics Book Shop. 117 S. Warren St., Trenton; (609) 394-8400. The business is about used and rare books, but the owner also hosts community events and Scrabble nights.

Culture Apparel. 439 S. Broad St., Suite 108, Trenton; (866) 966-9127; www.cultureapparel.com. This emporium carries Bob Marley wear, Rasta wear for men, women, and children, jewelry, gift baskets, and country logos for Jamaica, Mexico, Trinidad and Tobago, and numerous others. There are African musical instruments and plenty of other merchandise categories.

Cybis Porcelain Gallery. 65 Norman Ave., Trenton; (609) 392-6074; www.cybisporcelain.com. Based on the legacy of painter/sculptor/porcelain genius Boleslaw Cybis, a native of Poland, this studio/gallery/showroom opened in 1939 and it is the oldest porcelain art studio in America. Artists work on the premises, and seven galleries have thousands of works on display. The galleries are open by appointment.

Messy Klosets. 101 S. Warren St., Suite B, Trenton; (609) 695-7300. This boutique carries trendy clothes for women, as well as handbags and jewelry.

The Record Collector. 358 Farnsworth, Bordentown; (609) 324-0880; www.the-record-collector.com. This store is a short car ride from Trenton. The owners draw customers from all over New Jersey, from out of state and from other parts of the world. In business for decades, they carry new, used, and collectible music—CDs, DVDs, old and rare LPs and

45s. On the weekends, they host live entertainment. If you are a music buff or pop culture historian, check it out.

Stace of Cakes. 11 N. Willow St., Trenton; (609) 989-4701; www.staceofcakes.com. Trenton is a treat, and Stacey Reece's shop takes the cake when it comes to creative confection using natural ingredients. Specialty cakes and cupcakes are the focus, and you can find gluten-free items here as well. You also can stop in for a Continental breakfast or vegan lunch. Open weekdays from 7:30 a.m. to 4:30 p.m.

where to eat

The Mill Hill Saloon. 300 Broad St., Trenton; (609) 394-7222. Built in 1859 as a brewery, it now is a neighborhood pub, restaurant, and music venue. You can find a selection of beers on tap, and pub food. $–$$.

Trenton Social. 449 S. Broad St., Trenton; (609) 989-7777; www.trentonsocial.com. Opened in 2011, this trendy spot is across the street from the Sun National Bank Center arena. The concept is casual dining for lunch or dinner. The menu is eclectic, from tapas to burgers, cheesesteak egg rolls, pasta, and fabulous salads. One is accented with apples, dried cranberries, and almonds—a killer combination. $–$$.

where to stay

Element. 1000 Sam Weinroth Rd. East, Ewing; (609) 671-0050; www.starwoodhotels .com/element. Conveniently located near the Trenton Mercer Airport, this stylish, contemporary lodging is an appealing place to land. There is an indoor swimming pool and a fitness center. This relatively new property has comfortable, modern guest rooms with kitchenettes and seating areas, trendy design in the bathrooms, and beds made up for a great night's sleep. Choose among deluxe rooms, 1- or 2-bedroom suites, and executive suites. $$–$$$.

flag on the play

Before Betsy Ross could stitch together the so-called first American flag, a few someones created patterns for the Stars and Stripes that met qualifications set by the Flag Resolution of 1777. Philadelphia native Francis Hopkinson, a resident of Bordentown, NJ, and one of the signers of the Declaration of Independence, designed a flag that his supporters claimed to be the "first" Old Glory. Hopkinson's flag has 13 stars arranged in a staggered or quincuncial pattern that repeats a motif of five units. Another Hopkinson design arranged the stars in a circle. Although similar to Betsy Ross's flag, his design featured stars with six points.

titusville & hamilton, nj

It is here that you will recall a grade-school lesson about George Washington crossing the Delaware River with 2,400 soldiers, cannons, and horses to preempt a possible attack on Philadelphia. It was savagely cold and not at all certain they would succeed.

getting there

From Trenton, take NJ 29 northwest.

where to go

Washington Crossing State Park. 355 Washington Crossing-Pennington Rd. (Route 546), Titusville; (609) 737-0623; www.njparksandforests.org. The voyage took place Dec. 25, 1776, in the run-up to the Battle of Trenton. Each year on Christmas Day, there is a reenactment of the conflict.

worth more time

Grounds for Sculpture. 18 Fairgrounds Rd., Hamilton; (609) 586-0616; www.groundsfor sculpture.org. Since the mid-18th century, royal decrees held that there would be county fairs in this vicinity. On the site of the former New Jersey State Fairgrounds, the Grounds for Sculpture opened in 1992 as an outdoor venue for contemporary sculpture. The park displays more than 250 sculptures on about 35 acres of landscaped area, with thousands of rose bushes, hundreds of trees, and flowers and shrubs to accentuate the pieces—some with water features. There are courtyards, decorative walls, an amphitheater, and two buildings with museum exhibits and a cafe and shop. Rat's is a gourmet restaurant that overlooks the sculptures. To reserve a lunch or dinner here Tues through Sun, call (609) 584-7800. The facility suggests that Rat's is not a place to bring young children. From Trenton, take the East State Street Extension to Sculptors Way.

Six Flags Great Adventure Amusement Park, Wild Safari and Hurricane Harbor. Route 537, Jackson; (732) 928-1821; www.sixflagsnewjersey.com. This major fun zone is geared for families of all ages, with more than 100 rides, wild animals in their natural habitat, and water adventures. There are 13 roller coasters, including the new Green Lantern stand-up version, plus Kingda Ka and El Toro. The complex has three children's areas, interactive animal entertainment such as Dolphin Discovery, Safari Discoveries, and concerts. Adjacent to the theme park is the largest drive-through safari experience outside of Africa, featuring about 1,200 animals from 6 continents. Next door is Hurricane Harbor, a popular water park. Take the Garden State Parkway to exit 98; go west on I-195 to exit 16.

day trip 03

delaware river region

sewing symbols, reaping a republic:
philadelphia, pa; camden, nj;
cherry hill, nj

Patriotism is not puffed up here in the epicenter of national ideals. It is Colonial history on the hoof, and a visitor's main challenge is choosing among so many venues that deserve to be explored in depth.

Touring Philadelphia after any absence, you are struck by the simple clarity that regardless of what happens on any given day in Washington DC, citizens would do well to return here for a refresher course in the way things are supposed to work. It was here, after all, that President Washington took a crash course in transferring presidential authority to John Adams.

If you've already seen all the historic buildings and artifacts and have time for only one attraction, consider the only American museum devoted to the US Constitution. It is an organic space beating a drum for the continuity of a unique form of government—from the iconic parchment penned in 1787 to the precipice of the US presidential election in 2012.

Philadelphia architecture is a fascinating eyeful, and not just on the institutional side. Many old industrial sites have been adapted for residential use. These days The Chocolate Works, The Iron Works, and The Brass Works are residential addresses.

Make time for the Vietnam War Memorial and the Gloria Dei Church (Old Swedes Church), a National Historic Site.

When selecting a bridge over the Delaware River, the names of these spans make you want to slow down and ponder the matter a bit more, committing yourself to Walt Whitman, Betsy Ross, or Benjamin Franklin. The latter, nicknamed "Big Blue," is the most convenient to the Independence Visitor Center.

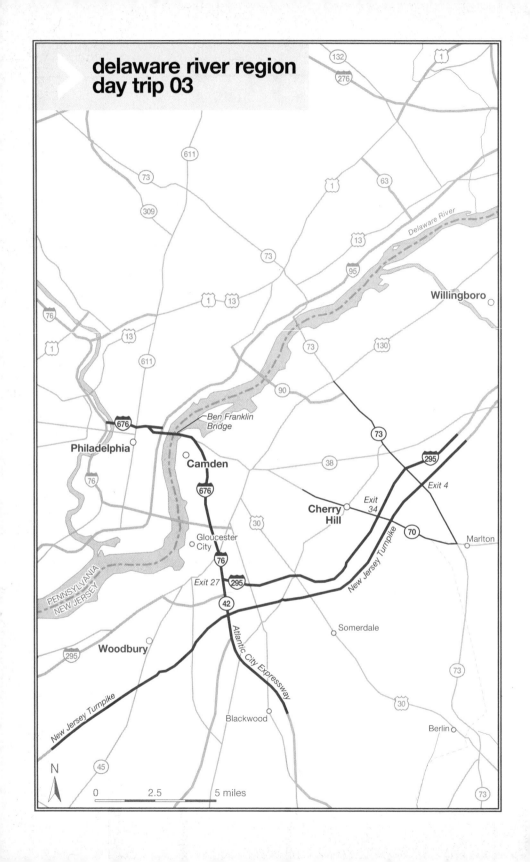

delaware river region
day trip 03

Parking in Philadelphia is a true challenge. Try the parking garage at One Independence Mall, an office building near all the action.

philadelphia, pa

getting there

Philadelphia is about 85 miles from Newark, and the ride is mostly on toll roads. From the north, take I-95 (the New Jersey Turnpike) to exit 4 (NJ 73 west). Go a short distance until you reach I-295 and head south to exit 27 (I-76); head north to the merger with I-676 North; then cross the Ben Franklin Bridge over the Delaware River into Philadelphia. From Atlantic City, take the Atlantic City Expressway to I-76, then I-676 and over the Ben Franklin Bridge.

where to go

The Independence Visitor Center. 599 Market St., Philadelphia; (215) 965-7676; www .independencevisitorcenter.com. This is the best place for reentry into the city's groaning board of visitor choices. Tour the center to determine the scope of your adventure for the time you have allotted to be here. This also is the place to buy tickets for many points of interest and to decide whether you want a bus tour, trolley ride, or horse-and-buggy outing.

Philadelphia Trolley Works. 5th and Market Street, Philadelphia; (215) 389-8687; www .phillytour.com. Given the city's parking shortage, throngs of pedestrians, and the fact that it's tough to sightsee and drive, we recommend this hop-on, hop-off option for a painless way to maximize your time. The mode of transportation is a restored Victorian trolley. These charming conveyances take you on a 90-minute tour with 21 stops. Our guide was most entertaining, and even provided helpful restaurant tips, along with historical anecdotes about the new republic. Stops include Independence Historical National Park, Benjamin Franklin Parkway, the Philadelphia Museum of Art, Antique Row, South Street, Society Hill, Penn's Landing, Liberty Bell, Old City, Avenue of the Arts, and the Pennsylvania Convention Center. Tours run daily except Christmas and New Year's Day. The cost is $27 for adults, $25 for seniors, and $10 for children ages 4 to 12.

National Constitution Center. 525 Arch St., Philadelphia; (215) 409-6600; www.constitu tioncenter.org. This center on Independence Mall is the only American museum devoted to the US Constitution. It is a multilevel cylindrical space, a "drum" displaying the text of the Constitution on lighted Plexiglas panels flanked with maps, sketches, posters, time-line murals—plus replicas of headlines about "secession" and "emancipation." There are audiovisual features and a scale model of the US Capitol. Amid stacks of actual court briefs brought before the US Supreme Court, you are invited to "put on a black robe and sit on the bench." American law books are displayed in towers, with the books stacked in spirals. You

face facts

One of the most interesting and innovative elements at National Constitution Center in Philadelphia is The American National Tree, a modernistic metal "trunk" and "limbs." Each "leaf" is the backlit face of someone whose life and work made a difference to this country. The exhibit is interactive, inviting you to simply "choose an American face and hear an American story." Push a button and a monitor reveals text about the person who made you curious to know more. Also, you are encouraged to suggest other faces that belong on the tree. The simplicity of the exercise is a foolproof circle: question, learn, teach.

see memorabilia such as Harry Truman's Panama hat and Hawaiian shirt. The exhibits guide you from Revolutionary times up to this minute, with more than 100 interactive, multimedia exhibits, film, photography, text, sculpture, and artifacts. Start your tour with the 30-minute theatrical performance, "Freedom Rising," which takes place in the DeVos Exhibit Hall of the Kimmel Theater. The center is open weekdays from 9:30 a.m. to 5 p.m., Sat from 9:30 a.m. to 6 p.m., and Sun from noon to 5 p.m.; closed Thanksgiving and Christmas Day. Admission is $12 for adults, $11 for seniors, and $8 for children; free with military ID.

Liberty Bell Center. 6th and Market Street; Philadelphia; www.ushistory.org/tour/liberty-bell.com. The site is open year-round, but the bell is visible around the clock. Inside the center, you will find a video presentation and exhibits on the bell's origins and its iconic role as an international symbol of freedom. Taped messages are offered in a dozen languages. The Liberty Bell is suspended in a glass chamber near Independence Hall. The site is a reminder of the days when William Penn orchestrated the colony's government, opting for people to shape laws and worship as they pleased. In 1751 the Speaker of the Pennsylvania Assembly ordered a new bell for the State House, inscribed with a Bible verse from the Book of Leviticus: "Proclaim Liberty throughout all the Land unto all the inhabitants thereof." Today, the State House is called Independence Hall. Admission to the center is free.

Marian Anderson House. 762 Marian Anderson Way (Martin Street, between 19th and 20th Streets), Philadelphia; (215) 732-9505; www.mariananderson.org. The famous contralto bought this home in 1924, and it was designated a historic site by the Philadelphia Historical Commission in 2004. It became a museum and is filled with photos and memorabilia of her life and career. The museum was founded by Anderson's protégé, classical pianist Blanche Burton-Lyles. Open weekdays from 11 a.m. to 3 p.m. or by appointment.

Independence Seaport Museum. 211 S. Christopher Columbus Blvd., Philadelphia; (215) 413-8655; www.phillyseaport.org. This entertaining and educational attraction on the

Delaware River includes a fascinating collection of exhibits about maritime history, especially the 1892 Cruiser, USS *Olympia,* a National Historic Landmark ship. The old gal is open for tours on a limited basis. See the website for the museum's newest exhibits.

Spirit of Philadelphia. 401 S. Christopher Columbus Blvd., Philadelphia; (866) 455-3866; www.spiritofphiladelphia.com. After a $1.5 million renovation, this cruising vessel is even more in demand. Leave the dock at Penn's Landing for lunch, dinner, holiday celebration, or maybe a walk down the aisle. Prices range from $38 for a weekday lunch cruise, up to $74 for a dinner cruise on Saturday. There are packages for groups of 20 or more.

Eastern State Penitentiary. 2027 Fairmount Ave., Philadelphia; (215) 236-3300; www .easternstate.org. A favorite lodging for Willie Sutton and Al Capone, among others, this historic site is a popular attraction just for the architecture, which is scary Gothic. It once was the most famous and expensive prison in the world, but today is empty of inmates. It's a popular place for visitors anytime, especially around Halloween. This was the world's original "penitentiary," a jail designed to make the inhabitants contrite, remorseful, or maybe just sorry for the jury pool they drew. To inspire penitence, the inmates spent 23 hours a day hooded, in solitary confinement, with a work bench, a Bible, and the "eye of God," a vaulted skylight over the cell. Many of America's most notorious criminals did time here. Tours include cell blocks, solitary cells, Al Capone's Cell, and Death Row. Open daily from 10 a.m. to 5 p.m., excluding Thanksgiving Day, Christmas Eve, Christmas Day, and New Year's Day. Admission is $12 for adults, $10 for seniors, $8 for students and children; no children under age 7.

Morris Arboretum of the University of Pennsylvania. 100 E. Northwestern Ave., Philadelphia; (215) 247-5777; www.morrisarboretum.org. Located in historic Chestnut Hill, this site has 92 acres of historic landscape, paths, gardens, brooks, and fountains. There are about 13,000 labeled trees, plants, and flowers. Open daily from 10 a.m. to 4 p.m. and until 5 p.m. on weekends from Apr through Oct. Admission is $14 for adults, $12 for seniors,

bringing home the bacon

You don't have to be 6 degrees separated from Kevin Bacon to appreciate a special site in Philadelphia. Just drop by LOVE Park (JFK Plaza) at the eastern end of Benjamin Franklin Parkway. The mixed-use urban hangout was founded by the actor's father, architect and urban planner Edmund Norwood Bacon (1910–2005). At the age of 92, Edmund skateboarded in the park as a protest against a city ban of the sport. He had designed the park in 1932 while attending Cornell University. It was built in the 1960s.

and $7 for students and children from ages 3 to 17. There are free guided tours at 2 p.m. Sat and Sun.

where to eat

La Scala's. Chestnut and 7th Street, Philadelphia; (215) 928-0900; www.lascalaphilly.com. This is a busy daytime magnet, obviously popular with businesspeople and professionals having a power lunch or break from the office. There are comfortable booths, Top 40 tunes in the background, and TV screens with financial and political news. We enjoyed the bread board with roasted garlic and balsamic vinegar. The Margherita pie was luscious, with a thin crust, tasty sauce, and cheese—no doubt similar to what you could get at Apollo pizzerias before the family expanded the business into a full-service restaurant serving Italian-American cuisine. In 2005 they also changed the name to show off the heritage of immigrant founders Frank Rocchino and Charles LaScala. The restaurant and bar are open for lunch, dinner, take-out, and delivery. $$.

Paradiso Restaurant & Wine Bar. 1627 E. Passyunk Ave., Philadelphia; (215) 271-2066; www.paradisophilly.com. We have close friends who visit the city a couple of times a year and rave about Paradiso, so we plan to go there on our next visit. It is a fine-dining establishment, casually elegant and crisply simple, with a small bar. It is open for lunch and dinner. The wine list is well-informed, and the menu has just the right number of appealing eclectic items. $$.

Radicchio Cafe. 402 Wood St., Philadelphia; (215) 627-6850; www.radicchio-cafe.com. This Tuscan trattoria is the gem of its neighborhood, and most patrons opt to walk there versus making futile attempts at finding a parking spot. We had to work for our dinner by circling the block numerous times, then asking the staff where to park. We learned that a neighboring church will not tow your car, so we parked there and walked a few blocks. And believe it—the results made the ordeal well worthwhile. Chef/owner Massimo Cosca from Southern Italy opened the restaurant in 2001. This BYOB cafe is open for lunch and dinner. $$.

Vietnam Restaurant. 221 N. 11th St., Philadelphia; (215) 592-1163; www.eatatvietnam .com. This family business began with immigrants opening a grocery store in West Philadelphia in 1982, and branching out into a restaurant in Chinatown. The "hole in the wall" grew into an eatery, which expanded and now has Bar Saigon on the third floor, adding another chapter to the legacy of Nhu Lai and Thuyen Luu, who fled Southeast Asia with their children. Stop in for some Tom Nuong Xa or Banh Cuon. We were pleased at this recommendation from our tour guide, whose heritage is Vietnamese. $–$$.

where to shop

Antique Row. Pine Street (one-way heading east), Philadelphia; www.antique-row.org. Just wander and enjoy the many antiques shops and merchants selling vintage treasures, from furniture to clothes, books, and crafts. Check out Russakoff's Book Store at 259 S. Pine St.; (215) 592-8380.

Gallery at Market East. 9th and Market Street, Philadelphia; (215) 625-4962; www.gallery atmarketeast.com. There are more than 100 stores in this multilevel urban mall. You can find apparel, shoes, accessories, books, gifts, and mall food.

Reading Terminal Market. 51 N. 12th St., between Arch and Filbert Streets, Philadelphia; (215) 922-2317; www.readingterminalmarket.org. This is one of the top 3 stops on any visitor's itinerary in the city. When this farmer's market opened in 1892, a lot of the vendors were from New Jersey, including fishermen and hunters who hauled their goods to the market. As the enterprise grew, each generation tried to keep up with its new features. Today, the market draws 100,000 visitors a week, with the aroma of baked goods, fresh produce, Amish specialties, meats, seafood, and poultry. Merchants here sell unique wares, from handmade pottery, jewelry, and crafts to cookware, flowers, clothing, and books. You also can find ethnic foods and specialties here, and a good mix of restaurants. Check out Miscellanea Libri for used books, get your loafers shined at The Shoe Doctor, and stop by the Pennsylvania General Store for gift baskets, chocolates, candies, and crafts.

Shops at Liberty Place. 1650 Market St., Philadelphia; (215) 851-9000; www.shops atliberty.com. A fine retail mix awaits you here, from Ann Taylor Loft to Jos. A. Bank and Victoria's Secret.

where to stay

Le Méredien. 1421 Arch St., Philadelphia; (215) 422-8200; www.lemeredien.com/Philadel phia. This 202-room boutique hotel is located in a 10-story historic building with a central atrium courtyard on the 5th floor with a 75-foot ceiling and skylight. There is a business center and a 24-hour gym. The Georgian-Revival–style building dates to 1912 and once was a YMCA. It was another hotel before Starwood did a makeover and reopened it in 2009. The new aesthetic balances the building's historic clubby-ness with crisp guest rooms in black and white with splashes of red. The in-house Amuse restaurant is open for breakfast, lunch, and dinner, featuring a French bistro menu. Le Méredien has a cocktail lounge on the lobby floor. $$.

camden, nj

Up from a down state is one way to characterize this city across the river from Philadelphia.

breakthrough broth

The first "condensed" soup was cooked and canned in Camden in 1897—well before the concept of alphabet soup, low-sodium stews, and chunky, all-vegetable gourmet varieties. Today, the Joseph A. Campbell Preserve Company uses the better-known moniker Campbell Soup Company.

Camden's waterfront readily shrugs off the negativity associated with urban crises getting so much ink in recent years. With performance arenas, parks, and marinas, this destination should not be shortchanged.

In addition, the town has historic sites well worth a look. One engaging opportunity is that families may opt to spend a night on a battleship.

getting there

Camden is about 75 miles from Newark, and the ride is mostly on toll roads. From the north, take I-95 (the New Jersey Turnpike) to exit 4 (NJ 73); go west a short distance until you reach I-295; and head south to exit 27 (I-76). Head north to the merger with I-676 North. From Atlantic City, take the Atlantic City Expressway to I-76 into Camden.

where to go

Adventure Aquarium. 1 Riverside Dr., Camden; (856) 365-3300; www.adventureaquarium .com. If you love sea creatures—and who doesn't?—this experience will be a highlight of your trip. The aquarium is very progressive when it comes to taking care of you, whether you are young, old, mobile, or not—and keeping you well-informed about the marine life you are here to enjoy. The attraction is open daily, year-round, from 9:30 a.m. to 5 p.m. Admission is $22.95 for adults and $17.95 for children ages 2 to 12. To avoid standing in line at this major draw, buy tickets online. The aquarium is situated on the Camden waterfront, at the north end of the Dr. Ulysses Wiggins Waterfront Park and Marina. It is close to other attractions here and easily accessible from Philadelphia; for details on the RiverLink Freedom Ferry from Penn's Landing, see www.riverlink.org.

Susquehanna Bank Center. 1 Harbour Blvd., Camden; (856) 338-9000; www.livenation .com. The global concert promoter presents top touring musicians at a 25,000-seat out-door amphitheater on the Camden waterfront. During fall and winter, the venue is a climate-controlled 7,000-seat theater for concerts and family-friendly entertainment. The center is just south of the Adventure Aquarium, where you can enjoy views of the Philadelphia skyline. See the website for the concert schedule. The center is close to other attractions on the waterfront and easily accessible from Philadelphia; for details on the Freedom Ferry from Penn's Landing, see www.riverlink.org.

Battleship New Jersey Museum. 100 Clinton St., Camden; (866) 877-6262, ext. 108; www.battleshipnewjersey.org. Located on the Camden waterfront across the Delaware River from Philadelphia, this attraction is a historic ship museum that offers guided and self-guided tours daily. Visitors should be prepared to climb ladders and navigate passageways, so wear flat, comfortable shoes. If you prefer, there are tours of the main deck sans ladders, and a video tour of the battleship in the main deck Wardroom Lounge. No strollers are allowed, so if there is an infant in your party, plan to wear a carry-on with the baby in front. The battleship *New Jersey* also lets youth groups and families reserve overnight encampments, weekends during the summer. You get to have dinner and breakfast from the crew's mess, tour the ship, ride the 4D Flight Simulator, and sleep in the bunks as the crew of the USS *New Jersey* once did. To reserve tickets online, see www.ticketweb.com.

Camden Children's Garden. 3 Riverside Dr., Camden; (856) 365-8733; www.camden childrensgarden.org. The Camden City Garden Club opened this 4-acre "horticultural playground" in 1999. It is designed for children and families to enjoy exploring the natural world. Indoor attractions include the Philadelphia Eagles Four Seasons Butterfly House, a tropical exhibit, Plaza de Aibonito, and Ben Franklin's Secret Workshop. There is a Dinosaur Garden, Maze, Tree House, Picnic Garden, CityScapes Garden, Storybook Gardens, and Fitness Garden, and rides such as a carousel, train, and butterfly. Open Fri through Sun 10 a.m. to 4 p.m. and Thurs by appointment. Admission is $6 for adults.

Walt Whitman House. 330 Mickle Blvd. (Martin Luther King Blvd.), Camden; (856) 964-5383; www.state.nj.us/dep/parksandforests/historic/whitman.com. The "Good Gray Poet," a tower of 19th-century American culture, moved to Camden after suffering a stroke and lived for a time with his brother. In 1884 Whitman bought this house and it was the only home he ever owned. Built almost 4 decades earlier in Greek-Revival style, this wooden-framed structure was where the author of *Leaves of Grass* received other famous literary figures—Oscar Wilde and Bram Stoker among them. He completed his last volume of poetry here, and today, the house is a state historic site and National Historic Landmark.

berry savvy

For almost forever, bruised cranberries got the round file. That is, until grower Elizabeth Lee of New Egypt decided to boil them. Delighted with the taste of the "jelly," Lee launched a business selling "Bog Sweet Cranberry Sauce." She is one of the founders of the Ocean Spray agricultural cooperative.

You will see the poet's original letters and personal belongings, the bed in which he died, and the death notice that was nailed to the front door. Also preserved is a collection of rare 19th-century photographs and an 1848 daguerreotype, the earliest known image of Whitman. The house is open for guided tours Wed through Sat from 10 a.m. to noon and from 1 to 4 p.m.; and Sun from 1 to 4 p.m. Admission is free.

cherry hill, nj

Booking a playdate is a natural in Cherry Hill, which is largely considered a bedroom community for people who commute to Camden, Princeton, Trenton, and Philadelphia. The township is home to 51 municipal parks, 3 county parks, and a working farm. One former mill and farm, which dates to the mid-18th century, is now a park with an arts center.

A major draw here is all about kids and is a national model for hands-on activities to make the whole family smile.

getting there

Cherry Hill is less than 80 miles from Newark, and the ride is mostly on toll roads. From the north, take I-95 (the New Jersey Turnpike) to exit 4 (NJ 73); go west a short distance until you reach I-295; head south to exit 34 (NJ 70).

where to go

The Garden State Discovery Museum. 2040 Springdale Rd., Cherry Hill; (856) 424-1233; www.discoverymuseum.com. *Parents* magazine calls this place one of the top 50 children's museums in the United States. It is an activity magnet for infants through age 10, with about 20 large interactive areas that invite children to touch, explore, and create. Exhibits include a 2-story unbuilt playhouse called "Under Construction," an animal clinic called "Vet and Pet," a rock climbing wall, a pretend doctor's office, a pretend boat "Down the Shore," a farm stand, nature center with tree house, puppets and a spider web, a backstage theater with costumes and sound system, a replica of a diner with kitchen and milk shake machines, a television studio, and a Subaru science lab and service station. The museum is open daily, 9:30 a.m. to 5:30 p.m., with later hours weeknights in July and Aug.

theme trips

day trip 01

a garden state of mind:
farms & markets

New Jersey's rich soil yields nature's bounty in almost three out of four seasons—
odds that most gamblers would embrace. According to officials with "The Garden State,"
there are more than 700 locations engaged in an agri-business.

With all 21 counties playing in the dirt, you will ride by a farm, an orchard, and many
farm markets in your travels. And wherever you dine out, chances are better than phenom-
enal that your plate has some snippets of regional goodies in the form of vegetable and
fruit side dishes, very berry accents, sauces from all of the above, and herbs perking up the
dish. In many cases, your meat or poultry entree is from a regional source, and the seafood
is likely local.

Exploring the state would not be complete without a taste of "Jersey Fresh," a phrase
you will see on colorful banners drawing your attention to tomatoes, sweet corn, bell peppers, eggplant, squash, lima beans, cranberries, blueberries, pumpkins, and more.

Other farms are all about trees, including those special evergreen tannenbaums in
demand during the holidays.

As for a "garden of Eden" experience, New Jersey grows about 30 varieties of apples,
and many ripen in September—encouraging you to "fall" hard for an orchard stroll. In The
Skylands region alone, you will find Winesap, McIntosh, Red and Golden Delicious, Granny
Smith, Cortland, Fuji, Gala, Empire, Stayman, Jonagold, Jonathan, and Macoun.

Many other chapters refer to farms of long-standing and farm markets laden with
temptation. Visit the State of New Jersey website to search for a complete list of farms and
information on agritourism: http://www.state.nj.us/nj/things/farms.

handy hostess

Several years ago, Wheelers Farm was located on Route 47 North near Goshen in Cape May County. The family's specialty was good produce in its own season: strawberries, asparagus, corn, tomatoes, peppers, melons, squash, and pumpkins. Sue Wheeler recalls raising three daughters there and working the farm with her husband: "We didn't need sons . . . the girls did everything, drove the trucks and equipment—they did it all." After her husband died in 1999, the Wheeler women stuck it out 2 more years. One year, they hired a corn picker and "bagged away," selling a dozen ears for $1. Health issues forced Sue Wheeler to find another liveli-hood, and she took a job as the "farm girl-hostess" at the Bellview Tavern in Cape May Court House. Not that she lost the 100 acres, however. Lindsay Clarkson signed a long-term lease on the land, where he grows trees for Tuckahoe Nurseries. Clarkson's wholesale company sells to landscaping contractors. And while the site is no longer open to the public, Sue says the land is in good hands.

DiMeo Fruit Farms & Berry Plant Nursery. 3101 Nesco Rd., Hammonton; (609) 561-5905; www.dimeofarms.com. The fifth generation of this farming family runs the century-old operation. The farm market sells fresh organic blueberries, pick-your-own organic blueberries, blueberry plants, raspberry plants, aronia berry plants, and other natural, non-genetically-modified berry plants. After picking berries, you also may enjoy a family picnic on one of DiMeo's nature trails.

Batsto Village. 31 Batsto Village Rd. (Route 542), Washington Township near Hammonton; (609) 561-0024; www.batstovillage.org. Located in the Wharton State Forest in Burlington County, this village dates to 1766, when Charles Read established an iron works on the Batsto River. Bog ore mined from streams was fashioned into iron for pots, kettles, and stoves. Iron workers and their families created the need for a farming village, which grew and lasted. Subsequent iron-works owners included John Cox, Joseph Ball, William Richards, his son Jesse, and Jesse's son Thomas Richards—all of whom lived in "the mansion." This 32-room residence sits in the center of the village, which includes a sawmill, glassworks, gristmill, a blacksmith shop, wheelwright, post office, general store, ice house, cottages, a nature center, a lake, a dam for moving bog ore boats, and an iron furnace. By the mid-1800s, mining declined; the village turned to making glass before falling on hard times. Joseph Wharton of Philadelphia took over the property, renovated the mansion, and lived there until his death in 1909. For almost half a century, Wharton's buildings and lands were held in a trust. New Jersey bought the properties in the 1950s, and the last villagers vacated the site in 1989. Batsto Village is listed on the state and national historic registers.

big on the blues

The cultivated blueberry originated in New Jersey, and there are two townships that host annual blueberry festivals in June: Browns Mills in Burlington County, and Hammonton in Atlantic County. Hammonton bills itself as the "Blueberry Capital of the World."

You may tour the village and portions of the mansion. The nature center on Batsto Lake has information on the Pinelands ecosystem, and there are canoes for guided nature tours. Farm buildings on display include a horse barn, circa 1830, built of Jersey ironstone, a piggery, a wood house, carriage house, horse stable, threshing barn, range barn, and mule barn. This destination is about 25 miles west of Atlantic City. Take the Garden State Parkway to exit 50 onto Route 9 North; proceed to Route 542, turn left, and ride about 12 miles to the village.

day trip 02

theme trips

>>> **the grape escape:**
wineries

If farms be here, can wine be far behind? Three and a half centuries ago, European settlers selected New Jersey geography for its rich soil. Some planted corn and apples; others cultivated grapes.

Having hit its stride and looking ahead to the enticing notion of "Napa" neighborhoods and wine trails on the East Coast, the 20th New Jersey Wine Festival toasted this mushrooming industry in August 2011.

The Garden State Wine Growers Association (GSWGA) organizes the festivals, where food and entertainment complement the main purpose of showing how far and "wine" New Jersey has grown.

The owners of New Jersey vineyards are quite a mix. Some followed after their ancestors, who knew nothing but the soil and its treasure; others are "retired" from professions and engaged in a new challenge—including one vintner whose day job used to be fighting with Green Berets in Afghanistan.

See the GSWGA website for information on its annual Holiday Wine Trail Weekend (usually the weekend after Thanksgiving) and other seasonal wine and food tastings. At most wine festivals, you are able to sample artisan crafts, food, and live music. Some wineries host art and music events, brunch, and master-chef meals with wine pairings. See www .newjerseywines.com for each winery's calendar.

Winemaking is hardly a cottage industry here. Bear in mind that a few environs merit an American Viticultural Area designation: Warren Hills, the Central Delaware Valley, and the Outer Coastal Plains.

In the school of pastoral precision, 14 New Jersey wineries brought home 62 awards from the 2010 Finger Lakes International Wine Competition. The annual sip-off drew competitors from all 50 states, nine Canadian provinces, and 13 foreign countries.

Gold-award winners were Sharrott Winery in Winslow, Alba Vineyards in Milford, and Heritage Vineyards in Mullica Hill. The 23 silver and 31 bronze award winners are cited next to their names.

Most New Jersey vineyards are in the milder southwestern counties. A few are in The Skylands region; the rest are "down the Shore." Here are some labels to whet your appetite for the joisey grape. They are grouped within regions, by county:

the skylands

sussex county

Cava Winery & Vineyard. 3619 Route 94, Hamburg; (973) 823-9463; www.cavawinery .com. Among those who presented at the inaugural New Jersey Wine Festival, Cava released its first estate wine.

Ventimiglia Vineyard. 101 Layton Rd., Wantage; (973) 875-4333; www.ventivines.com.

Westfall Winery. 141 Clove Rd., Montague; (973) 293-3428; www.westfallwinery.com.

warren county

Alba Vineyard. 269 County Route 627 (Finesville), Milford; (908) 995-7800; www.albavine yard.com (1 gold, 4 silvers, 1 bronze).

Brook Hollow Winery. 52 Frog Pond Rd., Columbia; (908) 496-8200; www.brookhollow winery.com.

Four Sisters Winery at Matarazzo Farms. 783 County Route 519, Belvidere; (908) 475-3671; www.foursisterswinery.com.

Villa Milagro Vineyards. 33 Warren Glen Rd., Finesville; (908) 995-2072; www.villamilagro vineyards.com.

hunterdon county

Old York Cellars. 80 Old York Rd., Ringoes; (908) 284-9463; www.oldyorkcellars.com.

Unionville Vineyards. 9 Rocktown Rd., Ringoes; (908) 788-0400; www.unionvillevine yards.com (5 bronze awards).

made in the usa

Real estate management keeps Anthony Tammaro plenty busy, yet he often thought that learning to make wine would be a kick. In 2010 he and his sister, Irene Tammaro, took a course at Vintner's Circle on Route 10 in Whippany. After participating in several classes, you pick your own wine to make, out of perhaps 100 varieties. Anthony chose two: an Italian Primitivo, which comes from the Puglia region at the heel of "the boot," and an Italian Amarone della Valpolicella, which is Venetian. His family helped with styling labels—one is Castello di Tammaro—and bottled the first case of limited-edition wines. The first Primitivo was uncorked in December 2011; the Amarone, in March 2012. The next step for "Anthony Tammaro Vintner" was expansion. He bought all the necessary winemaking equipment and has five new batches maturing. They will be ready by the end of 2012, which means Anthony has to draw up a new bucket list. In addition to Whippany, Vintner's Circle has winemaking locations in Andover, Easton, Hackettstown, Middletown, and Dickson City, PA. www.vintnerscircle.com.

the shore

monmouth county

4 JG's Orchards & Vineyards. 127 Hillsdale Rd., Colts Neck; (908) 930-8066; www.4jgswinery.com (silver award-winner).

Cream Ridge Winery. 145 Route 539, Cream Ridge; (609) 259-9797; www.creamridgewinery.com.

ocean county

Laurita Winery. 35 Archertown Rd., New Egypt; (800) 528-7482; www.lauritawinery.com.

delaware river region

mercer county

Hopewell Valley Vineyards. 46 Yard Rd., Pennington; (866) 488-9463; www.hopewellvalleyvineyards.com (3 silver awards, 7 bronzes).

Silver Decoy Winery. 610 Windsor-Perrineville Rd., East Windsor (Robbinsville); (609) 371-6000; www.silverdecoywinery.com (2 silver awards).

Terhune Orchards & Winery. 330 Cold Soil Rd., Princeton; (609) 924-2310; www.terhune orchards.com.

burlington county

Valenzano Winery. 1090 Route 206, Shamong; (609) 268-6731; www.valenzanowine .com.

camden county

Amalthea Cellars. 209 Vineyard Rd., Atco; (856) 768-8585; www.amaltheacellars.com.

Sharrott Winery. 370 S. Egg Harbor Rd., Blue Anchor; (609) 567-9463; www.sharrott winery.com (gold award-winner).

gloucester county

Cedarvale Vineyard & Winery. 205 Repaupo Station Rd., Logan Township; (856) 467-3088; www.cedarvalewinery.com.

Coda Rossa Winery. 1526 Dutch Mill Rd., Franklinville; (856) 697-9463; www.codarossa .com.

DiBella Winery. 229 Davidson Road, Woolwich Township; (609) 221-6201; www.dibella winery.com (no tasting room).

Heritage Vineyards. 480 Mullica Hill Rd., Mullica Hill; (856) 589-4474; www.heritagewinenj .com (1 gold award, 4 silvers).

Wagonhouse Winery. 1401 Route 45 at Marl Rd., Swedesboro (Mullica Hill); (609) 780-8019; www.wagonhousewinery.com.

salem county

Auburn Road Vineyards. 117 Sharptown Auburn Rd., Pilesgrove; (856) 769-9463; www .auburnroadvineyards.com (2 bronze awards).

Chestnut Run Farm. 66 Stewart Rd., Pilesgrove; (856) 769-2158; www.chestnutrunfarms .com. It has no tasting room, but knows the business (1 silver award, 1 bronze).

hops in hoboken

No surprise that New Jersey got in on the ground floor of suds. The first brewery in the state dates to 1643, in Hoboken. In the Shore-nuf spirits category, Laird & Company is the state's oldest commercial distillery—circa 1780. It is located in Scobeyville, near Colts Neck in Monmouth County.

greater atlantic city region

atlantic county

Bellview Winery. 150 Atlantic St., Landisville; (856) 697-7172; www.bellviewwinery.com.

Chateau Balić. 6623 Harding Hwy (US Route 40), Mays Landing; (609) 625-6166; www.balicwinery.com. The winery has special events, and its website invites you for free wine tastings any day of the week.

DiMatteo Vineyards. 951 Eighth St., Hammonton; (609) 704-1414; www.dimatteowinery.com (3 silver awards, 1 bronze).

Plagido's Winery. 570 N. 1st Rd., Hammonton; (609) 567-4633; www.plagidoswinery.com.

Renault Winery. 72 N. Breman Ave., Egg Harbor/Galloway; (609) 965-2111; www.renaultwinery.com (4 bronze awards).

Sylvin Farms. 24 N. Vienna Ave., Germania; (609) 965-1548; www.sylvinfarmswinery.com.

Tomasello Winery. 225 N. White Horse Pike, Hammonton; (800) 666-9463; www.tomasellowinery.com.

the southern shore

cumberland county

Swansea Vineyards. 860 Main St., Shiloh; (856) 453-5778; www.swanseavineyards.com.

cape may county

Cape May Winery & Vineyard. 711 Townbank Rd., Cape May; (609) 884-1169; www
.capemaywinery.com (3 silver awards).

Hawk Haven Vineyard & Winery. 600 S. Railroad Ave., Rio Grande; (609) 846-7347;
www.hawkhavenvineyard.com. The winery is new, but savvy (1 bronze award).

Natali Vineyards. 221 N. Delsea Dr., Cape May Court House; (609) 465-0075; www
.natalivineyards.com (1 silver award).

Turdo Vineyards & Winery. 3911 Bayshore Rd., North Cape May; (609) 884-5591; www
.turdovineyards.com.

worth more time

Old Mill Antique Center. 1 S. Main St. (Route 45), Mullica Hill; www.mullicahill.com. Gold
awards for wine are not the only reason to make the trek to Gloucester County (where you
will find Heritage Vineyards on a 100-acre farm on Mullica Hill Road). This gem of a town
was settled in the late 17th century, and much of what you see was developed during the
Civil War. Mullica Hill—the town itself—is on the National Register of Historic Places. It's a
dream trip for antiques lovers, as there are dozens of shops and antique buildings. The Old
Mill Antique Center is located in a former gristmill built prior to the American Revolutionary
War. It has a dozen dealers on three floors. Main Street has plenty of galleries, boutiques,
and cafes. The town has an Amish Farmer's Market, where you will find fresh produce,
cheeses, meats, baked goods, candy, and sandwiches.

day trip 03

DO NOT JUMP OR DIVE FROM PIER

>>> **train yourself:**
trains

Rail transportation made it possible for New Jersey to become the filling in a Manhattan-Philadelphia sandwich. So, is it better to be one of the bookends or the cheesesteak in between?

Depending on where you are and where you hope to go, try training yourself in the ways of past generations and current commuters.

New Jersey Transit. www.njtransit.com:

> **Hudson-Bergen Light Rail.** (973) 275-5555. This connects Bayonne, Jersey City, and Manhattan.

> **Newark Light Rail.** This underground line takes you from Newark Penn Station to Newark Broad Street Station, for connections to other points.

> **Morris & Essex Line.** Stops include Hackettstown, Dover, Morristown, Gladstone, Summit, The Oranges, Newark, Hoboken, Secaucus Junction, and New York Penn Station.

> **Far Hills Train Station.** US Route 202, Far Hills. This station is on the Gladstone branch of the Morris Line, and the building is listed on the National Register of Historic Places.

> **River LINE.** (800) 626-7433. This line goes to Camden and Trenton, and makes 20 stops.

Towaco Train Station. 632 Main Rd. (Route 202), Towaco; (973) 275-5555. As described in the day trip to Montville, this station is part of the Montclair-Boonton Line, with stops at Montclair State and New York's Penn Station. Commuters may now go from Towaco to Penn Station in Midtown Manhattan via a transfer in Montclair into Newark.

Port Authority Trans-Hudson (PATH). (800) 234-7284; www.panynj.info. Rail service from the Newark metro area into Lower Manhattan is courtesy of The Port Authority of New York and New Jersey. There are 13 stations spanning 14 miles, and trains run 24 hours a day. There are three terminals in New Jersey and two in Manhattan.

The Delaware River Port Authority. www.ridepatco.org. DRPA operates the PATCO Speedline between Camden County, NJ, and Center City in Philadelphia. There are four stations on the line in Philly and nine stations in New Jersey, where you will find park-and-ride facilities. A primary stop at Woodcrest Station connects you directly with I-295 exit 31. PATCO Speedline runs 24 hours a day.

Pennsylvania Station (Newark Penn Station). Raymond Plaza, between Market Street and Raymond Boulevard, Newark. An architectural gem built in 1935, the station is worth a visit just on its design merits alone. With Indiana limestone outside, the station is decorated with wall carvings of modes of travel—wagons, steamships, cars, and airplanes—and chandeliers inspired by signs of the zodiac. Newark Penn Station is served by Newark Light Rail, New Jersey Transit lines, Amtrak long-distance trains, and the PATH system. Designed by McKim, Mead and White, the station mixes Art Deco with Neo-Classical elements. The first regular train here was a New York-Philadelphia express. The tracks are above street level, except for the underground Newark Light Rail station. Newark Penn Station is the west end of the Newark-World Trade Center line of the PATH system.

Whippany Railway Museum. 1 Railroad Plaza, Whippany; (973) 887-8177; www.whip panyrailwaymuseum.net. As described in one of the day trips in The Skylands region, this attraction is a family-friendly outing to learn about New Jersey's "ties" to locomotive history. The passenger depot is an exterior landmark, and you will see countless examples of oldie "iron horses." Consider a ride on the restored Jersey Coast Club Car, built in 1927. It isn't open in the winter, except for the 10-mile Santa Claus Special.

day trip 04

theme trips

>>> **foray freely:**
ferries

A few of the Day Trip chapters explain that ferry rides are the sole option for certain attractions. They also can be a fun outing for any family member. Even in iffy weather, the vessels have enclosed salons that are comfortable and climate-controlled.

The crews are first-rate professionals and most ferries have a variety of amenities. Here are a few choices for relaxing water travel to get you where you want to go:

Statue Cruises. Liberty State Park; (877) 523-9849; www.statuecruises.com. This company operates ferries to and from Ellis Island and the Statue of Liberty National Monument. It also offers a Liberty Harbor Cruise, which includes those sites as well as Governors Island, the September 11 Memorial, the Brooklyn Bridge, and Battery Park.

New York Waterway. Port Imperial, Weehawken; (800) 533-3779; www.nywaterway.com. This agency for the Port of New York and New Jersey has several ferry terminals. The one at Weehawken is handy for a short ferry ride to West 39th Street in Midtown Manhattan. The terminal at Jersey City is described in the Day Trips to Ellis Island and the Statue of Liberty. Other terminals are located at Belford/Harbor Way, Edgewater Landing, Hoboken at 14th Street and at the Hoboken/NJ Transit terminal, Liberty Harbor/Marin Boulevard, Lincoln Harbor, Newport, Paulus Hook, and the Cape Liberty Cruise Port at Port Liberte. Manhattan terminals also are located at Wall Street/Pier 11, Battery Park City/The World Financial Center. Other Hudson River stops in New York include Beacon, Haverstraw, and Newburgh (see Gateway region day trips). The ferry company's website has information on shuttle buses at each terminal.

The Delaware River and Bay Authority. www.riverlink.org. This agency operates the RiverLink Ferry between the Camden waterfront and Penn's Landing in Philadelphia. This form of transportation is very convenient for the numerous visitor attractions located on both sides of the river.

Cape May-Lewes Ferry. 1200 Lincoln Blvd., Cape May; (800) 643-3779; www.cmlf.com. Drive on or walk on, as there are shuttle buses on both sides (see Southern Shore region day trips). Reserve in advance to take your car on the ferry; foot passengers may be walk-ons. The 17-mile ride across Delaware Bay takes 70 to 80 minutes. Terminals on both sides have restaurants, outdoor cafes, and gift shops. The ride itself is pleasant, although there can be a little wave action in the widest part of Delaware Bay, where it merges into the Atlantic Ocean.

Three Forts Ferry. Fort Delaware State Park, Pea Patch Island, DE; (302) 834-7941; www.destateparks.com. Ferry service is your only option to reach the island, which is in the Delaware River between Fort Mott State Park at Finns Point, NJ, and Fort DuPont near Delaware City, DE. A passenger ferry, *Delafort,* brings you to the island for a day of living history, including highlights from the Civil War. The area is ancient, having been settled by Finnish farmers in the 1630s. You can explore soldiers' quarters, ramparts, parade grounds, and gun emplacements.

SeaStreak. 2 First Ave., Atlantic Highlands; (800) 262-8743; www.seastreak.com. The company's 7 high-speed catamarans take you from Central New Jersey to Wall Street and other points in Manhattan (see Shore region day trips). Vessels have a capacity for 149 to 400 passengers, with daily year-round service from Atlantic Highlands, Conners/Highlands, and South Amboy to Pier 11, East 35th Street, and the World Financial Center via shuttle. *SeaStreak* also offers ferry service from New Jersey to the new Yankee Stadium in the Bronx for selected home games. Babe Ruth Plaza is located outside the stadium, and the New York Yankees Museum is on the Main Level near Gate 6.

festivals & celebrations

New Jersey loves to party, celebrate and/or just hang out to people-watch, soak up the atmosphere, sample the food, engage in historic and cultural treasures—and count one's blessings. No reason is necessary for a festive gathering or commemorative event, although there are countless good ones.

The following schedule of festivals and special events is based on plans in place at the time of publication.

january

Hoboken Food Tour. River Street and Hudson Place, Hoboken; (800) 595-4849; www .hobokenfoodtour.com. Every Saturday year-round, rain or shine, this gastronomic exercise takes about 3.5 hours. The walking tours start from the main entrance of the Hoboken PATH train station. It features a stop at Carlo's City Hall Bakery, home base for master baker and *Cake Boss* TV personality Buddy Valastro. Other stops usually include Lisa's, Fiore's, and Grimaldi's.

february

Wine & Chocolate Wine Trail Weekend. (609) 588-0085; www.newjerseywines.com. Garden State Wine Growers Association. This event takes place in each region. Participating wineries are listed on the website.

march

Garden State Film Festival. Paramount Theatre, Asbury Park; www.gsff.org. Screenings of more than 100 films take place over 3 days.

North Jersey Gem and Mineral Show. Pope John Paul II Center, Clifton; www.nojms .webs.com. The annual show, now in its 23rd year, draws rock hounds and those curious to see the gems, fossils, jewelry, and books on display.

april

Cherry Blossom Festival. Branch Brook Park, Newark; (973) 268-2300; www.branch brookpark.org. An annual celebration of the park's 2,000-plus cherry trees. When in bloom, they dress the park like pink snow.

Cape May Jazz Festival. Cape May; (609) 884-7277; www.capemayjazz.org. This event is held in the spring and fall, presenting mainstream jazz over a 3-day run.

Mullica Hill Antiques Street Fair. Mullica Hill; www.mullicahill.com.

Spring Plant Sale & Earth Day Celebration. Layton Road, Far Hills; (908) 234-2677; www.somersetcountyparks.org. The event takes place at the Leonard J. Buck Garden.

may

Spirit of the Jerseys State History Fair. Washington Crossing State Park, Titusville; www .state.nj.us/dep/parksandforests/historic.

Mother's Day Wine Trail Weekend. (609) 588-0085; www.newjerseywines.com. Garden State Wine Growers Association. This event takes place in each region. Participating wineries are listed on the website.

Annual Wine & Beer Expo. Tomasello Winery, Hammonton; www.tomasellowinery.com.

trailblazers

Steve Marano in Newark and David Brickley in Virginia are aligned in pieces of a common cause—the September 11 National Memorial Trail. Most trails go from point to point, in either a sloppy line or a lazy circle. This route is unique, in that it clearly triangulates the World Trade Center Memorial in Manhattan, the Pentagon Memorial in Washington DC, and the Flight 93 National Memorial in Shanksville, PA. And it does this by crossing New Jersey twice—along the East Coast Greenway via Trenton and down to Philadelphia; and along the 130-mile Liberty Water Gap Trail across five counties. Brickley spearheaded this work-in-progress. Marano, through the New York-New Jersey Trail Conference, is working on the fledgling Liberty Water Gap Trail, which runs from Liberty State Park in Jersey City to the Delaware Water Gap; from there, the National trail continues to Shanksville. When completed, the intent is for Sept. 11 observances, taking in the Lenape Trail in Essex County, Patriots Path in Morris County, the Paulinskill Valley Trail, and the Sussex Branch Trail. In a bit of serendipity, Marano's day job is about to land right in the lap of the Lenape Trail. He is director of business development for Panasonic, which is preparing to move its North American headquarters to a building on Raymond Boulevard in Newark, where the Lenape Trail winds along the Passaic River. For updates on trail progress, see www.libertygap .org and www.911memorialtrail.org.

Family Fun Day. Lord Stirling Stable, Basking Ridge; (908) 766-5955; www.somerset countyparks.org. An annual event since 1981, the festival involves pony rides, tractors pulling wagons for hayrides, arcade games, face painting, and other family activities.

Blues & Wine Festival. Natirar County Park, Peapack-Gladstone; (609) 588-0085; www .newjerseywines.com. Garden State Wine Growers Association.

Suningive Gardens. Browns Mills. (609) 893-4646; www.whitesbog.org. You need reservations for this tour of the gardens treasured by Elizabeth White, the woman who first cultivated the blueberry. The event is coordinated by the Whitesbog Preservation Trust.

june

Annual Rose Day. Colonial Park, Franklin Township; www.somersetcountyparks.org. The celebration of peak bloom at the Rudolph W. van der Goot Rose Garden dates to 1974. The garden displays more than 3,000 roses in hundreds of varieties.

Jersey Seafood Challenge. Drumthwacket, Princeton; www.nj.gov/seafood. The annual competition encourages chefs to create dishes using local ingredients. In 2011 it took place at the governor's mansion, and the host was First Lady Mary Pat Christie.

Whitesbog Blueberry Festival. Browns Mills; www.whitesbog.org. Historic Whitesbog Village in the Brendan T. Byrne State Forest is the birthplace of the cultivated blueberry, which is New Jersey's official state fruit. Elizabeth White gets credit for persevering when all around her had eyes only for cranberries.

Gooch's Garlic Run. The 2011 event was its 24th, coordinated by the Blue Knights NJ IX Chapter of law enforcement officers from Sussex County. Hundreds of them ride motorcycles to benefit children's charities, and the event is named in honor of Al "Gooch" Monaco, a retired lieutenant from Andover PD. The run terminated in Newark's Ironbound.

Puerto Rican Day and Festival. Haverstraw, NY. Other Hispanic cultures celebrate the day, too.

North Rockland Community Family Day. Haverstraw, NY; www.townofhaverstraw.org. This event usually involves a 3-mile run/fun walk.

Red Bank Jazz & Blues Festival. Red Bank; (732) 933-0541; www.jsjbf.org. The event is presented by the Jersey Shore Jazz & Blues Society.

Milford Music Festival. Milford, PA; www.milfordpa.us. A fun outing in this quaint town just across the Delaware River.

Cape May Forum. Cape May; (609) 770-2626; www.capemayforum.org. Chatauqua-style gatherings participate in discussions on topical themes.

Newark Black Film Festival. 49 Washington St., Newark; (973) 596-6550; www.newark museum.org. The Newark Museum is the venue for this annual festival, which has showcased independent films for almost 4 decades.

Red, White & Blueberry Festival. Hammonton; www.hammontonnj.us. The 25th annual tribute to New Jersey's official state fruit took place in 2011, with music, crafts, food, a display of classic cars, and amusement rides.

State Fair Meadowlands. Meadowlands Sports Complex, East Rutherford; www.njfair .com. This family-oriented event runs for more than 2 weeks.

Artist Visions Film Festival. Lambertville; www.nj.com. In 2011 the event combined the Princeton Student Film and Video Festival. It shows the work of filmmakers and visual artists in and around Hunterdon County. Previously a weekend affair, it has expanded into a summerlong series. There are free outdoor screenings and live music.

july

Oceanfest. Long Branch. An all-day event on the Fourth of July, held every year since 1990, it incorporates crafting, sand sculpture, food vendors, hundreds of thousands in the crowds, dancing, music, carnival acts, and clowns.

Feast of St. Ann. Hoboken. This is an Italian festival with time on its side and authenticity to back it up. Dating to 1910, it runs for several days and nights, and the food is superb.

New Jersey Sand Castle Competition. 18th Avenue Beach, Belmar; www.njsandcastle .com. This down-the-Shore annual event has been drawing entrants and spectators for a quarter of a century. These castle-dreamers' masterpieces take up about 5 blocks.

Barrel Trail Wine Trail Weekend. (609) 588-0085; www.newjerseywines.com. Garden State Wine Growers Association. This event takes place in each region. Participating wineries are listed on the website.

Kaboom! Fireworks on the Navesink. Red Bank; www.kaboomfireworks.org. Held every July 3 for more than half a century, this burst of drama takes place at Riverside Gardens Park.

New Jersey State Ice Cream Festival. Downtown, Toms River; (732) 341-8738; www .downtowntomsriver.com/icecream. Families come in droves for the games, rides, food, and entertainment.

Native American Festival. Sussex County Fairgrounds, Augusta. This event features songs, food, crafts, and art.

Quick Chek New Jersey Festival of Ballooning. 39 Thor Solberg Rd. (Solberg Airport), Readington; (800) 468-2479; www.balloonfestival.com. This annual up-and-away dates to the 1980s. You can reserve a sunrise balloon ride, or be a spectator at dawn and dusk ascensions. Traffic tends to build up around 4:30 p.m. Sat, so to avoid traffic, plan to arrive a bit earlier. You will have time to walk the festival grounds, enjoy the crafters and vendors, and scout the entertainment. This is the largest summertime hot-air balloon and music festival in North America. Here you will see more than 100 sport and novelty hot-air balloons from around the world. The event lasts for 3 days, draws more than 165,000 people, and raises money for charities. You can go up, up, and away, or simply marvel at the color-splashed skies. There are live concert series featuring top entertainers, fireworks, a nighttime balloon glow, aerial performers and other attractions, the "Running with the Balloons" 5K Race and Family Fun Run, children's amusement rides, interactive exhibits, arts and crafts, and food vendors.

Warren County Farmer's Fair. Harmony Township (north of Phillipsburg); www.warren countyfarmersfair.org. The fair got official in the 1930s but began in the 19th century when farmers planned family get-togethers. In 2000 the event added a hot-air balloon festival into the 8-day mix. There is food, entertainment, and displays of vintage cars.

august

Thunder Over the Boardwalk. Atlantic City; www.atlanticcitynj.com/acairshow. This perennial crowd-pleaser features the precision skills of pilots with the US Air Force, Army, Navy, the Coast Guard, and the Canadian Skyhawks parachute team.

New Jersey State Fair/Sussex County Farm & Horse Show. Augusta; www.newjersey statefair.org.

LBI Longboard Classic. Ship Bottom, Long Beach Island; www.livingocean.org. This event toasts the legendary surfboard and incorporates an environmental fair.

september

AP IndieFest. 708 Cookman Ave., Asbury Park; www.apindiefest.com. Founded in 2010, this film festival is a joint venture among ArtsCAP, the Asbury Park Film Initiative, and The ShowRoom.

Feast of the Madonna Dei Martiri. Hoboken; www.hobokenitalianfestival.com. This cultural festival dates to the 1920s. It goes on for days, featuring food, music, and fireworks.

Jazz It Up Wine Festival. Allaire State Park, Farmingdale; (609) 588-0085; www.new jerseywines.com. Garden State Wine Growers Association.

Oysterfest. Lake Avenue, Asbury Park; www.nj.com. Get out of your shell; take in the bands, the beach, the food, music, and amusements.

John Basilone Parade. Raritan; www.basiloneparade.com. This annual tribute recalls the heroism of Raritan native John Basilone, a US Marine Corps gunnery sergeant who was killed at the Battle of Iwo Jima during World War II. This happened after he had received the Medal of Honor for heroic service in the Army. He was heralded in a homecoming parade in 1943 and later reenlisted in the Marines.

The Garden State Rainbow Pride Festival. Paramount Theater, Asbury Park; www.gsrainbowpride.com. The event attracts gay and gay-friendly businesses.

Peters Valley Fine Craft Fair. Layton; (973) 948-5200; www.pvcrafts.org. The Peters Valley Craft Center is your host, and its annual fair has been a tradition since 1970.

Annual Giant Craft Show. Central Avenue and Ocean Pathway, Ocean Grove; www.oceangrove.org. This event has taken place every Labor Day weekend since 1981.

Island Beach State Park Beach Plum Festival. South Seaside Park; (732) 793-5525; www.friendsofislandbeach.com. This celebration of the resource takes place at Ocean Beach Swimming Area No. 1; there is beach plum picking and jelly making, bird-banding demonstrations, exhibits by environmental and nonprofit groups, arts and crafts, children's games, a kayak raffle, food, and live entertainment.

South Orange International Blues Festival. South Mountain Reservation, Essex County; www.southorangebluesfestival.com. Mike Griot of PWI Entertainment organizes the all-day rain-or-shine event, which had its first sound check in 2010.

Ship Bottom Irish Festival. 10th Street and Shore Avenue, Ship Bottom, Long Beach Island; (609) 494-6301; www.lbiaoh.com/ifest. Hibernians, and those who wish they were, gather each year at the Ship Bottom Boat Ramp Parking Lot.

The Red Bank Guinness Oyster Festival. RiverCenter, Red Bank; www.onlyoneredbank.com. This street festival is patterned after the Galway Oyster Festival, which has a 60-year tradition. There are two stages, food, and music, from Irish folk to blues, funk, and rock 'n' roll, plus children's activities. Red Bank restaurants participate in this fund-raiser.

Ocean County Decoy & Gunning Show. Tip Seaman County Park, Tuckerton; www.tuckertonseaport.org. The 2-day event celebrates the culture of game-hunting, with demonstrations, contests, seminars, a decoy auction, crafters, carvers, vendors, food, refreshments, music, and entertainment. Some events are held at the Tuckerton Seaport Museum.

october

Autumn House Tour. Lambertville; (609) 397-0770; www.lambertvillehistoricalsociety.org. In 2012, the Lambertville Historical Society will host its 30th house tour.

Far Hills Race Meeting. Mooreland Farms, Far Hills; www.farhillsrace.org. Founded more than 90 years ago, the annual steeplechase event is a fund-raiser for the Somerset Medical Center Foundation.

Cape May Wine Festival. North Cape May; (609) 588-0085; www.newjerseywines.com. The venue is the Cape May-Lewes Ferry Terminal.

Grand Harvest Wine Festival. Fosterfields Living Historical Farm, Morristown; (609) 588-0085; www.newjerseywines.com.

Governor's Surf Fishing Tournament. South Seaside Park; www.state.nj.dep. The annual event takes place at Island Beach State Park.

Arts & Main Fall Festival Street Fair. Grove to Doughty Streets, Somerville; www.find somerville.com. Music, crafts, and artists cause a stir downtown.

Black Bear Film Festival. 115 Mill St., Milford, PA; (570) 409-0909; www.blackbearfilm .com. The event offers interesting, thought-provoking indie films, including full-length feature films. The festival acknowledges the independent film world, and the venue is the historic Milford Theater.

Cape May/New Jersey State Film Festival. Cape May; (609) 884-6700; www.cape mayfilm.org.

The Lord Stirling 1770s Festival. Basking Ridge; www.somersetcountyparks.org. The manor estate and grounds of Lord Stirling take on a Colonial atmosphere, with pre-Revolutionary crafters and a militia conducting maneuvers.

Chowderfest Weekend. Ship Bottom, Long Beach Island; www.visitlbiregion.com. The chow-down follows the annual showdown as entrants compete for the best New England and Manhattan-style clam chowder.

The Country Living Fair. Batsto Village, Hammonton; www.batstovillage.com. Crafts, exhibits, music, old-time engines and cars, food, antiques, pony rides, farm equipment, chain-saw art, and quilting.

november

Cape May Jazz Festival. Cape May; (609) 884-7277; www.capemayjazz.org. This event is held in the spring and fall, presenting mainstream jazz over a 3-day run.

Holiday Wine Trail Weekend. www.newjerseywines.com. Statewide events include the Sussex Wine Trail, Warren Hunterdon Wine Trail, Cumberland Wine Trail, Gloucester Salem Wine Trail, Atlantic County Wine Trail, Shore Wine Trail, and Cape May Wine Trail. See www .newjerseywines.com for the dates and host vineyards in 2012.

Fall Oyster Harvest. Mullica River, Nacote Creek; (609) 748-2040; www.state.nj.us/dep/fgw.

december

Annual Gingerbread Wonderland. Frelinghuysen Arboretum. 353 E. Hanover Ave., Morris Township; (973) 326-7601. The 20th exhibit of more than 200 edible "structures" was held in 2011. The event coincides with a Holiday Craft Show, where you can find handmade holiday gifts.

Holiday Crafts Fair. 1301 Hudson St., Hoboken; (201) 656-2240; www.hobokenhistorical museum.com. Local artisans and crafters sell their jewelry and decorative items in time for Christmas.

A Victorian Christmas to Remember. Batsto Village, Hammonton; www.batstovillage .org.

Christmas House Tours. Mullica Hill; (856) 881-6800; www.mullicahill.com.

First Night. Red Bank. Held on New Year's Eve in numerous locations around the United States, this art and entertainment festival celebrates alternatives to alcohol-related events.

index

Getaway ideas for the local traveler

Need a day away to relax, refresh, renew?
Just get in your car and go!

Regional Travel at Its Best

To order call 800-243-0495 or visit www.GlobePequot.com